Down Jersey Cooking

Bonnie)
Let's share our
Down Jersey table
with family and friends!

Joe Colanero
6-18-04

Down Jersey Cooking

Celebrating our Heritage from Past to Present

by
Joe Colanero

Down Jersey Press...Woodbury, New Jersey

Down Jersey Press
706 Lancing Road
West Deptford, New Jersey 08096-4004

ISBN 0-9753696-0-1
Library of Congress Control Number 2004092549

Printed in USA by
Cadmus Communications
Port City Press Division

Cover graphics courtesy of Anthony Colanero
Maurice River cover photo courtesy of and by Jody Carrara
Chioppino photo by Joe Tierno, courtesy of Dill's Seafood

Dedication and Gratitude to:

My forever thanks to my wife, Loretta, and our children Catherine, Ann and James for their suffering during recipe testing, proof reading, and my rantings about our Down Jersey Heritage. Also, of course, to my Mother and Father, Louise and Ralph Colanero, for their courage in leaving a tiny village in Abruzzi, Italy, in the early 1900's to give their six children a future in America.

Also, I remember the encouragement and nurturing of my Buck Street Grammar School teacher in Paulsboro, Ms. Mary Taylor, and my early mentor, Mrs. Hanna Bostwick, a fellow member of the South Jersey Organic Gardening Club.

Finally, my deepest appreciation to all the gracious and sharing Down Jersey friends who willingly contributed to the collection of foodways, sketches and family traditions that fill this work.

Down Jersey

The gray area depicts a rough representation of the full region that has become known as Down Jersey. It's heart, though, lies near the meadows and breezes along the Delaware Bay.

Contents

Introduction—VIII

*****

To the Farm Market—*19*

*****

Tomato Cooking Savvy—*27*

*****

Soups Grandma Might Have Made—31

*****

Light and Easy Fare—*47*

*****

Vegetables from the Garden State—*63*

*****

All Together at Main Family Courses—*93*

*****

Our Own Seafood Seafare—*133*

*****

Vegetarian and Vegan for Everyone—*173*

*****

Fresh Salads & Tomatoes, of Course—*187*

*****

Dessert & Pastries with Love—*201*

*****

Sauces We Have Come to Know—*227*

*****

Our Lenni Lenape—*239*

*****

Jerseyspeak Glossary—253

*****

Index for the Serious—*255*

Introduction
There *is* a Down Jersey Cuisine

It is understandable that, at first glance, the culinary foodways of our Down Jersey region might appear unremarkable. Yet, the mention of noodle-style chicken pot pie, a pepper 'n eggs sandwich or a church oyster and ham supper would soon awaken anyone to the possibilities of a distinctive cuisine that lies deep within the heart of southern New Jersey.

It has been said that great cuisines come from a land abundant in foodstuffs, the infusion of many diverse ethnic groups and the wealth to support development of aristocratic food.

We have two of the three, and are all the better for it. Ignoring the last supposed requirement, a wealth of regal chefs clamoring to make a name for themselves, we instead are able to hold onto the practical, nutritious and downright home-doable recipes that rise among the noblest of fare. As to foodstuffs, we are unique in having favorable soils and mid-Atlantic weather in which we can grow the hardiest of northern vegetables and fruits as well as all southern crops, save the tropicals. Going from the land to the sea, we harvest a wide range of seafood from blue crabs and oysters in the Delaware Bay to fish and shellfish in the Atlantic Ocean just off the Jersey coast. Anyone in Down Jersey takes it for granted that one either has a producing vegetable garden or a variety rich farm market nearby, and is only minutes away from a fresh seafood shop. In our early history an observation by a Scotsman that we are worthy of being called "The Garden State" put into words the promise of a bountiful land. This promise drew the early settlers, and later, many diverse immigrants from nearby Ellis Island in the Upper Bay a few miles off New Jersey.

The rich traditions of the past, from colonial beginnings of our native Lenni Lenape, through numerous ethnic groups and up to present, all have tossed their culinary inheritance in the pot that we are rediscovering today. In this work, I will attempt to share with you the recipes and remembrances that our grandparents would have wanted us to pass on to our children. As a practical consideration, recipes that suit today's cook are included as well and that, while not linked to a particular ethnic past, are closely tied to the provisions and seasons of Down Jersey.

In searching for the foodways of our past, our grandparents are often a rich resource to mine. Today's expanded awareness of nutrition and health compels us to offer updated variations, but by going back to the origins of our cooking, we can understand the foundation of where we are. Just as food itself sustains life, the foodways of our past sustain our culture. In Down Jersey, there is a wealth of ethnic diversity to share in all of that.

The Scope of Down Jersey

This land we refer to as our Down Jersey region now begs for a definition as to the length and breadth of its scope. If there were an epicenter, it would be close to the Delaware Bay, where there have been the strongest and purest influences of the melting pot that we now know. Its western boundaries would thin out at Salem, while the eastern reaches would begin to flirt with the cuisine of the seashore. The northern range would weaken as you travel into the bedroom communities that serve Philadelphia and Northern New Jersey, which is to say the communities of Camden County near Philadelphia and those of western Burlington County. As to Philadelphia itself, many of its popular foods have impacted on us and, where the dishes have become part of us, we have included them.

The cuisine of the shore, which has grown by leaps since the 1980's when the casinos began to leave their mark, would be considered outside of Down Jersey for the purposes of this book. Serving the "shoe-bees," as the day-trippers are called, brings about a whole different approach to restaurant fare. As for home cooking down at the shore, any visit to a shore farm market shows that the visitors are interested in a day off from cooking. Fine. But that's not us.

As much as we respect our culinary traditions, we felt compelled to include more recent contributions of cooking that are so Down Jersey, we could not fail to include them. We have attempted to sidestep the passing fads and recognize the worthy, more recent recipes, those that we are likely to do again. In that way, perhaps they will be those that will also be passed down to future generations.

The Garden State

In this region so fittingly within the Garden State, the waves of immigrants coming ashore found what we now take for granted: a most hospitable climate for growing a wide range of northern and southern crops, and favorable soil to nurture them. A Japanese-American residing in Seabrook in Cumberland County would have no less trouble finding suitable ingredients for a sukiyaki than would a Mexican-American seeking hot peppers.

With an average 190-day growing season and an agreeable soil range from sandy loam to clay, our Down Jersey gardeners and farmers can supply us with a wide range of produce over a long season. Growing season temperatures peak at an average in the 80's for most of southern New Jersey. Rainfall, averaging in the range of 42 to 46 inches per year throughout the region today is supplemented with drip irrigation favoring economy of water usage, moisture control and high product quality. Because of this pastoral hospitality, immigrants found it easy to locate or adapt their old-country recipes to what was available.

The heart of Down Jersey lies well within what geologists call the inner and outer Coastal Plain, which was brought about by the rise and fall of oceans thousands of years ago that left deposits of sand, silt and clay. The inner plain, which parallels the Delaware River, is somewhat more fertile, but both zones are amenable to fertilizer and so they have been rewardingly productive for farmers and gardeners alike. Down Jersey is in what horticulturists refer to as growing zone 7, because of this we are able to grow most temperate crops of fruits and vegetables.

Mention the summer season to anyone in Down Jersey and the response will surely draw a personal reminiscence of our crowning vegetable, the Jersey tomato. With improved season extending methods, growers are giving us tomatoes earlier and earlier in June, and stretching the other end into November. Going past our beloved tomato, the full season brings diverse fresh produce to our tables from late winter on to late fall.

The season kicks off with dandelion cutting in late March, nudged forward by use of plastic culture. Celebrated by its major growing region, Vineland, which proclaims itself as the dandelion capital of the world, its devotees go beyond the braggadocios Italian community and on to the Germans and Greeks in our area.

Over wintering spinach harvested in April four years out of five, will encore with a spring crop in May and return again in October for yet another cut. It's only natural that spinach and oysters found themselves paired in many of our dishes.

A modest crop of broccoli rabe satisfies the demand in April, with out of state supplies filling the breech until our major rabe season starts in the fall.

Asparagus, once a major crop that was hurt by a disease, fusarium crown rot, has been returning to our fields due to improved disease resistant varieties bred by Rutgers Cook College, and by more vigorous hybrids. The latter part of asparagus season that lasts until early June happens to coincide with our blue crab catches, both delicate items that belong on a serving plate together.

June strawberries bring delight to farm market shoppers who savor the true fruity sweetness of local-grown, full-flavored berries. The Quakers and the Germans instinctively knew how to pair them with rhubarb, another sister season crop.

Improved season-advancing methods utilized by farmers bring more and more once summer crops to the market early. Squash, zucchini and early maturity corn now regularly appear in June, along with the more traditional cabbage and lettuce.

Down Jersey boasts being a white corn market. Our long growing season has hooked us on the white varieties that happen to be of longer maturities. Silver Queen still reigns as the king of corn to shoppers, though farmers have switched to varieties that are far easier to grow than the fickle Silver Queen, and have done well with introductions that may actually be superior in taste.

The Fourth of July marks the day we expect to have our Jersey tomato appear at local marts. Of course, weather gets in the way with delays and shortages that distress the would-be shoppers. In recent years, newer varieties bred for shipping and cosmetics rather than for taste have had a dampening effect on our tomato reputation, but we all pray this trend is short-lived. But don't blame it on the farmers alone. Marketers know that people talk taste but select firmness. Gardeners have sensibly been loyal to old standards, and, with the help of the hype on heirloom tomatoes, have been accessing more of the softer heirlooms that bring a tomato to its highest glory.

The full bounty of summer production hits the markets with sweet peppers, zucchini, other summer squash, eggplant, okra, cabbage, plum tomatoes, and cucumbers. The former abundance of Down Jersey factories turning the small cucumbers into pickles gave coinage to the name *pickles* that other regions call *kirbies*.

The major crop portion of white potatoes grown by potato farmers are destined to travel to the processors for products such as potato chips, though early July brings us a great variety, Superior, with a wonderful taste and excellent keeping qualities.

Peaches and nectarines, some types of which are ready for picking in early July, are highly prized for their deep color and sweet juiciness. Shipments travel to foreign countries that value their goodness. Apples, too, are choice for the odd reason that the production quantities don't economically justify long-term storage. Hence, Jersey apples are picked from the tree closer to maturity and are far sweeter for it. Their color doesn't deepen as well as those grown in the cooler western states, but savvy shoppers know our apples exceed in flavor and skin-deep eye appeal.

Our fall season is where the land and the weather collaborate in harmony to bring about a rich, extended season. As summer crops give way, the cold tolerant autumn crops of broccoli, broccoli rabe, various greens, pumpkins and other winter squash, spinach, leeks and more continue the parade until the heavy frost arrives in late October and early November. Crop protection and sheltered sites in the vicinity of the slow-to-chill Bay often extend harvesting for several more weeks. As a food writer, I often prod readers not to give up so soon when the first chill arrives. I suggest continued scouting for fall crops, pointing out that many of them become all the sweeter as an adaptation to the colder temperatures. We all know that we shouldn't bother with Brussels sprouts until they have been kissed by several frosts, but we need reminders that other fall crops share in that sweet touch of nature.

Backing up somewhat, pole lima beans come in a close second as a Down Jersey specialty crop, immediately behind our beloved tomato. Farmers that deliver huge truckloads to the processors survive by growing the bush varieties that are far less labor intensive. As good as they are, they are no match for pole lima bean varieties, which happen to be the original growth habit before hybriders coaxed them into machine-harvesting bush sizes. Other than home gardeners, few farmers have been successful in commercially growing pole limas, but those that have are doing well, thanks to loyal local customers.

Pole limas hit the farm markets in mid-August as they demand a long, warm growing season, but not too hot either. For that reason, pole limas are not viable grown as close as 50 miles away in slightly colder northern New Jersey or Pennsylvania. Because the blossoms abort, hence no pods, in days of temperatures reaching the mid to high 90's, pole limas don't fare well a mere hundred miles south of us. Southern growers favor the more heat-tolerant sivvy or butter beans. Good as they are, they are not the pole limas that we cherish. Pole limas can be found until the daytime fall weather chills into the 50's, with some revival if the weather warms somewhat.

Sadly, the interest in sweet potatoes is easing, perhaps due to the time constraints of today's homemaker. Brought up into the south by the Native Americans from central America, sweet potatoes find agreeable growing conditions in the sandy soils of Down Jersey and into the broader reaches of southern New Jersey. "Fresh-dug" sweet potatoes arrive at our markets in mid-October with the cured, sweeter tasting sweets filling the bins in mid-November. The lucky shopper is the one who finds a local heirloom sweet potato, such as Jersey white or Nancy Hall, that can't make it to the price-competitive supermarkets, but anyone with a memory knows they are worth the extra pennies.

The Mid-Atlantic Coastal State

In Down Jersey, because of our proximity to the Atlantic shoreline, Delaware Bay and River, we enjoy an abundance of fresh fish and shellfish. This compliments the large variety of fresh vegetable crops indigenous to this region. For over 300 years, New Jersey commercial fishermen have been going out to sea and returning home with some of the finest, freshest seafood caught anywhere in the world. The port of Cape May/Wildwood has, for over 20 years yielded the highest value per pound of fish on the East Coast. As a result, hardly anyone in this area lives more than a few minutes from a fresh seafood market.

Already the Garden State, New Jersey could just as well be called the Coastal State. With 108 miles of shoreline in Cape May County alone, it's no wonder that southern New Jersey has such a reputation with seafood lovers. The nearly million anglers who love the sport and its delicious rewards keenly know this. This may sound a bit promotional, but due respect to our seafood heritage is long overdue.

To continue our maritime culinary history, southern New Jersey—all of whose counties border on shoreline—has access to a wide variety of both northern and southern fish species. To the surprise of many, trapping for lobster occurs offshore, resulting in top value ranking each year. Formerly lowly regarded squid yields major boatloads harvested for locals for use in gourmet recipes. Conch, usually identified with Caribbean cooking, is caught regularly along the Cape May ocean coast and in the Delaware Bay. Flounder and fluke (known locally as summer flounder) are big sellers at nearby markets. Filling out the dockside iceboxes are swordfish, black sea bass, tuna, whiting, mackerel, porgies, butterfish, monkfish and skate.

Clams are a major shellfish harvest in southern New Jersey along the ocean coast, back bays and sounds. In the last decade, the technology of aquaculture has aided in seeding clam beds for even higher production from the back bays. Tons of ocean quahogs and surf clams dredged by ocean going craft plus hand-worked garveys in the shallow bays tonging hard clams have deeply influenced our culinary traditions. Hardly a diner or restaurant could escape omitting a signature dish of clam chowder as a regular item. Our seafood chapter contains tips for clam cookery as well as an explanation of the different species and fisheries.

Sailing into the Delaware Bay, a large funnel-shaped estuary from the tip of Cape May to Salem County, the lauded eastern oyster harvesting continues as it has for centuries.

Late 19th century photos, now on display at the Port of Call Restaurant in Port Elizabeth, attest to the hundreds of schooners once needed to haul huge quantities of oysters from our waters. Diseases have since decimated an industry that once harvested millions of dollars in oysters. In the late 1950's a parasitic disease called MSX devastated the oyster beds, leaving the future of Delaware Bay oystering in doubt. Those oystermen who once depended on this rich source are now struggling to stay afloat. With the aid of scientific research efforts in culturing and harvesting techniques, catches have slowly increased. It's a complex area needing more explanation for those seeking a full understanding, but is outside the scope of this book.

In a recent commercial venture that shows promise, faster growing, disease resistant triploid oysters are being grown in protected mesh bags on metal racks. These cultured oysters, now marketed to exclusive restaurants, will be available soon to a much wider market. These Cape May Salts have received rave reviews from oyster fanciers as they are salty, as the name implies, plump and, thanks to the racks, grow faster and have excellent marketing qualities. The racks not only keep the oysters off the sandy bottom, they protect them from predators. The resulting oyster sounds perfect for upscale local restaurants serving oysters on the half shell.

In the cold months, multi-story stacks of crab pots are a common sight in the backyards of the watermen along the Delaware Bay. Once the waters warm and the blue crabs emerge from the mud of their winter hibernation, these traps will be set to collect their luscious prey. Usually occurring in May if the weather is so inclined, the watermen haul out up to three hundred or more pots in long rows marked by their individual numbered, colored buoys, much to the dismay of sport fishermen.

In the midst of the season that stretches into October, again with the cooperation of the weather, crabs that are ready to toss off their old shells, called shedders, are set aside for special treatment. Shedders are turned over to soft shell shedding operators for monitoring 24 hours a day. Once they shed, they are vulnerable to cannibalism from other crabs, so they must be separated over to safe holding areas. Premium grades with their full attachment of claws and legs are quickly transported to the large markets in Philadelphia and New York. Down Jersey restaurants eagerly anticipate them, too. Locals, who don't fret if a leg is missing, feast on the downgraded culls at bargain seafood counters in back road crab shacks.

Before the blue crab season begins, the annual shad run draws a keen interest from sportsmen and serious commercial waterman. They lay out their nets to catch the upriver spawning run, much like the Lenni Lenape natives had done before the settlers arrived. These fish contain multiple layers of fine bones, which require the skill of a deft hand to remove. In mid-May, as our waters warm in the Delaware River, other shad continue their spawning runs farther north in New York State and Canada.

Weakfish, also known as sea trout, are popular with sport fishermen and those who are familiar with its delicate meat.

Granted, New Jersey fisheries are not clothed in the mystique that other regions enjoy, but they provide excellent quality and variety of choice to world-wide markets as well as our local seafood merchants.

Although our dairy industry constitutes an important segment of our agricultural economy by providing fresh milk for nearby markets, there hasn't been enough excess milk production to drive producers to create notable cheeses or other products from milk on a large scale. But dairy farmers are looking into this possibility. Nearness to the markets of the Northeast has provided the market shopper with wide varieties of cheeses fueled by the demands of many ethnic groups within our region.

Let us now turn to the work we are presenting to you, the culinary heritage of the southern area of New Jersey I have tried to define as Down Jersey. Revealed through recipes published for the first time ever in one collection, we can share with you the foodways from those who have graciously passed along family treasures, often initially unaware of their worth to the rest of us.

Pulling together all of our cooking lore these past seven years has taken countless "road" days pursuing anything remotely springing from our region. Visiting historical societies, family kitchens, church suppers, upscale restaurants and cozy neighborhood eateries, butchers, and fish retailers, I pursued leads to consider what might be worthy to gather and pass along to you.

If you bear with me through the next few sections covering the recipes themselves, our farm markets, vegetables, and seafood, then you will reach the heart of my work, the treasures of Down Jersey. We cherish our part of the world as a great place to live and, hopefully through this effort, a place where we can better recognize our common, yet distinctive, culinary heritage.

Take the opportunity to spend time with your family or friends at the table while appreciating our local foods. It won't be a waste of time.

About the recipes

The foundation for recipes in this book lies with those prepared by our grandparents and parents, and continues on to where they are currently respected: in area home-style restaurants, and sometimes at delicatessens, sandwich shops and even pub fare. The highest regard will be given to those family recipes so familiar that they are often passed down phrased as, "All you do is…"

While honoring the old ways, and with our increased awareness and knowledge of nutrition, recipes have been adapted reluctantly and cautiously. So, choices of healthy alternatives as well as variations will be suggested.

Our abundance of farm markets offering fresh produce over a long season give us a welcome break from the convenience of purchasing prepared foods. However, where an item's use merits its inclusion, such as canned baked beans or frozen spinach, they will be suggested.

While not formatted by seasons, our recipes will relate to vegetables and cooking according to season. You may have noticed that summer's vegetables have a natural affinity with other summer crops, tomatoes with basil, corn with beans and so on. Winter calls for heartier pairings, like hearty winter soups laden with kielbasa, bacon or root vegetables.

Each recipe has been tested and, above all, had to taste good. It had to show a combined delivery of flavor, texture and appearance that makes it all worth doing again and again. Those that, by their very nature, are more elaborate or time consuming, are those that merit the effort. For example, making a long-simmering mincemeat stuffing may ask for a stint at the stove, but this keeping-quality recipe done in a large batch makes it one to consider doing when time allows.

There are recipes that for so simple a prep, are amazingly good. Others may ask for more ingredients and time. I have come to the conclusion that the genius in cooking is knowing when to stop. As an artist must put down the brush at some eventual point, so must a chef lay down the knife and spoon. As part of that thought, by suggesting ingredients in the variations, not only do I intend to suggest a variety of approaches, but offer the basic recipe that is well enough as it is. One sauce might call for a lengthy list of ingredients, each contributing to the final taste, yet another might call for surprisingly few and shouldn't be tampered with. The heart of cooking is to have a sense of taste to adjust the seasonings for the intended, and to maintain an intensity of attention to details, large and small.

This drawing by the late Turnersville artist, **Al Foster**, shows what might possibly be the **first tractor** used for farming in Salem in 1904.

I cannot over-stress the importance of quality ingredients, including fresh and dried herbs, in the final outcome of your efforts to deliver a dish that represents Down Jersey cooking. A fresh farm-market apple just off the tree without waxing or storage, or a fresh summer sweet corn has no equal. Herbs that bring out the best with their small but powerful additions should be the freshest they can be, fresh or dried. Most containers of dried herbs we purchase hold far more than we can use before they lose their freshness and become stale. It is far better to share a newly bought jar of herbs with family and friends than to sit on it till they detract, rather than add, to your preparation.

It is our hope that you first enjoy a trip to your nearby markets bearing fresh produce, seafood or meats fitting the season. Scout and select the best of the fresh. Then return to seek a selection from *Down Jersey Cooking*. The chosen recipe might be one that your grandparents would have made, or it could be a recipe that is simply Down Jersey.

In 1992, the late Margaret Louise Mints, along with Alex Ogden, published their work, *Man, the Sea and Industry: A History of life on the Deleware Bay from 1492 to 1992.* Traveling from Salem to Cape May they recorded the history of the waterman, mainly oystermen and crabbers, by writing down for us the stories of the hardy seafarers and their boats. As much of the ways of the past have gone by, their book gives us a glimpse of how the working life used to be along the Delaware Bay.

Farm Market Shopping

Seasons and Reasons

The foundation of great cooking calls upon the freshest of quality ingredients before the chef applies his skills and creativity or a home cook scans a cookbook for that must-do recipe. To that end, cooks are encouraged to shop at local markets for the freshest of the best first, that is, let the choice selections of the day at the market drive the menu choices, not the other way around. Not only that, but the forces at the market that drive the highest quality vegetables and fruits in their high season also drive down the prices for the smartest buying opportunities. So, symbolically, we are reminding you of the prime seasons and helpful shopping hints in this section of the book before you delve into the recipes.

Look for this logo for **Jersey Fresh** fruits and vegetables.

Of course weather will push harvest times ahead or behind according to our particular year, though the range usually doesn't go beyond several weeks. Fall crops that can resist light frosts (our average first serious frost date is in late October), however, can extend well into December in mild years.

Don't hesitate to call ahead to your farm marketer. Due to the variability of each season, they understand that you desire to be informed on availability. It's a pity when someone misses the last pick of the season.

I don't suggest that you should ignore or side-step the produce at supermarkets entirely. The science of shipping and handling has vastly improved the quality of produce in the bins, allowing purchases of favorites when a year-round farm market is simply too inconvenient to travel to. Still, by setting our sights on farm markets, we are aiming for the best of the freshest.

On a seemingly odd bit of advice, there is no substitute, even in the smallest of gardens, for growing your favorite vegetables at least once, no matter how few of them you grow. In the process of growing them from seedling to harvest to use, you will learn more about each one's season, ripeness or maturity and prime qualities than from any other source. Just as a seafood fancier learns to select the freshest, you will develop that savvy that helps you at the market to make wiser, timely selections.

Arugula: A quick grower, this peppery green can be found in early spring or fall when cool weather favors its growth. Growth in warm weather renders arugula more bitter. When selecting, favor the smaller, younger growth leaves.

Asparagus: In season from late April to mid-June in southern New Jersey. Early cutting is advanced by faster soil warming so temperature, sun, clouds and rain all have their impact. At the other end of the harvest season, hot weather in June dramatically diminishes field cutting, so early warm-ups will shorten the local season.

Basil: This heat-loving and frost-tender herb will be in season for us from July through to September and early October from fields, and throughout the year from greenhouses, though some greengrocers believe greenhouse basil has less flavor.

Green (Snap) Beans: In season from late June until early October. Bean crops could be harvested a bit later, but the farmer's expense of keeping them free of diseases limits the fresh season for us. Beans are warm season lovers, yet they suffer when our temps stay in the upper 90's for more than a few days. That causes the blossoms to drop, resulting in no bean development until temps moderate. During these exceptionally hot periods, local green beans may be scarce. That's ok, for then the eggplants will thrive.

Beets: Though it gets scant attention, quite a bit is grown in southern New Jersey. The best quality of beets at the market, will be in the fall and winter when they are the sweetest, and that's also when we desire them most for warming winter salads, stews and soups. Do consider using beet leaves for cooking as greens, and the smaller, interior leaves in salads.

Pak Choy (Bok Choy): This Asian cabbage with thick stems and mustardy-tasting leaves is a relative that has become popular with us is in season in the cool of spring and fall. Spring and summer harvest can occur within days for the farmer as it can lose its prime quickly. Fall is their best season for us. Recently, a miniature form, often called Shanghi Bok Choy with green stems, has been at the markets. Pak Choy has a delightful mustardy bite with crunchy lower stems that add texture to dishes.

Broccoli: Broccoli is a cool-season crop, and though it fares well in home gardens for those who start it early, the predominant local farm market season is during our extended fall. Broccoli in the fields will handle light frosts, so check with your greengrocer on availability. Some farmers will extend harvests further by covering the crops with plastic.

Broccoli Rabe: In prime season in late winter and fall. This cousin of broccoli that is delightfully bitter has a narrower prime season as hot weather or other stresses will make it unbearably bitter. Due to the ups and downs of our temps, broccoli rabe will vary, so taste a bit of the stems to determine if it's to your liking. Many recipes rely on blanching in copious amounts of water to reduce its bitterness. Before you start your cooking, take a sample bite to test its sweetness, then proceed to cook accordingly. It has become available year round from other growing regions.

Brussels Sprouts: Not a major crop in New Jersey. You should know that it takes several frosts to bring extremely hardy Brussels sprouts to their sweetest. Avoid those that are harvested in summer months as they will taste cabbagy. Unfortunately, Brussels sprouts have a long shelf life, beyond the freshness they can deliver when harvested and used straight away.

Cabbage: Home gardeners will have crops in early summer, but most of the season's crops from farmers arrive later in the season when the weather is cooler and they have longer shelf life. Fresh cabbage will tolerate light frosts so they will be available through fall, and with storage, it's available year round. Be more careful when buying cabbage in the winter to insure that the cabbage has been stored properly. In other words, it shouldn't smell cabbagy, it should give off a sweet and spicy aroma.

Carrots: Available year round at markets from other growing regions. Though grown by home gardeners and ready for harvesting in the fall—in fact it can be kept in the ground for harvesting all winter—few area farmers grow carrots commercially. Excessively warm soils can impart a turpentine taste, as well as conventional chemical growing methods. We recommend the purchase of organically-grown carrots when available; the extra cost is worth it.

Celery: Though once a major crop in the early days of the last century, New Jersey farmers no longer grow this labor intensive vegetable. Available year round from other regions, mainly Florida and California.

Sweet Corn: Our season has been earlier and earlier, both due to faster-maturing varieties and to soil-warming techniques such as plastic row covers used by farmers. The trade off in getting earlier corn is that the ears are smaller and the flavor is compromised. It pays to be patient. As long as the corn receives sufficient irrigation, hot weather bothers it not at all. Our season should last into late September when the demand drops, not the ability of farmers to extend the season. Due to the numerous new varieties and the introduction of supersweets, we suggest you try an ear or two before buying large quantities.

Collards: A sweeter, more tender kin to kale. Somewhat less hardy to cold, it is also best in the cooler months of the fall. Collards are not generally overwintered, while winter hardy kale suffers minimal damage and recover quickly in the spring.

Cucumbers: As a warm-season crop, cucumbers bear prolifically when the temps warm in July and continue yielding until early September when cool nights halt their growth.

Bear in mind that in southern New Jersey the small cucumbers that we call pickles are seldom waxed (it's done to extend shelf life, all the better for home cooks who rather not peel the skins anyway), so they are great for salads.

Dandelion: Extremely popular from early times with both the Italian, Greek, and German farmers, dandelion is available amazingly early due to its early emergence and soil warming plastics used by local farmers. With the cooperation of favorable weather, expect to see local dandelion as early as March. By the way, the cultivated varieties now grown by farmers are superior to the wild-harvest dandelions.

Eggplants: Another warm season lover, eggplants begin to bear in July and continue into September, though some will hold in the fields into October, weather permitting. There are subtle differences in the numerous varieties now sold, so check with your farm marketer as some are less bitter and some have more tender skins, making them more suitable in certain preps. Prime quality eggplants will give somewhat in the hand and will have a shiny skin.

Endive and Escarole: Though they could be grown in the spring, they are desired as fall crops when the cool weather brings out their best flavor. They're available until October from local farms. Endive is the frilly, toothy type, while escarole is the broad-leafed type from the same family of chicory.

Fennel: Not a significant local crop, somewhat available year round.

Garlic: Grown by gardeners, but not in significant quantities by farmers.

Kale: The ultimate hardy and fully-flavored green, kale is grown for fall harvesting and is available well into the winter months when the quality is supreme. However, harsh winds can sometimes dry the leaves.

Kohlrabi: This underappreciated bulbous vegetable thrives during cool summers and in the colder days of fall. Available from mid-summer through fall, though not grown in significant quantities by local farmers. Very popular with Northern Europeans and Asians. The leaves of kohlrabi are rather good as cooked greens.

Leeks: Extremely hardy to cold and requiring a long season to mature, leeks continue to be available at local farm markets from the fall throughout winter as long as the ground permits harvesting, that is, it hasn't frozen. Late winter also brings in a flush of harvests.

Lettuce: Though area farmers will grow a range of crisphead to Romaine and looseleaf types, Romaine is by far the prominent crop. Looseleaf lettuce acreage has been expanding due to improved heat-tolerant varieties being developed. Romaine and looseleaf types are available from June through to October. Cooler weather delivers higher quality lettuce.

Melons: Cantaloupes and watermelons mature in abundance during August and early September. Their flavor is best when rainfall is scant during the final maturing period. As warm-season crops, the warmer the season, the longer the harvests.

Onions: Not a major crop in New Jersey. Available, of course, year round from many growing regions. Check with your greengrocer for differing levels of sweetness and storage qualities. The rule of thumb is the sweeter the onion, the shorter the storage life.

Green Onions (Scallions or Scullions): Grown locally and available throughout the year.

Parsley: Available from local fields from August through October and November. Very cold tolerant.

Peas: Since they thrive in the cool weather of spring before our heat arrives and they become starchy ever so fast, almost everyone has resorted to using frozen peas. Seabrook Farms, a major processor of peas, contracts with farmers and arranges harvesting in such a way that they are frozen within minutes from the field. A few gardeners, however, manage to grow peas for a spring crop, fewer yet for fall.

Peppers, Sweet: Bear in mind that all peppers initiate growth in some shade of green and mature to red, orange or other colors. Green peppers are available from local fields in July and green and reds are available in August and continue until mid-October.

Peppers, Hot: As the "heat" of hot peppers is influenced by the intensity of sunlight, temperatures and moisture levels in the soils, hot peppers can vary widely in hotness. Warmer temps, bright sunlight and low moisture levels draw out the hottest peppers. That said, more and more New Jersey farmers are growing them and they should be in season from July through to October.

Potatoes, White: Many potato varieties in New Jersey are grown specifically for processing, but some are quite good as "table stock." Check with your greengrocer for varieties that suit you. Available from early July to November, and longer from storage.

Potatoes, Sweet: Available from late September through Christmas and sometimes through to Easter. Southern New Jersey farmers grow a lot of sweet potatoes, some of them are wonderful heirloom varieties not found outside of farm markets. The first dug sweet potatoes are usually not cured and are not for storage, so buy small amounts for immediate use. By November most sweet potatoes available will have been cured, are sweeter tasting and will keep well if kept above 55 degrees with moderate humidity. Though sweetness levels vary greatly at harvest time, it is generally agreed that all will be at their sweetest by Christmas time.

Pumpkins, Edible and Carving: The edible smaller pumpkins will mature earlier in the fields and can be available as early as late July, but light demand keeps them from showing up in the bins. All pumpkins will begin to fill the bins in September and will be offered through and somewhat past Thanksgiving. While the large, carving types are too fibery for cooking use, smaller pie pumpkins have much less fiber, are sweeter and have more edible flesh. As a member of the squash family, pumpkins and squash can be used interchangeably.

Radishes: Best in the cool seasons, especially our fall, but not a major crop locally. Though we often think of radishes as those cute red spicy bulbs, there are many other varieties that come onto the market. Color, size and sharpness vary greatly. Daikon, a Japanese radish, for example, is much sweeter than American standards. In Down Jersey, the immigrant Russian Jewish population has brought about demand for Black Spanish, a large, black-skinned crisp, hot radish that keeps well and is suitable for Russian winter salads.

Radicchio: Once grown as a new venture, local growers for the most part have opted out of this relative in the chicory family due to its low tolerance for our warm weather, which causes it to color poorly and become too bitter.

Rape: Also called Hanover salad and smooth kale, this cousin of kale has a loyal following in the African American communities. It is remarkably hardy as is kale, and lends itself to use in many dishes. By the way, a version of rape happens to be the source of rapeseed oil, marketed as Canola oil.

Spinach: A major crop in southern New Jersey as it will overwinter here four winters out of five, and the spring cutting makes it worthwhile for the farmer. It's available fresh from late September until a hard feeze covers the field, often sometime in December. Spring cuttings happen in late March until early May.

Squash, Winter: There are a number of species of winter squash including pumpkins, which are the ones with a hard skin and store, in varying degrees, much longer than summer squash. By far the most popular winter squash is Butternut, which is available from September through November and beyond if the farmers place them in storage. Check with your farm marketer for the specifics of other worthwhile varieties.

Swiss chard: Able to tolerate heat and cold, Swiss chard is available from July through to October from local fields. It's a great addition to salads, soups and often included in a pot of greens.

Turnips: Though handy year round, production and use occurs more often in the fall with availability from local fields well into November. They bring an earthy flavor to many dishes, especially soups, stews and boiled dinners.

Tomatoes: The interim quality of southern New Jersey greenhouse tomatoes can be found from March through early June, and in lesser quantities throughout the summer. Far less pricey and the queen of our summer fields, summer, field grown and vine ripened Jersey Tomatoes start to appear in late June. Early-maturing field tomatoes may be somewhat compromised in flavor and a bit pricier, but are still far ahead of "gassed" imports. Full production of our tomatoes commences in July with availability till September and October. Plum tomatoes, though are available in July, are more abundant in the fall months when home cooks want them for their canning and freezing.

Zucchini: A summer squash, now also available as yellow-skinned, zucchini will be in season locally from late June until September, perhaps longer if the season remains warm for this heat-loving vegetable. At the market, select the smallest specimens since they are the most tender. Zucchini rarely requires peeling.

Fruits

Apples: Summer eating apples arrive at local markets as early as mid-August, followed by eating and cooking apples, which will be harvested by the first week of October. Jersey apples are exceptionally sweet and juicy as they are not waxed for shipment and they don't undergo long term storage. They should be available until late December.

Blueberries: Available from mid-June to mid-August. Recent new introductions have extended the season somewhat.

Cranberries: Fresh cranberries are available from early September to early November.

Nectarines: The same season as peaches.

Peaches: Weather permitting, the traditional first day of picking is the Fourth of July, and should continue until the first week of September. Many local orchards continue to grow the long-popular white peaches, which are particularly sweet and juicy, but don't travel as well as the yellow-fleshed peaches. Newer varieties of white-flesh peaches are coming in to the market, but I haven't determined their quality compared to the old timers.

Pears: Virtually the same season as apples, starting with Early Summer Barletts and ending with Brown Bosc.

Plums: Virtually the same season as peaches, with Early Asian plums arriving first, followed by European and Italian plums.

Strawberries: The strawberry season begins at the end of May, peaks during June and ends in mid-July. Extreme heat and excess rainfall can have significant impact on the length of the season and the fruit quality. As our farmers are close to major urban markets, they favor the more flavorful, somewhat more tender strawberries not found with trans-continental shipping varieties. Smart shoppers carry coolers in their cars as they travel and shop.

Tomato Cooking Savvy:

Honoring Down Jersey's Famous Summer Vegetable

Though grown in all but the most extreme climates, tomatoes grown in New Jersey are blessed with favorable weather and soil, such that our tomatoes garner praises worldwide. Their rich color and powerful tangy taste ooze with a juiciness that commands premium prices at the markets, and they are worth it.

Doubtful myself of the Jersey tomato's exceptional qualities, I relay this experience, though it is but one test, it convinced me. I had grown a popular Jersey Tomato variety, Ramapo, from seed to seedlings in my hobby greenhouse during early spring. At the seedling stage, I shared those seedlings with my cousin, Maryann Vettese, who lives in Ambler, Pennsylvania, about 50 miles due west of our homesite in Woodbury. At a family get  together later in July, we both brought vine-ripened tomatoes from those same Ramapo seedlings. The difference was immediately apparent. The Ambler grown-where days and nights are cooler and the soil is heavier---were decidedly of a darker, less appetizing color, and the taste proved less desirable as well. Indeed, we are fortunate to have great tasting tomatoes here.

There is more than weather and soil that brought us such good fortune. Thanks to the research and releases from Rutgers University and the skill of local farmers, full advantage was given to the tomato. First, Rutgers released the now well-known Rutgers tomato, then later brought out the Ramapo tomato, destined for a more local audience, but another bright red contributor to the cause. Starting out as field workers, immigrant Italians went on to purchase farms in the then-affordable acreage surrounding the region of Vineland. Combining their native skills in farming and their heritage of tomatoes in cuisine, tomatoes received yet another boost.

The prominence of Jersey tomatoes, both from the farmer's fields as well as home gardens, has greatly influenced our food customs. As with the watermen's use of fresh seafood, when the tomato is out of season it's use declines dramatically. But when they are available locally from late in June through to the end of November, there is no tolerance for anything but a Jersey tomato.

Round, or slicing tomatoes, come to mind when we think of summer tomatoes. They possess the brightest, fullest tomatoey taste with a pleasant balance of sweetness and tartness. Round tomatoes shine when they are served uncooked, as in salads and sandwiches.

When cooked, the instructions for round tomatoes often call for peeling and seed removal. Peeling would be naturally understood, but in the process of removing the seed, the squeezing also rids the tomato of much of its juice. It so happens that the juice is the most acidic portion of the tomato and some cooked recipes strive to lessen its acidity. You might also note that round tomatoes with a high portion of liquid between the locules, or walls, are the least tasty. Most early-maturing tomatoes share this trait.

Plum tomatoes go by a number of aliases: plum refers to their size, paste refers to their frequent use in sauces, and pear comes about from their bulbous base like a pear, at least with the heirloom varieties. In any case, they differ not only in their smaller size, but in that plum tomatoes have a higher content of solids desirable for sauces and are less tart, another benefit for use in cookery. Because of their sturdiness, plums are choice for make-ahead salads where they undergo a madman's tossing, and in salsas where they keep their hold up to the tossing and marinating. You might call them the all-purpose potatoes of the tomato set.

Cherry tomatoes in a way are the newest kid on the block from the marketing standpoint. They have been around a long time as cherry tomatoes, but now are appearing in smaller sizes, some so small that they have picked up the name grape tomatoes. Whereas the long-popular cherry tomatoes about the size of walnuts haven't rated highly with most fanciers, they have found a home in restaurant salads, and more recently, in plate presentations by creative chefs. Slight improvements in their flavor has come about, but a recent introduction of a hybrid Grape Tomato has brought ecstatic raves from diners and therefore raising the bar. Expect to see more improvements all along this diminutive class of tomatoes. I'll go so far as to forecast these little delectables being commonplace in fruit compotes. Unless your small tomatoes are single-bite size, do your guests a favor, cut them in half.

Fresh Market Season In March, greenhouse-grown tomatoes begin to appear at local markets, both those grown hydroponically, rooted in water instead of soil, and the soil-grown. Most assuredly they are not equal to the summer, field-grown

tomatoes, but for some they ease suffering from the late fall and winter abstinence. Surely, they are preferable to the green-picked, hard, artificially gas-ripened tomatoes from California. Because they are pricey, locals use greenhouse tomatoes sparingly, such as the center treat in a green salad. Depending on cooperating weather, the first tomatoes appear at farmstands in late June. Patience, however, rewards you with lower prices. From the practice of canning in September when the kids are back in school, plum tomatoes are more plentiful later in the season. Weather again decides when the season shuts down, usually in late October. But, bear in mind that when the night temperatures head down into the mid 40's, the major tomato flavor component is lost.

If you must know, it's (Z)-3-dexenal. That's why summer tomatoes that haven't been so harmed, are mentioned as the best of the best.

Selection at the Market As far as greengrocers go, *thumb* is a bad word. Picking up every tomato for a thumb squeeze has to leave each tomato the worse for it. Instead, after looking at the tomato of your choice, grasp the whole tomato and gently feel it for firmness and lack of soft spots. More fortunate are those who trust their greengrocer to select the best. When purchasing more than a few, consider a mix of those fully ripe and ready to eat and those which will mature in a few days or more. If they feel cold, they may have been stored in a chilled area, a sure sign they won't be at their flavor peak. Bear in mind, too, that once a tomato has begun to show color on the vine, there is little flavor improvement after that, although the ripening continues. It's when picked green for long distance shipment and forced into a pinkness with ethylene gas that they disappoint us with minimal flavor.

Tomato Storage: From the moment you make the selection, handle them gingerly as they bruise easily, and that shortens their shelf life. As you already know, cold storage harms their flavor, so treat them as you would bananas; keep them out of the refrigerator. Storage around 50 degrees F. is ideal, so aim for that. Once they are stressed by low temperature at 45 degrees F. or less, chill injury occurs; they don't ripen after that. They simply rot instead. At the other temperature range, avoid a sunny location where they would ripen too quickly. It's preferable to wash tomatoes immediately before use as any lingering surface moisture increases chances of spoilage before use.

Cooking with Tomatoes: First, become aware of what you have at hand. As tomatoes ripen, they lower in acidity and thus the sugars become more assertive. Ripe tomatoes may call for less sugar adjustments at the final taste test. Whereas plum tomatoes have the firmness for fried tomatoes and other dishes where sturdiness is a plus, barely pink tomatoes can be used as well, but with a touch of sugar to compensate for their higher acidity.

A sharp knife, or better yet, a serrated knife, permits slicing and dicing of the tomato with a minimum of liquid loss and crushing of the pulp.

Pay heed to a recipe's call for ripe tomatoes, especially with sauces. Sugar can balance the tartness of an unripe tomato, but it's still preferable to start with natural sweetness.

The most common method to peel a tomato is to cut an "x" opposite the stem end and place them in boiling water for about a minute. When cool enough to handle, the skin slips off easily.

Growing Tomatoes in the Home Garden

Tomatoes are the universal favorite of home gardeners because they are productive through most of the summer for fresh and canning use, and no tomato tastes as good as the one you grew yourself. They can be allowed to sprawl on the ground, or you can grow them on a wire trellis or stake supports that fit into small locations.

Normally ground tomatoes yield 8 to 15 pounds per plant, whereas staked tomatoes normally average seven pounds per plant. This information can be misleading since you can stake more plants in a given area than if they were grown on the ground. So you increase the overall yield. You also have a better chance of growing higher quality tomatoes on stakes than you do in the sprawling plants.

If you plan to prune and stake plants, make certain varieties are not a "determinate" type or they will stop growing when you pinch out the side shoots. Indeterminate varieties, the ones that keep growing and bearing fruit all season, are the ones to stake. If you grow determinate varieties, plant a range of early, mid-season and late varieties. Seeds should have been started by mid-April.

Normally, May 10 is the frost-free date in southern New Jersey. If cold nights threaten, cover them overnight with wooden baskets or boxes to protect them.

For ground culture, they should have at least 10 to 12 sq. ft of space per plant. If staking or wire trellissing, space 16 to 18 inches apart in rows 3 to 4 feet apart.

A liquid fertilizer can be applied at planting to jump-start them. You can use high phosphorous houseplant fertilizer mixed according to directions. Tomato feeder roots develop close to the soil surface. Never cultivate too deeply near the plant. After the roots start spreading out, hoeing the soil more than one inch deep can be injurious.

For "ground culture" plants, feed when the first cluster blooms and repeat every three to four weeks until early September. Use three cupfuls of the liquid starter solution mix per plant at each feeding or use one pound 10-6-4 per 100 square feet. For staked tomatoes, use the same rate of fertilizer on a 2 to 3 week schedule.

Just before the first fruits set, mulch around the plants with salt hay, straw, or other weed-free natural mulch to a depth of 4 to 6 inches. Mulching prevents weeds, conserves moisture, and keeps the soil cooler for better root growth. If used on ground tomatoes, mulch will also keep the fruit off the ground to minimize rot.

Black plastic, newspaper, and other artificial mulch can also be used but they are not as effective in absorbing moisture or allowing you to fertilize effectively, unless you couple mulch with trickle irrigation.

Tomatoes need a constant supply of moisture. When rains are not adequate, and especially if you don't mulch, a soaking of five to six inches of soil depth is important every 5 to 7 days. This is important for staked tomatoes in particular. Under mulch, watering intervals can be lengthened.

Wait until the tomatoes are nearly full ripe before picking them for home use.

—Adapted from an article by Charlene H. Costaris,
Atlantic County Agricultural Agent

Chapter 1
Soups Grandma Might Have Made

If there is a soup that belongs in Down Jersey, it would be clam chowder. We highlight first a chowder from a restaurant in Dennis Township that has long been closed, but the style is alive in the originating family. This version is neither tomato or cream based, it's simply clam based.

We present a few more versions that bring together both corn and clams, then move on to asparagus soup. From the Polish immigrants we have a borscht that adopts our beloved pole lima bean. From the Japanese in Seabrook we have miso, then we move to a sauerkraut soup from an Estonian contributor, also from Bridgeton near Seabrook, and more.

Where soups once brought sustenance to the family tables of immigrants low on the economic ladder, we now turn to their nourishing warmth and practicality. Though soups may ask for a stint at the stove, tending to them requires little more that a watchful eye and a stir. What's more, soups are eminently doable in large batches for freezing.

Among the dishes one could prepare, soups lend themselves to easy changes from the original recipe. Tasting as you go along, indulge in adding ingredients that you or your family favor or that inspiration simply drives you to do. Usually though, it's advisable to follow a recipe the first time according to script.

A few general guidelines are in order to help you master the craft of soup making. First, try to use low-salt ingredients if you can. Broths, butter and the like will add salt whether you desire it or not. You lose control of the amount of saltiness that suits you, or the amount that your doctor advises. Check the freshness and taste of every ingredient. Even if the ingredient is primary, it will ruin your efforts if the vegetable, meat, and commonly, your spices, have taken on off-odors from being on the shelf too long. Also, bear in mind that in a large soup pot there is considerable residual heat after you turn off the heat source. For example, in the case of spinach with oysters, the spinach should be stirred a few moments after the heat is turned off in order to keep the spinach's firmness.

We would all lose the opportunity to bring more soups to the table if we on relied on recipes alone. When you consider that our first greens, dandelions, start in March and continue with a parade of other vegetables through to winter when temperatures dip into the teens, we have a lot at hand. Take that as an opportunity to add any of them to a soup stock and you have a fresh, vibrant greens soup to savor. The tenderest are not even cooked. They are added after the soup stock has been brought to a light simmer. The heat source is then turned off: the tender greens will finish "cooking" in the hot stock.

Soups..... 31

Springtime Asparagus Soup

Serves eight to ten

Always welcome in spring, asparagus soup can also be frozen for a light, first-course soup enjoyed into the summer months. Our farm production is off from earlier highs in the 1970's, but we still have hundreds of acres of asparagus grown by local farmers. If you are lucky enough to live near a farm marketer that grows it, ask for the tough ends that have been trimmed off. Too fibery for the soup itself, they are great for soup stock.

The stock:

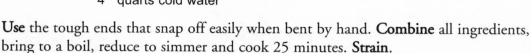

2	pounds asparagus ends, cleaned, cut in 1-inch pieces
2	medium onions or equivalent of leeks
2	bay leaves
2	carrots, peeled and chopped
1	teaspoon salt
4	quarts cold water

Use the tough ends that snap off easily when bent by hand. **Combine** all ingredients, bring to a boil, reduce to simmer and cook 25 minutes. **Strain.**

The soup:

2	pounds asparagus, tips cut off and set aside
4	tablespoons butter
2	medium onions, or leeks, diced
1	teaspoon salt
2	tablespoons parsley, chopped
	Approximately 4 quarts of stock
2	cups cooked rice
	Freshly ground black pepper
3	eggs beaten with 1 tablespoon vegetable oil
	Parmesan or Romano cheese for garnish

Cut remaining spears into 1/2-inch pieces. **Melt** the butter in a soup pot, add onions; cook for 2-3 minutes until clear, stirring occasionally. **Add** asparagus pieces, salt and parsley. **Pour** in stock and cooked rice, bring to a boil and reduce to simmer. **Cook** until asparagus is tender, about 5 minutes. **While** the soup is simmering, slowly pour in beaten eggs while stirring at the same time. **Add** reserved asparagus tips and simmer for 3 minutes more. **Add** Parmesan cheese and check for salt. **Add** black pepper and serve. **Variations:** For a smoother blended soup, after the asparagus pieces are cooked tender, either insert an immersion blender to puree or allow to cool somewhat and puree in a blender. Also, instead of rice, or in addition to, pour in about 1/2 cup of heavy cream to thicken the soup. **Note:** The residual heat in the soup will likely dull the asparagus to an olive green. For a brighter garnished soup, quickly blanch the tips separately in boiling water for a minute, then scoop out into a bowl of iced water to stop further cooking.

Laird Family Black Bean Soup

Serves eight

This Laird family recipe dating back to the 1700's was served in 1980 at the bicentennial celebration dinner for Laird's Applejack, the "Oldest native spirit beverage in the United States." The recipe is excerpted from Laird's Applejack Cookbook, "AppleJack: The Spirit of America."

1   pound dry black beans, picked over
2   quarts water
1   large onion, sliced
3   green peppers, diced
2   cloves garlic
1/2 cup extra-virgin olive oil
1/4 ham bone, or 1/4 pound ham, diced
2   bay leaves
1   ounce white bacon or fatback
1   teaspoon salt
1/2 cup vinegar
1/2 cup Laird's AppleJack

The evolution of the Laird's AppleJack Bottle

Wash beans thoroughly and soak overnight in water, or add to a pot with water to cover, bring to a boil, turn off heat and set aside for one hour. **In** 4-quart soup pot, sauté onion, green pepper and garlic in olive oil. **Combine** all ingredients except vinegar and AppleJack. **Simmer,** stirring occasionally, until beans are tender and liquid is of thick consistency, about 1-1/2 hours.

Add vinegar and applejack; simmer for 10 minutes more, stirring occasionally.

Toad-In-a-Hole

1 cup flour
½ teaspoon salt
1 teaspoon Rumford
    Baking Powder

1 egg
1 cup milk
6 sausages
2 tablespoons drippings
    or bacon fat

Sift together the flour, salt and baking powder into a bowl, make a hollow in the center, break the egg into this and add half the milk.   Mix and beat to a smooth batter, adding the remaining milk gradually.

Parboil the sausages, skin and split them, then place in a roasting pan in which the drippings have been melted and heated.   Pour the batter over them and bake in a moderate oven—350-375° F.—about half an hour.   Cut into squares for serving and serve plain or with brown gravy or tomato sauce.

The **Rumford Chemical Works** of Rhode Island, manufacturers of baking powder, published over 50 cookbooks in the early half of the 1900's. In one if them, we have a scanned copy of a recipe that appeared in The Rumford Complete Cookbook. Their books were so popular that no doubt Down Jersey cooks relied on their recipes.

Polish Country Borscht

Serves six to eight

Immigrants from the colder northern regions of Eastern Europe and Russia are fond of their local variations on beet soup, a warm, tangy soup welcome in the winter months.

Carrying forward their customary use of beets that thrived in colder climates, local Polish cooks soon adopted and added the use of our warm-season pole lima beans. Although a summer crop, lima beans freeze and dry well. If you can't get local pole limas, use frozen beans, which will likely be bush lima beans, but understand that they are not the same.

The key to this soup is the ham used for the stock. The first choice would be the cooking water from a country ham, next would be sautéed cubes of country ham itself. Smoked pork bones would be too strong flavored for this traditional soup.

> 2   red beets
> 2   tablespoons butter
> 1   medium onion, diced
> Salt and pepper to taste
> 5   cups ham stock, or
>   5 cups water and 1/2 pound diced country ham
> 2   cups fresh lima beans, pole beans preferred
> 3   medium boiling potatoes, peeled, 1/2-inch cubed
> 3   tablespoons sugar
> 3   tablespoons white vinegar
> Sour cream for serving

Boil the beets in water until tender, about 25 to 30 minutes. Remove, and when cool enough to handle, peel the skin and dice. Set aside.

In a 6-quart soup pot over medium heat, add the butter and sauté the onions, and, if using, optional ham; cook until onions are soft.

Add water or stock, potatoes, and lima beans.

Add salt and pepper to taste, being mindful of the saltiness of the ham.

Bring to a boil; reduce to simmer and cook until beans and potatoes are tender, about 15 minutes.

Add set aside beets, sugar and vinegar; give a stir and adjust seasonings.

Serve with a dollop of sour cream in each bowl.

Variations: Shredded cabbage and diced carrots are common additions, as is a pinch of allspice for more seasoning zip. Those whose babci (grandma) served this Eastern European mainstay might want to increase the sugar and vinegar to 1/4 cup each for a more assertive sweet and sour borscht.

Creamed Corn and Chicken Soup
(or, Corn and Crab Soup)

Serves six to eight

Historically speaking, corn arrived relatively recently into Asian cooking. Since its introduction, though, Asian cooks have created wonderful adaptations with corn into their cuisine, including this soup. In Down Jersey, there is a bonus for us. Our region's corn harvest coincides with our blue crab season, and what a match they are. The basic recipe calls for chicken, but crabmeat would be a welcome alternative. In that case, omit the marinating process that would have been done for the chicken.

For the budget minded, consider crab claw meat instead of jumbo lump or lump. Claw meat, although darker and coarser texture, is sweet and full of flavor.

Marinade:
2   tablespoons of cornstarch and 1 teaspoon sherry,
      or dry white wine , and 1 tablespoon soy sauce
Soup:
16   ounces creamy corn, uncooked
6   cups chicken stock
1   chicken breast, uncooked, or 1/2 pound crabmeat,
      picked over
1   egg, beaten with 1 tablespoon of vegetable oil
1/4 cup green onions, chopped
1/4 cup cornstarch mixed with 1/2 cup water

Finely chop chicken breast; marinate 20 minutes. Save skin and bone for stock. **Bring** chicken stock to a boil. Add creamed corn, reduce to simmer; cook for 1 minute. **Stir** in chopped chicken or crabmeat; cook 3 minutes more, but if using crabmeat, it only needs warming because it has been steamed. **Give** the cornstarch and water mixture one last stir, and stir into soup to thicken. **As soup** returns to a simmer, stir in egg in a circular motion to create ribbons of egg. **Simmer** for 1 minute more. **Add** the green onions, adjust for salt, and serve hot.

Steamed Crabmeat or Pasteurized?

Understanding which is which can be confusing, and can make quite a difference. In order to be picked from the shell, crabs must be **steamed,** which also helps to preserve the meat for a short time as it is highly perishable. Traditionally sold in plastic tubs with a removable lid, the freshest and best grades are usually sold steamed. Don't ever hesitate—asking permission, of course—to lift the lid to check for a fresh aroma. Also, if there appears to be water in the base of the container, it probably was frozen, not a good practice for a product priced and sold as fresh.

Besides steamed crabmeat, it is also sold **pasteurized,** which is crabmeat further heated at a precise higher temperature and time for longer keeping. Usually sold in cans, some brands pack it in sealed tubs that appear to be the steamed version. Either way, pasteurized crabmeat places the burden of trust on the buyer as it cannot be checked for freshness. Brands of pasteurized crabmeat often list use-by dates of up to six months, but unless the packer's code is known, who knows when it is packed? But since pasteurized crabmeat may be up to half the price of steamed, do consider it at times, but rely on a trusted fish purveyor, and one that has fast turnover. Once again, read the label.

Virginia Dare Clam Chowder

Serves four to six

From the late 1920's to the early 1940's, a small restaurant named Virginia Dare situated on Delsea Drive near Dennis Creek, earned a reputation for its clam chowder. Although the restaurant is a distant memory for Robert Whittick, son of the founders, he still enjoys preparing this family heirloom. In true down-by-the-bay fashion, Whittick shuns use of canned clams, or clams shucked at fish markets. "I'd rather shuck my own. In that way I am sure that I will have fresh clam juice to enrich the chowder." Note that, although the Whittick recipe doesn't call for Jersey red tomatoes, nonetheless it does call for a scant 4 tablespoons of milk, so it is neither a Manhattan nor New England style of clam chowder, either. It's downright Down Jersey.

1   teaspoon cornstarch, mixed with
     4 tablespoons milk
1   dozen chowder clams, well scrubbed
4-5 medium potatoes, 1/4-inch cubed, red
     preferred
1/4 small onion, diced fine
2   celery stalks, diced fine
Fresh ground pepper to taste
Old Trenton Oyster Crackers, optional

Mix the cornstarch and milk until dissolved. **Set** aside. **Shuck** clams over a container to catch released clam juices. **Carefully** remove clam meat from its shell, checking for any clinging shell fragments; place in a food processor. **Pulse** until clam meat is coarsely puréed. **If not using** a food processor, lift and squeeze the clam meat free of some of its juices and dice meat with a knife. "Decant" the juice by slowly pouring the juice into another container, stopping before the grit pours. Allow the grit to settle a few minutes; repeat the process. **Place** potatoes, onions and celery in a 4-quart soup pot; add just enough water to cover. **Bring** to a boil, reduce to simmer; cook until potatoes are almost tender. **Add** the clams and 1/2 of their juice; cook 3 more minutes. **At that time**, the potatoes should be fork-tender. **Add** remaining clam juice to the potatoes only if stock isn't too salty. **Stir** in the cornstarch and milk mixture. **Add** desired amount of fresh ground pepper; cook for one minute more. **Serve** warm with Trenton Oyster Crackers.

> **Clam shucking:** Holding the clam over a bowl to catch the juices, set it in the palm of your left hand, the hinge end with its indention towards you. Hold the clam knife in your right hand, its blade poised between the shells at the opposite end, and guided by the fingers of your left hand, force the blade between the shells, then cut around under the top shell to release the muscle. Run the blade under the body of the clam to release and remove it. If that doesn't work, set the clams in the freezer for 20 minutes to relax the muscles.

Corn and Clam Soup

Serves four to six

While my research has not uncovered Native American Lenni Lenape use of corn and clams together in a soup, it is highly likely that they did. Clams, of course, are abundant along our seacoast and we know the Lenape used them. Though we have scant archeological evidence of the Lenape as cultivators of corn here in southern New Jersey, the Lenape did bring a variety, "Delaware Blue Corn," with them during the trail of tears to Oklahoma. Of course, today's sweet corn isn't the corn of the Lenape.

If using canned clams, this soup is a quickie to prepare. Most of us who dig for clams, however, have a supply of frozen clams, for they freeze well. Paprika or curry seasoning suits corn and clams, but omit or reduce if they are not your choice. Notice that no salt is added, because salty clams take care of that.

```
2    tablespoons vegetable oil
1    small onion, diced
Pepper to taste, no added salt
1    teaspoon paprika or curry, if desired
2    cups home-frozen corn, or store package
         equivalent
7    cups of water if using fresh clams with its
         clam juice or, with use of canned clams,
         1 (14-ounce) can chicken broth, plus
         6 cups water
2    tablespoons rice or cider vinegar
6-8  chowder clams, or 2 (6.5-ounce) cans
         minced clams, sea clams (surf) clams
         preferred
1/4 cup parsley, chopped
```

If using live clams, clean carefully, shuck and mince the meat, reserving the clam juice in a separate bowl.

In a 4-quart soup pot, sauté onions in oil until golden. Add pepper to taste, plus paprika or curry, if desired. **Stir** in corn to coat, and add broth or clam juice, and water. **Bring** to a boil. **Reduce** to simmer and cook for three minutes for fresh or home frozen corn, or according to package instructions. Fresh clams are added at the last 3 minutes to avoid toughness; canned clams are added at any time during simmering because they are already tender from processing.

Add parsley, stir and serve.

Variations: For those preferring a thicker broth, you may stir in 1 to 2 tablespoons of flour with the onions. Cooked lima beans in small quantities, about a cup, can be added as well.

Note: Surely, our Lenni Lenape would not have used curry or paprika, but they would have used a wide number of native herbs and spices foraged from the wild.

Curried Dried Corn and Clam Soup

Serves four to six

I was asked by Noel Margerum from Margerum's Old Fashioned Corner at the Reading Terminal Market (now closed) in Philadelphia to prepare a soup using local ingredients along with dried corn. In soups, dried corn delivers a nice bite and doesn't intrude with a cloying taste. Curry, from the colonial period when spices came up from the Caribbean in sailing ships, has a history of use in our region, as of course, Jersey shore clams. In this case, canned clams are used in the interest of convenience, but by all means choose fresh shucked and minced clams if you can.

```
1    small onion, diced
1    garlic clove, minced
1    teaspoon curry, adjust as desired
1    (14.5-ounce) can chicken broth, plus 4 cups water
1    tablespoon cider or white wine vinegar
1/2  cup dried corn, or 1-1/2 cup fresh
 2   (6-ounce) cans chopped clams
1/4  cup fresh, chopped parsley, or 2 tablespoons dried
```

In a 3 or 4-quart soup pot, sauté onions until clear, then add the garlic and curry, cooking for about one more minute, stirring occasionally.

Add the chicken broth, 4 cups of water, vinegar, and dried corn.

Bring to a boil, lower heat to a simmer, and cook for 30 minutes, 10 minutes if using fresh corn.

Add clams, can liquid, and parsley. Stir and simmer for 3 minutes and serve.

Cook's Comment: How do you keep clams from getting chewy? Well, clams, like their mollusk, squid and conch brethren, are cooked either a quick 2 or 3 minutes, or are slowly cooked in moist heat for 30 to 45 minutes, such as in stews or chowders.

Canned clams, due to the heat required for sterilization, are already tenderized, so they can be added at any time during the cooking. Fresh, however, should be cooked for at least 30 minutes, or added during the last 2 minutes.

Chowder clams are tougher than the smaller clams, but they deliver more taste and more meat per clam, so chowder lovers prefer them. Chopping the chowder clam meat and simmering until tender takes care of any possible chewyness.

Escarole Soup
(Italian Wedding Soup)

Serves six to eight

While the author hasn't identified this extremely popular Italian soup as to its native region, there is no doubt it was famously popular in the town of Paulsboro. Escarole, and its frilly cousin, endive, are both hardy chicories that will hold up in home gardens and local farm fields well into November, and sometimes with weather permitting, until December. The fall season also happens to be when the best chicken stock was possible from full-flavored old stewing hens.

For special occasions, the extra treat of including tiny meatballs or chicken will be worthwhile. Then it's worthy of being called Italian Wedding Soup.

1   head escarole
2   tablespoons olive oil or butter
1   medium onion, diced
1   clove garlic, minced
Salt and pepper to taste
3   cups homemade (preferred) chicken broth, plus 5
       cups water
1/2 cup long or short grained rice
Parmesan or Romano cheese for grating
Optional: 1/2 pound small meatballs and or 1/2 pound
       of shredded chicken

Cut away the butt end of the escarole head and any yellowing or browned leaves. **Wash** thoroughly in a deep pot filled with tepid water. **Repeat** for a second time. **Drain,** cut escarole into 1/2-inch strips and set aside. **In a soup pot,** heat oil or butter over medium low heat; sauté onions until golden. **Add** garlic; sauté 1 minute more. **Add** escarole, salt and pepper, and toss to coat with oil. **Add** stock and water, plus rice and the tiny meatballs and or shredded chicken, if using. **Give** the pot a good stir. **Bring** to a boil, reduce to simmer, stir, and cook for 18 minutes. **Adjust** seasonings and serve with Parmesan or Romano cheese for sprinkling.

Escarole soup meatballs:

1/2 pound ground beef, or butcher
       mix of beef, pork and veal
1   egg, beaten
1/2 teaspoon salt
1/2 cup bread crumbs, moistened
1   clove garlic, minced
2 Tablespoons grated parmesan,
or slightly less Romano cheese

Mix all ingredients. **Pinch** an amount sufficient to make a meatball about the size of a marble (3/4-inch round) by rolling in the palms of your hand. You may want to sauté a sample meatball or two to adjust seasonings, perhaps a bit more salt than the saltiness of the cheese. **Bake** in a 375- degree F. oven for 15 minutes, shaking the pan occasionally, or skip if time is short.

Lima Bean Soup

Serves eight

Our uniquely favorable growing weather for pole and bush lima beans has gardeners and farm marketers growing more of them than any surrounding region. The State of Delaware, though, comes in at a close second in production. It's no wonder then that the abundance has taken them into many heirloom Down Jersey dishes. Dr. Frank De Maio has graciously passed along this recipe that he received from Terri Reale-Trongone. Terri said this recipe reminds her of the old days when her mother's native Napoleatan cooking would fill the house with appetizing odors when she came home from school. According to Dr. De Maio, the ingredients given makes about four quarts, enough to feed 8 normal people or 4 Napoletani.

> 1   pound of dry lima beans, washed
> 1   large ham bone, 1 ham hock, or 1/2 pound of cured
>   bacon
> 3   medium all-purpose potatoes, peeled, cut into 3/8"
>   cubes
> 1   chopped onion
> 1/2 cup celery, diced
> 2   cloves garlic, minced
> Salt and pepper to taste

In a 6 to 8-quart soup pot, add the dry lima beans and cover with water.

Bring to a boil and cook for two minutes.

Remove from the heat and set aside for two hours.

Save the liquid, adding enough water to measure five quarts.

Return the beans to the kettle, add the five quarts of stock and ham bone; bring to a boil.

Reduce to a simmer and cook until tender when tested with a fork, about 2 hours.

Add the remaining ingredients, lightly salt and pepper; simmer for one hour more.

Remove the ham bone, and when sufficiently cool to handle, pick off the meat, dice and return to the soup kettle.

Check for salt and pepper adjustment, and serve.

Author's note: Anyone who has ever grown pole lima beans in a home garden admits to skipping at picking time more than a few pick-ready beans. They love to hide in among the poles and strings, so they are easy to miss. That's ok, for they go on to mature on the vine, become dry in their pods and then are picked, shucked and stored as a dried bean. Dried limas are super for soups like this one.

Miso Soup

Serves two

What we may see as an essentially instant soup of intriguing flavor, to the Japanese in and around Bridgeton, miso soup has been a mainstay in their diet. This recipe from my friend Bonnie Schaffer, is rich and robust in flavor. Miso, a paste made from fermented soy beans, rice or barley and salt, forms the basis for the soup, along with the dashi. As such, it should not be heated more than is needed to warm the broth, lest it lose its flavor. Although the Japanese have found miso in nearby markets in Bridgeton, we can now expect to find it at many common and upscale markets throughout Down Jersey.

    3   cups instant dashi stock package mix, or soup
            stock, see note
    5   tablespoons white miso
    1/4 tofu cake, cut into small cubes
    2   tablespoons chopped scallions

In a saucepan over medium heat, add the dashi stock.

When the dashi is heated through, add the miso, stir to melt and heat just to boiling.

Add the tofu and green onions and taste for adjustment and serve. If a stronger flavor is desired, add additional dashi powder a little at a time because the taste should be subtle. **Likewise**, add the miso for added flavor a tablespoon at a time.

Variations for taste and color: Kamaboko, Japanese fish cakes, sliced thin, may be added at the last minute since they are already cooked and only need warming. Chopped N apa, an Asian cabbage with its mild flavor, can be added with only minimal blanching. Thinly sliced carrots, if desired, would be tossed in at the beginning. One tablespoon of soy sauce, preferably Japanese soy, will deepen the flavor and the color.

Note: Instant dashi, known as dashi-no-moto, is a Japanese soup stock sold in packages that mainly has dried bonito flakes and kelp; it simply requires addition of water. Generally, 2 teaspoons are used for three cups of stock. The dry mix is added to water brought to a boil, and the dashi is stirred in.

The long, thin **Asian cucumbers**, shown here, are much crisper and sweeter than common types, and they grow well in Down Jersey.

Estonian Sauerkraut & Barley Soup

Serves eight to ten

Eve Trume, a WWII refugee who came to America to live in Seabrook when she was eight years old, still cooks the dishes of her Estonian homeland. This sauerkraut soup is one she would like us all to know as it represents the use of meat and vegetables used in Estonia. Though the usual meat flavoring comes from pork neck bones, Trume says that all-beef hot dogs can be substituted as an agreeable alternative.

1-1/2	pounds of pork neck bones, or country-style spareribs
1	teaspoon each of salt and pepper
2/3	cup barley
1	carrot, diced
1	small cabbage, shredded
1	medium onion, diced
1	teaspoon caraway seeds
1	(16-ounce) can or package of sauerkraut

Place the neck bones in a 8 to 10-quart soup pot with water to cover; bring to a boil for 2 minutes. **Remove** surface scum; add 4 quarts of water, salt, pepper, barley and carrot. **Bring** to a boil, reduce to simmer; cook for 1-1/2 to 2 hours until the neck bone meat is tender when tested with a fork. **Remove** scum as more surfaces. **Remove** meat and set aside.

Add cabbage, onion, caraway and boil for 20 minutes.

Drain the sauerkraut liquid from the can and add to the soup and cook for 5 minutes more.

The pork meat, which should now be cool enough to handle, can be picked from the bones and added back to the soup.

Adjust for seasonings and serve. Bear in mind that sauerkraut will be salty to varying degrees depending on the brand. Eve Trume highly recommends that this soup be served with a quality rye bread, preferably homemade.

Buying cabbage at the market: Unless you are buying cabbage at a farm market where it is either locally grown or has been personally selected from wholesalers by the farmer, be more cautious. Perhaps because cabbage stores well and keeps its fresh look for a long period—it's invaluable distinction to earlier generations—it is often sold out of storage far past its prime for eating. Select cabbage at the market that has a fresh, spicy aroma (not cabbagy) and sort of squeaks when held and twisted tightly.

Snapper Soup

In pursuit of a snapper soup recipe, I learned that it's virtually impossible and impractical to make it at home. That's sad considering how esteemed this Down Jersey specialty is revered. Unless someone in the family continues to "poke" for the snappers as they hunker down in the mud along our creeks, the only recourse is to find them at the wholesalers. There, the snapper turtles weigh a minimum of 6 or 7 pounds and are priced at $4 to $5 a pound. Not only that, but it's almost a two-day process. No wonder that we all relish the treat of finding fresh-made snapper soup at restaurants from the few that make it fresh, and not from canned soup.

In that regard, I have taken the stories of two Down Jerseyans for you to read and muse with pleasure. Maybe the few lucky ones out there might have the wherewithal to make their own.

At Gloucester City's O'Donnell's Restaurant, which rates as an institution after having served millions since its opening in 1922, Chef Dannis Ekimaglou carries on thire traditions, one of which is their made-from-scratch snapper soup made in 15-gallon batches. Here is his method as graciously relayed to me:

Place onions and their skins (for color) along with chopped celery, carrots and tomatoes and, of course, the snappers in whole (they were gutted and cleaned at the wholesaler's). Add in 2 or 3 cinnamon sticks and 10-15 whole cloves. This 15-gallon pot filled with water is brought to a boil, reduced to a simmer and cooked for 5 hours. The snappers are removed and set aside.

In another large pot, Dannis melts 4 pounds of margarine and an equal amount of flour to make a roux. This is stirred and cooked for 10 to 15 minutes, then a can of tomato puree and 6 ounces of beef base (no salt is added as the beef base is sufficiently salty) is added and mixed in.

Back at the first pot, the whole pot is strained of its vegetables and the roux is then mixed in with the stock. A gallon of sherry is added along with several heaps of white pepper. While that is simmering, Dannis hand picks the snapper meat away from the bones and fat (most of it is dark meat), chops it and returns the meat to the main pot that is then simmered for 2 hours more. Then, it's done!

Dannis suggests adding chopped boiled eggs directly to the soup bowl for a special touch. He also recommends use of a double boiler when re-heating for a gentler heating.

Elnora Gardenhire from Pine Hollow near Newfield, on the other hand, recalled her father's famous snapper soups. Regretfully, she does not have the recipe, yet she recounts this remembrance:

My father was an ordained minister who worked at the Pennsylvania Railroad Seashore Lines in the 1950's. At 5' 7", he became quite muscular as he labored to lay tracks. Along the tracks, he would see and catch the snapper turtles. We remember seeing them in the backyard where he would keep them until they were killed. Having learned to cook when he was inducted into the Civilian Conservation Corps (CCC) in the late 1930's, my father knew how to make snapper soup. He would sell bowls of it to fellow workers for 10 cents a bowl. When he made it for us eight kids, it fed the whole family.

Sweet Potato Soup

Serves four to six

The requirement of sweet potatoes for a long, warm growing season has found them in their practical northern commercial limits here in southern New Jersey, though they can be grown farther north by gardeners. Our favorable climate and soil for growing sweet potatoes and the influence from southern immigration to Down Jersey has kept us stuck on sweet potatoes, which includes heirloom varieties. It would be easy to specify an heirloom variety such as Nancy Hall with its maple syrup like taste, but that might deter someone from trying this soup. Do call ahead to your sweet potato grower or farm marketer to secure your order for one of their heirloom varieties.

2	slices bacon
1	medium onion, diced
1	cup celery, diced
2	garlic cloves, minced
1/4	teaspoon cumin
1	bay leaf
3	cups chicken stock
3	cups dry white wine
3	large sweet potatoes, peeled and thinly sliced
2	large baking potatoes, peeled and thinly sliced
2	cups light cream (or less as desired)
	Choice of garnish

In a soup pot, render bacon over low heat until bacon is crisp.

Remove bacon and set aside.

In the bacon drippings, over medium heat sauté the onions and celery until translucent.

Add the garlic and cumin and stir in for 30 seconds.

Add the bay leaf, chicken stock and wine. Bring to a boil and reduce to a simmer.

Add sweet and white potatoes and cook until tender, about 25 to 30 minutes.

Discard bay leaf and either puree soup in a blender or use an immersion blender.

Return soup to pot and stir in cream, if using.

Garnish and serve soup. Choices of garnish are coconut flakes, minced green onions or a dollop of whipped cream or yogurt.

A Dutch tin-lined caldron by Peter Goebel. The Dutch were setting the standards for cookware and trading it throughout the world. This piece would be appropriate in almost any kitchen circa 1600-1800.
Dated: 1657
—Drawings courtesy of Goosebay Workshops

Tomato Egg Drop Soup

Serves eight to ten

Our discriminating Chinese have learned that Jersey tomatoes enable them to create a variation of simple egg drop soup that we have found in their restaurants. This recipe, adapted from cookbook author Angela Chang's "Chinese Home Cooking," is quite easy to prepare. The creative cook is encouraged to add seasonal and local ingredients such as corn, crabmeat or chopped clams.

2   medium round tomatoes, peeled and seeded, cut
     into chunks
6   cups water
2   (14.5 ounce) cans Chicken broth or stock
2   teaspoons cornstarch mixed with 4 teaspoons water
3   eggs, beaten, with a dash of salt added
1   tablespoon green onions, minced
1   teaspoon sesame oil
Salt to taste

Bring water, chicken broth, and tomatoes to a gentle boil.

Cook for 3 to 5 minutes until the tomatoes have softened; blend well.

Reduce to low, pour in cornstarch mixture while continuing to stir.

Turn off heat, hold the bowl containing the eggs about 8 inches above the pot and slowly pour the beaten eggs in a wide circle into the soup in a circular motion, stirring continuously for 1/2 minute. This will cause the egg drops to turn into ribbons and large flakes. **Add** the scallions, sesame oil and salt. **Serve** hot.

Variations: Very thinly sliced sweet onions can be gently added to the surface of each soup bowl as a garnish.

CURRY OF CHICKEN

Here's a chicken feast for "chicken feed." You have all the ingredients right in your pantry except the chicken and perhaps the curry powder, which can be obtained quickly at your grocer's.

2 lbs. chicken   2 teaspoons curry powder
2 small onions   1 tablespoon flour
1/4 cup butter (or margarine)   1 egg yolk

Have your butcher cut up the chicken as for fricassee. Wash it well and place in stew pan with enough water to cover it. Cover pan and let boil slowly until chicken is tender. Now add a heaping teaspoon of salt and boil a few minutes longer. Remove chicken from pot, but save the liquid. Now cut up the onions and fry them in the butter. When the onions are brown, remove them from the frying pan and put in the chicken. Fry the chicken for 3 or 4 minutes, then sprinkle it with the curry powder, and pour over it the liquid in which the chicken was boiled. Add the brown onions, stir thoroughly and stew for five more minutes. Now mix in a tablespoon of flour which you have thinned with a little water and stir in the beaten egg yolk. Remove from the fire and that's it!

This recipe from the **Baltimore & Ohio** at the early part of the 20th Century points out how railroad dining cars were leading the way to introduce worldwide cuisine to their travelers.

Pumpkin or Butternut Sage Soup

This recipe was offered to tasters with an alternate choice of a traditional pumpkin soup, and interestingly, the tasters preferred this different soup half the time. Perhaps it might be your choice.

2-1/2	pounds pumpkin, butternut or other winter squash
1/4	cup olive oil
12	whole sage leaves, or 2 tablespoons crushed
2	onions finely chopped
1/4	teaspoon dried thyme
1/4	cup chopped parsley
	Salt and pepper to taste
2	quarts water
	Grated cheddar cheese for garnish

Preheat the oven to 375 degrees F.

Cut squash in half, brush with olive oil and bake, face down, for 30 minutes, or until tender.

Meanwhile, in a skillet, add the olive oil and heat until quite hot. Add the sage and cook until the leaves turn dark, about 1 minute. If you are using leaves, scoop out and set aside.

Add the onions and cook until they turn slightly brown, about 10 minutes.

When the squash is out of the oven and cool enough to handle, scoop out the flesh and add to the soup pot along with the olive oil from the sauté pan and the onions. **Add** the water, salt and pepper; bring to a boil and simmer for 25 minutes. Serve with portions of the set aside sage leaves in each soup bowl. Garnish each bowl with a generous serving of cheddar cheese.

Note: This soup will have a rustic texture. If you want a more refined soup, pass the broth and ingredients through a food mill.

Chapter 2
Light and Easy Fare

Today's cooks appreciate having the chance to look over recipes that are both easy to do and light on the digestion. Sure enough, going back to Down Jersey's culinary heritage, we have light courses to offer. Since we have included updated preparations that draw upon our regional ingredients, we can bring them to you as well. Dietary confusion aside, most of us would agree that smaller meals are becoming the recommended way. Less food is easier for our bodies to handle.

As with most small meals, by adding more meat or cheese, the meal can be made substantial and thus fit for the biggest meal of the day. I would think it's easier to notch up a sandwich perhaps than to downscale a large dinner portion. In the other direction, most can be scaled down to make interesting appetizers. While some of these recipes are already vegetarian, we present them here for all rather than in our vegetarian and vegan chapter.

In this chapter we celebrate one of the hallmarks of our champion vegetables, the Jersey tomato, with a recipe-if we need one at all--for the ritual of our first-of-the-season tomato sandwich.

Asparagus and eggs are so much a part of Down Jersey that it is a common sight to see posters such as this one advertising a breakfast. In earlier times the poultry industry was as prominent at the asparagus crop is today. The combination of using them together in dishes lingers in home kitchens and community get togethers.

First Tomato Sandwich

Makes one sandwich

Anyone outside of Down Jersey could hardly be expected to understand our eagerness for the first real, juicy field-or garden-grown tomato. For a blissful moment, this annual ritual could easily qualify, in our minds, as a true holiday to celebrate.

While there is a common perception of remembering in our youth the practice of eating a sun-warmed, shaker-salted Jersey tomato, my amateur historical research has proven beyond a doubt that the first tomato is most often consumed in an uncomplicated sandwich. And, as Evelyn Clifford, from Thorofare, has said, "I don't care what you might think about nutrition, but I like my first tomato on soft, white bread!"

The two top favorite "first" versions are given here.

1	fully ripe Jersey round tomato
	Salt to taste
2	slices soft white bread
1	thin slice American cheese
	Mayonnaise, full fat, to spread
	Leaf lettuce, such as Romaine, optional

Wash and trim away top and bottom of the tomato. Cut thick 3/8-inch round slices and salt to taste.

Place tomato on sandwich bread, topping with a slice of cheese.

Lightly spread the second slice with mayonnaise; add lettuce, if using. **Prepared** correctly, this is a juicy, two-napkin sandwich.

Variations: Some prefer to lightly toast the bread, others may choose a light hamburger bun, also lightly toasted. Also, balsamic vinegar and extra-virgin oil may be substituted for the mayo.

Why are Jersey tomatoes so revered?

Some would say that a Jersey tomato's color and tangy taste comes from Jersey's sandy soil, some would say it comes from the varieties introduced by Rutgers, others, the weather. This author ventures to opine that, mostly, it's the weather. Grow a Jersey tomato in a pot in artificial soil, or in the garden or field, and the same full satisfying flavor is there. Of course, varieties leave their mark, too.

Culturally, tomato plants feel comfortable in a fairly narrow temperature range. At low temperatures in the 40's, especially in the evening, the rich summery flavors are lost. Too high daytime temperatures bring about odd-looking orangey fruit, at least those that are on the vine. At temps in the high 90's, the flowers abort and tomato production shuts down. Southern New Jersey is fortunate in having relatively few days in the high 90's. Due to the influences of moist air coming from the southwest over the Delaware Bay, evening temperatures remain high, with high humidity to boot.

Jersey Style Garlic Bread

Makes two dozen

This version of ever-popular garlic bread evolved over the years using mostly local ingredients. As excellent quality French or Italian bread has become readily available at our supermarkets, you can still make a tasty garlic bread even if you don't have access to an artisan baker. Unlike most garlic bread recipes, this is not toasted or baked. With the inclusion of the red peppers or paprika, it has an appealing color and delightful flavor.

- 1/3 cup extra-virgin olive oil
- 4 cloves garlic, minced
- 1/4 red bell pepper, finely minced, or
     2 tablespoons good quality paprika
- 1/2 teaspoon red pepper flakes
- 1/4 cup fresh parsley, chopped
- 3 tablespoons Romano cheese
- 1 baguette loaf, sliced 1/2-inch thick across

In a skillet, heat olive until hot. **Add** the garlic, peppers or paprika, and after 30 seconds, turn off heat. **Add** the garlic to the still hot oil; stir in. **As** the oil begins to cool, add the Romano cheese and parsley; stir in. **Spoon** or brush onto the sliced bread.

Bruschetta

Makes two dozen

Jersey plum tomatoes are preferred, since they have the flavor and the sturdiness to hold up. Besides, they are not usually waxed as are shipped-in plum tomatoes.

- 8 medium plum tomatoes, 1/4-inch diced
- 2 tablespoons extra-virgin olive oil
- 1/2 mild medium onion, 1/4-inch diced
- 2 cloves garlic, minced
- 1/4 cup freshly chopped Italian (flat leaf) parsley
- 2 tablespoons Parmesan or Romano cheese
- Salt and pepper to taste
- 1 baguette loaf, sliced 1/2-inch thick across

Use a sharp knife, preferably serrated, to slice off both ends of the tomatoes, and to dice them while maintaining their shape and avoiding losing much of their juice.

In a small bowl, fold in ingredients carefully with a spatula; allow to rest for a half hour, if you can. **Test** for seasoning adjustment; top bread slices with portions from a spoon. **Serve** at room temps. It's an excellent conversation starter.

Asparagus and Eggs Sandwich

For two sandwiches

Few matches are as comparable as asparagus and eggs. Here in Down Jersey it is hard to say one word without saying the other. The combo of them in a sandwich, on a light roll preferably, brings the marriage to ultimate bliss. As with any preparation combining few ingredients, its the quality and technique that matters.

      1/2 pound asparagus, tender portions only, cut in 1-inch
              lengths
        4 eggs, beaten
      Dash of hot pepper flakes, optional
      1/2 teaspoon salt, plus black pepper to taste
        2 tablespoons grated Romano or Parmesan cheese
        2 tablespoons extra-virgin olive oil
        2 cloves garlic, cut in half lengthwise
        2 sandwich rolls, preferably light crumb

Wash and inspect the triangular bracts (leaflets) on the asparagus carefully. If you have any suspicion or see any grit, remove each one and wash carefully. If the asparagus is thick, cut in half lengthwise to insure even cooking. Set aside.
Combine the eggs, hot pepper flakes, salt and pepper and Romano cheese; set aside.
In a large sauté pan over medium heat, add the oil and slices of garlic; sauté until golden, about 30 seconds. **Remove** garlic and discard. **Add** the asparagus, stir to coat with oil and sauté over medium heat, covered, for 4 minutes, stirring occasionally.
Pour the egg mixture over the asparagus; move asparagus to evenly disperse in eggs.
Cook undisturbed for 30 seconds, then push the mixture toward the center with a fork to allow the uncooked eggs to reach the outside edges and cook.
When the underside is cooked, cut the mixture in quarters with a spatula, permitting each quarter to be flipped to cook the other side. Otherwise, preheat the broiler and finish cooking the surface under a broiler, about 4-6 inches below the heat element.. Be sure to use a sauté pan with an oven-safe handle; use protective material when grabbing the handle. Broiling time is about 2-3 minutes. **Fill** rolls with asparagus and egg mixture. Serve with Romano cheese as a side.

> **Asparagus history:** Southern New Jersey's climate and sandy soils have been favorable for growing asparagus. With considerable acreage in production, the 1970's brought elevated levels of diseases that devastated yields. After leading research by Dr. Ellison at Rutger's Cook College, new hybrids were introduced that were resistant to the disease, fusarium crown rot. The hybrids also were selected to breed only male plants, which, since they are not burdened with seed production, are more vigorous. Despite the advances, production levels are still below earlier days. **Tip:** To the home cook, asparagus at the market is now much thicker, sometimes calling for them to be cut in half for even cooking.

Sausage Biscuits and Gravy

Serves six

As you approach the Delaware Bay, the influence of southerners becomes more apparent, such as with the southern version of chipped beef on toast, which is sausage, biscuits and gravy. You will find this offered at restaurants near Route 40 and farther south. The key to this dish is that it must be greasy without being too greasy.

2	tablespoons vegetable oil
1	pound bulk breakfast sausage
3	tablespoons all-purpose flour
1-1/2	cups milk

Salt and generous black pepper to taste

Preferably in a cast iron pan, heat oil, add sausage, brown over medium-low heat, breaking sausage into small pieces as you stir. **Remove** sausage and set aside; spoon out all but 3 tablespoons of fat.

Stir in flour, cooking over medium-high heat for about one minute. **Remove** from heat and slowly add milk, stirring constantly and until smooth..

Return to heat and cook until thickened, about 2-3 minutes. Return sausage to pan; add salt to taste and warm. **Pour** over baked biscuits and grind a generous amount of fresh black pepper over it all.

Biscuits

Serves six

Buttermilk brings out a superior tangy taste in biscuits, but the Easy Mix recipe is commendable as well.

Easy Mix Biscuits

2	cups flour
2	teaspoons baking powder
3/4	teaspoon salt
1/3	cup vegetable oil
2/3	cup milk

Combine oil and milk and set aside. **Sift** flour and mix in baking powder and salt. **Pour** oil and milk over dry ingredients and mix and knead lightly. **Roll** out dough on a floured counter and cut, with a drinking glass or biscuit cutter. **Bake** at 450 degrees F. for 12 to 15 minutes, or until lightly brown.

Basic Buttermilk Biscuits

2	cups all-purpose flour
2	teaspoons baking powder
1/2	teaspoon baking soda
1/2	teaspoon salt
6	tablespoons butter
1	cup buttermilk

Proceed as with the Easy Mix recipe, except break the butter into small pieces as you mix in the dry ingredients. **Also** bake at 450 degrees F. for about 15 minutes.

Cheese Balls

Makes two or three round balls

Dodge's Market, a country store that served customers back in the nineteenth century, has long since been a Down Jersey institution. Years ago, as you approached Dodge's on Route 40 in Elmer, a large sign could be seen that read "Headquarters for Sharp Cheese." This recipe given to us by the current owner, Donna K. Guarrera, comes from Dodge's files of stored recipes ready at hand to give customers over the counter.

1	small onion, chopped
16	ounces softened cream cheese
8	ounces blue cheese, room temperature
8	ounces sharp cheese, grated
8	ounces softened Wispride Brand cheese
2	tablespoons Worcestershire sauce
8	ounces crushed pecans

In a large bowl, mix all ingredients, except the crushed pecans, until smooth. **Form** into round balls.

Pour the pecans in a flat tray or baking pan, and roll the cheese balls to coat with the pecans, pressing the nuts with your hands to stick them to the balls.

Serve at room temperature with crackers or bread. The cheese balls can be made four to five days ahead and kept in the refrigerator, covered, until ready to serve.

Corn Fritters

Corn fritters might be your memory of grandma's kitchen. Most often made from leftover corn, we suggest you use fresh or frozen corn, and varieties that still have that old fashioned creaminess. We hope that our fresh farm market corn will prompt you to keep the family tradition.

2 cups all-purpose flour
2 teaspoons baking powder
1/2 teaspoon salt
2 eggs, beaten
1 cup milk
1/4 cup melted butter
3 ears fresh corn kernels, stripped, corn milk saved (1 1/2 cups frozen)
Powdered sugar, syrup or salsa for serving.

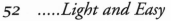

Mix dry ingredients of flour, baking powder, salt and sugar. Mix eggs and milk together. Fold into dry mixture, stir in corn. Add more milk if needed for a smooth, thick batter. Either deep fry at approx. 370deg. until nicely browned, or pan fry with ¼" deep oil, turning once. Place on a paper towel to absorb oil, serve warm. You may prefer to separate the yolks from the whites in order to beat the whites until stiff, adding last, after the corn, making it lighter.

Courtesty of your New Jersey Farm Marketer

This is an example of one of the recipes you might find at a member market of the **New Jersey Farmers' Direct Marketing Association.** They offer easy to do recipes that celebrate use of local vegetables.

Laird's Chicken Liver Paté

Serves eight as appetizer

France has their paté de foie gras, a goose liver specialty renowned around the world. We have our rival chicken liver paté, and a fine one at that. Chicken livers, particularly when in a paté, ask for other ingredients to moderate the full flavor.

Laird's has helped us by publishing in "Applejack, The Spirit of Americana," their paté version that uses, of course, AppleJack as a key flavor booster. Laird & Company, from Scobyville, New Jersey, is recognized as the oldest operating distillery in the country.

I have adapted Laird's recipe somewhat to add cream for a smoother texture.

4	tablespoons (1/2 stick) butter
1	medium onion, finely minced
1	pound chicken livers, connecting threads removed
1/4	teaspoon salt
1/8	teaspoon pepper
4	tablespoons heavy cream
2	tablespoons Laird's AppleJack
	Fresh parsley for garnish

Melt the 1/4 cup of butter in a large pan over medium heat.

When the foam subsides, add the chicken livers, onions, salt and pepper. **Cook** for about 3 to 5 minutes while chopping the livers with the tip end of a sturdy spatula so as to cook the livers evenly. **Sauté** until the livers begin to lose their pink color; avoid overcooking.

Remove livers and pan juices from the pan and pour into a blender; blend at low speed until smooth.

Using the same pan in which the livers were cooked, add the heavy cream and AppleJack, bring to a low simmer and cook for 3 to 5 minutes, until most of the alcohol is evaporated.

Add cream and AppleJack to blended ingredients. **Blend** well and place in covered bowl or bowls.

Refrigerate, preferably 24 hours or overnight.

Garnish with parsley and serve with toasted rye, white bread triangles or crackers.

APPLEJACK: THE SPIRIT OF AMERICANA

LAIRD'S APPLEJACK COOKBOOK

Fried Rice

Serves four

Down Jerseyans of all ethnic groups were among the earliest to embrace Chinese cooking, perhaps due to its reliance on a wide variety of vegetables, most of which found accommodating growing conditions in our weather and soils. The recipe, though it breaks no new ground, bears repeating for its usefulness today.

2	tablespoons vegetable oil
1/2	cup frozen peas
1/2	cup finely diced carrots
1	small onion, finely diced, optional
1/2	pound ham, finely diced
1	tablespoon soy sauce, dark preferred
	Dash of hot pepper sauce, optional
4	cups cooked rice
2	tablespoons rice or cider vinegar

In a large pan or wok, sauté peas, carrots and onions in oil for about five minutes over medium heat, stirring occasionally.

Add ham, soy sauce, and stir. **Stir** in cooked rice and vinegar.

Heat until thoroughly warmed, taste for seasoning adjustment and serve in deep bowls, which keep the fried rice warm longer than the flat plates.

Variations: Any number of vegetables can be added if desired: cabbage, broccoli, red or green pepper, corn and green onions. Cut them into small dice and allow sufficient cooking time for each vegetable.

Vegetables for fried rice: Although there are traditional vegetables that go with fried rice, such as carrots, peas and onions, we should take advantage of those in season when they are at their best. In the spring it could be fresh spinach that's added, in the summer it could be squash or eggplant, and so forth. As you noticed, for fried rice the vegetables are cut fine. All you do when you do a change up is to add the differing vegetables at the time they take to cook and yet not overcook.

One further note, when selecting at the market, keep in mind to bring a pleasing color variation to the final dish. Not only would it be more appealing to the eye, but also the varieties will heighten the nutritional value with added antioxidants.

Open Faced Grilled Tomato and Cheese

Perhaps the popularity of pairing cheese with tomatoes is that the cheese gives body to the light but tangy tomato. Tasters usually prefer mild cheeses, such as sliced American, so as not to outshine the super taste of our Jersey tomato. Then again, it's your call.

For each sandwich:
1   tablespoon butter or olive oil
Round tomato, sliced 1/4-inch thick or more across
1   slice sturdy sandwich bread, trimmed or untrimmed
Salt to taste
Dash of dried oregano
Thick slices of American or mild Provolone cheese to
cover

Assemble sandwich, salting and adding oregano on tomato slices before topping with cheese.

In an ovenproof pan over medium-low heat, melt two tablespoons of butter or oil.

Add sandwich to pan and cook until lightly browned on the bottom.

Place the pan 4 to 6 inches under the broiler element until the cheese melts and browns slightly, about three to four minutes. **As** an alternative to finishing by broiling, before the bread browns, the pan can be covered, although the cheese itself won't develop that delightful browning.

As an additional flourish, drizzle extra-virgin olive oil over the sandwiches.

What's with staking tomatoes? Most gardeners have resorted to staking tomato plants for a number or reasons, even though it takes more material and time to stake and tie them as they grow.

The benefits to staking are that the tomatoes do not rest on the ground as they mature, and by staking, the vine can be more easily pruned for earlier and larger fruit. Tomatoes that contact the soil are prone to transfer soil organisms to the fruit, causing earlier decay. And by being shaded at the contact area, the sun does not permit even ripening of the tomato. Gardeners have long ago learned that by pruning off extra "suckers" the vine will put its energy stores into the fruit already on the vine.

The staking could be a short one in the case of tomato plants that are more of a bush than a lanky, tall-growing vine, or a tall stake for the longer bearing plants that need a tall stake. As an alternative to staking, gardeners often choose to use cages that keep the fruit off of the ground, and are not pruned.

For years, the bulk of the tomatoes grown by farmers were bush types without staking, which was the norm. In the 1980's, customers increasingly asked for higher quality tomatoes, so the farmers responded by offering staked tomatoes with their even, attractive appearance, longer shelf life, and, at a somewhat higher price that customers were willing to pay.

Port of Call Oyster Stew

Serves four as a first course

Oyster stew boils down to a very few basic ingredients, or as a cook once said, "Don't love'm to death with seasonings." True, for oysters themselves should shine with few other enhancements. Still, there are stew variations that respect the bright and briny zest of oysters, which we will list for you. But first, among many excellent versions, we have chosen to share the style by Chef Harry Whitelam at Port of Call Restaurant in Port Elizabeth. He serves gallons of oysters every week, so he must have many addicted customers. For sure, never overcook oysters, for they then become too chewy.

```
1   pint Delaware Bay oysters, about 16-20, (freshly
        shucked, if possible) with liquor
2   cups scalded half and half, or milk if you prefer
2   tablespoons butter
Dash of paprika and cayenne pepper, optional
Salt and pepper to taste
Trenton Oyster Crackers for garnish
Condiment jar of horseradish
```

Drain oysters from their liquor. Heat oyster liquor in a saucepan and bring to a boil, reduce to simmer, and skim off surface matter. **Add** oysters, and just as their edges begin to curl, about two minutes, add the half and half and stir. **When** the half and half is heated through, taste for seasoning adjustment. **Serve** with a dollop of butter in each soup plate. **Serve** with Old Trenton Oyster Crackers, along with a nutcracker to crush them, and horseradish.

Down Jersey Oyster & Spinach Stew:

Use Port of Call's recipe, except add 6 to 8 ounces of spinach to oyster liquor and simmer till tender, then add half and half. Substitute a grating of nutmeg for paprika.

New England Style:

Fry 4-8 slices of bacon until crisp, drain on absorbent paper, crumble and add to stew with the milk. Also, 1/4-inch diced potatoes can be added to the oyster liquor; cook until tender, with a little water added, before adding the oysters, lest the oysters overcook.

Southern Style:

Lightly sauté one quarter of a medium onion, chopped, before adding the oyster liquor. **Oyster sizes**: Commercial oysters are graded in various sizes, but it is sufficient for cooks to know that, in general, the larger oysters are preferred for frying and the smaller oysters are optimum for stewing. Also, when the intent is to stew them, if sold by the each, ask your fishmonger to spoon extra liquor into the container.

Barbecued Oysters

Serves four to six

When the weather is suitable for grilling, barbecued oysters from the Delaware Bay sure are welcome. Excellent as appetizers, they can be a second serving or part of the main meal.

Don't fret about the "R" months; see our comments below. Your only question is how many oysters to buy. Not all seafood stores will have in-shell oysters at hand, so call ahead to be sure they have them, or order ahead.

    2 dozen in-shell oysters
    Your favorite barbecue sauce

Preheat the grill. **Scrub** the oysters well under cold water, set aside in a cool location until ready to be grilled. **Once** the grill has reached a medium level of heat, place the oysters, flat shells up, directly over the heat. **Close** the cover and grill for 4-5 minutes, removing those that open. Some will open earlier than others. **Remove** top shell from opened oysters; try to not spill the juice in the bottom shell half. **Dab** your barbecue sauce on the oyster and serve.

Is it safe to eat oysters in months without an "R" in the spelling?

Many of our food habits are a carry-over from European customs. There, the flat oyster, *Ostrea edulis*, is quite unpalatable during the summer reproduction season, since it broods the tiny shelled larvae in the mantle cavity until they are quite large. There was also a belief that harvesting at the time of spawning would interfere with recruitment of young oysters. During the summer spawning season, our oyster, *Crassostrea virginica*, due to the presence of ripe gonad, has a somewhat different flavour, but it remains quite palatable though a bit thin following spawning. In our area of the northeast, the traditional oyster culture community was preoccupied with collecting seed for planting, staking up their leases and spreading shell to catch spat during the early summer; later in the summer the vessels were being hauled out for repairs and painting. Prior to the widespread use of mechanical refrigeration, the practical time for storage and transport of both live and shucked oysters in warmer seasons was-limited to a few days unless a copious supply of ice was available. This restricted the distribution of oysters during summer to the immediate area of production. These practical considerations supported the old custom of limiting harvesting to months with an "R". Today, however, oysters are harvested and available for consumption throughout the year.

—Excerpted from The New Jersey Aquaculture Association's
Questions About Shellfish

Pepper and Eggs Sandwich
Home Style Version

Makes two or three sandwiches

I recall how my mother would make her pepper and eggs sandwiches for me on thick slices of Italian bread, probably from Fiorile's Bakery (or was it Blum's then?) in Paulsboro. Taking it to work in my lunchbox, it would ooze with olive oil. How I felt sorry for fellow workers chowing down on a dry buttered ham and cheese on fluffy white bread!

2   small bell or 4 frying peppers, green or red
3   fresh eggs, beaten
Salt and pepper to taste
Hot red pepper flakes, optional
2   tablespoons olive oil
1   small clove garlic, minced
6   thick slices Italian bread

Wash, core and slice the peppers into roughly 1/2-inch by 2-inch strips.
Beat eggs and add salt and pepper, and pepper flakes, if desired. **Coat** a non-stick pan with the olive oil, or a lesser amount if you use an oil spray, and sauté the peppers over low heat, stirring occasionally.
When the peppers are soft, stir in the garlic and sauté for another 30 seconds, being careful not to burn the garlic.
Add the eggs and draw up the firming eggs, tilting the pan to spread the eggs. It's done when the eggs are slightly brown.
Test for seasoning and serve. Some prefer to add grated Romano cheese.

Pepper and Eggs
Deli Style

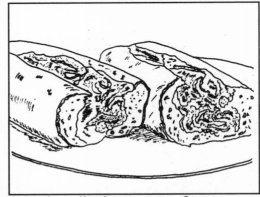

In the deli style, switch to jarred or frozen roasted peppers and skip the pan-frying; add them directly to the beaten eggs. Instead of slices of Italian bread, use the softer choices of sub (hoagie) rolls.

If these are not going to be eaten right away, cut the roll, place a strip of wax paper in the cut and fill with the pepper and egg mixture and wrap the whole sandwich. When the sandwich is later unwrapped, the wax paper can be gently "rolled" away from the filling. By the way, these sandwiches, either style, are absolutely delicious eaten *al fresco*.

Hot Pepper Appetizer

Serves six

Although listed as an appetizer, sautéed hot peppers are also pleasant for nibbling throughout the meal. Serve with ample crusty bread, for that's why there is a generous amount of oil and salt. It's another example of our good fortune to have thin cooking peppers available at local markets. Use of hot red peppers and green sweets helps you to control the hotness level.

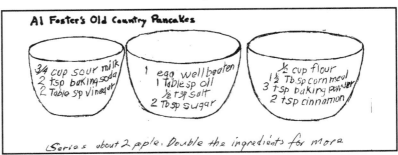

- 3 tablespoons extra virgin olive oil
- 6 long, thin hot peppers, red preferred
- 6 long, thin sweet peppers, green preferred, or 3 Cubanelle peppers
- 3 celery stalks, cut same as peppers
- 2 garlic cloves, smashed
- 3 tablespoons olive oil
- Generous sprinkling of salt

In a sauté pan, add oil and toss in garlic. **Remove** when garlic begins to lightly brown, about 2 minutes. **Add** celery, peppers and salt. **Lower** heat to a slow simmer to retain the peppers' sweetness and avoid bitterness from burning. **Sauté** for 10 minutes, stirring frequently. **When** transferring from the pan to the serving dish, transfer as much flavored oil as possible. **To cut** the hotness, add sweet peppers of a different color.

Note: Frying peppers are ideal for this dish, though bell peppers can be substituted.

Old Country Pancakes

The late **Al Foster,** from Turnersville and contributor of several drawings in this book, sent in this recipe for Old Country Pancakes in his own stylish way.

Al Foster's Old Country Pancakes

3/4 cup sour milk	1 egg well beaten	1/2 cup flour
2 tsp baking soda	1 Table sp oil	1 1/2 Tb.sp corn meal
2 Table sp Vinegar	1/2 tsp salt	3 tsp baking powder
	2 Tb sp sugar	2 tsp cinnamon

Serves about 2 pple. Double the ingredients for more

1) If the milk is not sour, make it luke warm and the vinegar will make it sour. Add the soda to this and it will make a foamy light mixture.

2) Pour this mixture into beaten egg mixture.

3) Gradually stir in the flour mixture with an extra teaspoon, more or less, to make a nice consistency.

4) Cook in cast iron pan for even heat. Serve directly off the stove with your favorite butter and syrup. Bacon optional.

Light and Easy.....

Cajun Portabella Sandwich

This recipe garnered first prize in the professional category at the 1994 National Mushroom Recipe Contest held in Kenneth Square, Pennsylvania. Cape May reared Chef John Jester passes this along to us to introduce a great way to enjoy portabellas. Some would venture to say that this sandwich tastes like a juicy, tender steak sandwich.

For each sandwich:
1   Portabella mushroom, stem
      removed

Seasonings:
   Cayenne pepper
   Black pepper
   White pepper
   Garlic powder
   Salt
   Paprika

Butter and oil for sautéing
Slices of tomatoes
Slice of American cheese
Kaiser roll or sesame seed bun

In a mixing bowl, add together equal parts of seasoning ingredients, except the cayenne, which should be added gradually as you test for spiciness.

Remove stem from portabella mushroom, save for other uses.

Wipe mushrooms (one for each sandwich) with a damp towel. Leave damp. Dust on seasonings, cover both sides well.

In a sauté pan over medium-low heat, add sufficient butter and vegetable oil in equal amounts for the number of mushrooms sautéed. Cook each side for two minutes until lightly browned, pressing each side down firmly with a spatula.

Serve on a light sesame seed bun or Kaiser roll with a slice of cheese, tomato and lettuce in the style of a hamburger.

Variation: Add mayonnaise or other sauce as you prefer. If it's more convenient, consider one of the prepared seasoning blends used for crab boils or steaks.

> **Portabella** mushrooms are a larger relative of the common white button and crimini mushroom. They have a meaty texture and fuller flavor due to a longer growing period. The stems, though tougher, can be used, but cut away the gritty root end if it is still attached.

Ratatouille

Our local abundance and quality of the essential ingredients of eggplant, zucchini, onions, peppers and tomatoes makes this famous Provence dish perhaps even better here. Although some consider peppers a part of the usual recipe, I have found that they are optional, and therefore one step easier. Traditional approaches may call for separately sautéing the vegetables, but it isn't necessary.

The distinctive flavor of this recipes uses anisette liqueur to add that fennel touch without having to buy the bulb, but if you choose to add fennel slices instead of anisette, that's fine, too.

Note that because most of us don't get around to making this dish as often as we would like, it's safer to get around possibly burning the garlic by infusing its flavor into the olive oil and then discarding. I don't believe that today's improved varieties and sweeter eggplants need that step of salting to remove bitter juices.

6-8	fresh ripe plum tomatoes (preferred), or 4 medium round tomatoes, peeled
3	tablespoons olive oil
3	garlic cloves, smashed
1	eggplant, your favorite type, peeled and 1/2-inch diced
3-4	medium zucchini, 1/2-inch diced, unpeeled
1-2	large onions, sliced
6-8	fresh basil leaves, or 2 teaspoons dried
2	tablespoons Anisette liqueur
	Salt and pepper to taste
1	bell pepper, red or green, optional

Bring a 2-quart pot of water to a boil, immerse the tomatoes, several at a time, for about one minute each, and peel when cool enough to handle. Dice into 1/2-inch pieces and set aside.

In a large sauté pan over medium heat, add the olive oil and the smashed garlic. **Sauté** until lightly browned and discard with a fork or slotted spoon.

Add the eggplant (white oriental eggplants may not require peeling), zucchini, onions, and 1 sliced bell pepper, if desired. Toss in the basil and a light amount of salt; sauté for five minutes, stirring occasionally. **Add** more oil, if needed.

Add the tomatoes and Anisette, if using, and simmer for 10 minutes, stirring occasionally. The sauce should be finished when the tomatoes begin to turn a darker color and at that time the whole ratatouille should be finished, too.

Adjust salt and pepper, and serve with a crusty French or Italian bread.

Butter-Browned Ravioli

Serves four

The popularity of Italian provisions through-out all communities in Down Jersey presents the opportunity of shoppers to purchase pasta products at fresh and fresh-frozen purveyors. This has been a boon to time-short home cooks who want to prepare meals in a straight forward manner. Ravioli (though we habitually say raviolis, ravioli is already plural), are excellent served in a manner similar to pan-sautéing perogi. Thus, ravioli are first boiled, and then sautéed with butter, and in Italian style, with a bit of extra-virgin olive oil added. Sauces and garnishes can be added, but this simple method is as good as it is.

> 1 (1-pound) package of ravioli, cooked in salted water
> 1 tablespoon butter
> 1-2 tablespoons extra-virgin olive oil

In a large pan, heat olive oil and melt in the butter. **Sauté** ravioli over medium heat until lightly browned on one side, then turn over and repeat. **Add** more oil or butter as needed. **Variations:** While the ravioli are boiling, you may want to sauté a batch of onions to add to the pan of ravioli mid way in the sautéing. Also, a toss of oregano or basil while sautéing, or tossing in parsley a few seconds before the finish would heighten the seasoning.

Omelette

The secret of light omelettes is beating. Beat eggs until they are fluffy and your omelette won't fall. The pan should be fairly hot, but not hot enough to burn the edges of the omelette. Remember to stir a little when you pour the omelette into pan--until it begins to rise. Turn it over once. Then roll when done. Serve immediately on warm plate. All hot foods taste better on warm plates.

A recipe instruction from the **Baltimore & Ohio Railroad** for omlettes served in their dining cars in the early part of the 20th Century.

Chapter 3
Vegetables from the Garden State

If there is a mantra associated with vegetables, it's that freshness is everything. That implies that we pay attention to the season when we get to choose locally grown tender vegetables. Vegetables bred for shipment and grown elsewhere are inferior imposters compared to locally grown, tender veggies. To drive that point home, I'll recall this story that happened at a family dinner a few years ago:

> My wife, Loretta, served a fine meal highlighted with broiled steak as the main event. As it happened to be in mid-summer, the fresh vegetables side dishes were sweet corn from the garden, green beans picked minutes earlier and fresh-dug new potatoes. In relishing each vegetable, with return visits to each platter, I couldn't have been more pleased. Then my wife said, "Don't you like the steak?" I had forgotten about the steak.

What a revelation. Never before had I realized that we relegate vegetables as second class to meat. It is, I reasoned, because the vegetables we have become accustomed to were less than what they could be. In my case, the vegetables were essentially organic, home grown varieties chosen for their reputation for flavor, not cosmetic beauty or shipping qualities. In a region where farm markets abound and supermarkets often bring in fresh from the farm produce, getting them isn't limited to gardeners. When vegetables are given due respect, they rise to first class status.

Adding to our good fortunes in Down Jersey, our growing season is reasonably long as seasons go, plus we have the added bonus of great Indian summer harvesting. It's that time after the first frost when some tender crops remain around a few more days for harvesting, and hardy crops resume growth. Besides, a number of the hardiest will continue to be cut from the fields well into winter, weather permitting. Fields of leeks, spinach and cabbage are common wintertime sights for us.

Prominent among the vegetables hereabouts is the lauded Jersey tomato, so prized that it is synonymous with our State name. Besides the proliferation of recipes that draw on our tomato as the defining ingredient in this vegetable chapter, you might have noticed how tomatoes earned their way into soups, sauces, and salads as well.

Abruzzo Style Oven Green Beans

Serves four to six

This might appear to be just another baked green bean dish, but don't be misled. Today's chefs might call this a roasted dish, though roasting usually implies meat. I learned this dish from my Mother, Louise Colanero, who in turn brought this recipe from her birthplace in the province of Abruzzo, in central Italy. Perfection in this dish means achieving that intense richness from browning the top layer of beans and some of the potato bits. That is why they are cut in small cubes. This winter season dish relies on green beans that have been fresh-frozen, which calls for par-boiling for three minutes. However, should you have fresh beans, add seven minutes to the oven cooking time.

8 ounces frozen green beans, cut to
    bite size pieces, about 1 1/2-2 inches
1 small onion, cut into 1/4-inch cubes
1 medium peeled all-purpose potato,
    cut into 1/4-inch cubes
2 cloves garlic, minced
3 tablespoons olive oil
2 dried hot pepper strips, optional

Preheat oven to 375 degrees F.

Pour and coat olive oil on bottom and sides of an oven-proof casserole dish, about 8 x 11 inches, then add garlic, onions, potatoes, green beans, salt, and black pepper. **Mix** thoroughly. If slight hot pepper tang is desired, place on top of mix at this time. **Cover** with aluminum foil and bake in a 375 degree F. oven for 1 hour. **Uncover** and bake for another five minutes to develop browning of ingredients. **Serve** from the casserole, adjusting final salt and pepper to taste. **Remove** hot pepper, if using.

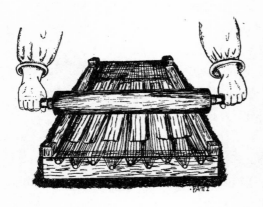

The use of the chitarra, or guitar, has been popular with spaghetti makers in the Province of Abruzzo in central Italy. Many Italian immigrants from that region continued the practice of using the chitarra before the pasta machines became affordable

The flat pieces of pasta are placed on the tightly laced thin steel strings and pressed upon by the wooden roller with a back and forth motion. As invariably parts of the pasta stick to the wire strings, the chitarra is then "played" by drawing one's thumb across the strings to have the remaining portions fall into the tray below. The resulting spaghetti has a unique square cut. Drawing thanks to Patti Levering.

South Philly Asparagus

Serves six

We have to admit that south Philly's Italian community, a major buyer of southern New Jersey's farm produce, returns the favor with great recipes. You may have noticed that after years of sending their specialties over to us, they relocate and become part of us.

Mariella Giovannucci passed this recipe from her mother-in-law along to me during the Book and the Cook Festival held in Philadelphia a few years ago. Catch Mariella at Fonte's in South Philadelphia.

    1   bunch asparagus(about 1-1/4 pounds), lower
           portions snapped off
    3   tablespoons butter
    1   cup bread crumbs
    Salt and pepper to taste
    1/4 cup pine nuts or slivered almonds

Steam the asparagus until tender, about 12 to 15 minutes. Set aside.
Melt butter in a sauté pan and add breadcrumbs. **Sauté** over medium heat until slightly browned.
Layer breadcrumbs and asparagus in an oven proof serving dish, top with pine nuts or almonds and warm thoroughly in a 350 degree F. oven, about 10 minutes.
Serve with a drizzle of olive oil and or a sprinkling of Parmesan cheese if you like.

Woodbury Daily Times May 18, 1922— The first shipment of asparagus by air was from Mullica Hill to Boston from the fields of S. M. Carter, Kerby, Moore, Tomkin, Borden, Brown, White and Iredell. A motion picture machine captured the flight. A Fokker plane piloted by Bert Costa left at 9:30 a.m. with 1,000 fancy asparagus in a five-hour flight to Framingham Field in Boston. Constant radio communication was maintained. The flight was intended to demonstrate the feasibility of ultimately putting into general use selected farm products. After flying 300 miles, Costas arrived shortly after noon.

10 crates sold for $12.50. They would have gotten more but the market was flooded.

Stir-Fry Asparagus

Serves six

It's quick and easy. No wok? Then use the largest sauté pan you have. Do use a naturally fermented soy sauce.

1-1/2 pounds asparagus, cut to 1-1/2-inch lengths
2   tablespoons vegetable oil
2   tablespoons soy sauce
3   tablespoons chicken stock or water mixed with
      1 tablespoon cornstarch

In a wok over medium heat, add oil and asparagus. **Cover** and steam-cook for 4 minutes.

Remove cover, raise heat to high and add soy sauce, stirring frequently.

Cook for another minute, then add chicken stock and cornstarch mixture, stirring regularly for another minute.

Remove and serve alone or over rice. Sesame seeds make a great garnish.

Variation: Reduce soy sauce to 1 tablespoon and add 1 tablespoon of oyster sauce.

Roasted Asparagus

When the shine of your favorite recipes has worn off and you yearn for variety, try the robust flavor of roasted asparagus; some days in May are still agreeable for having the oven on. **Preheat** oven to 425 degrees F. Toss asparagus to coat with olive oil, season with salt and pepper; add a few tablespoons of water in a roasting pan and roast for 15 minutes, covered. **Uncover** and bake for another 10 minutes, testing for doneness with a knife. **Serve** with grated Parmesan, garlic-enhanced mayonnaise or a salsa. This adaptation was inspired by Deborah Madison, author of several vegetarian cookbooks, including "Vegetarian Cooking for Everyone."

Other Ideas:

·   **Make** an omelet with cut and pre-cooked asparagus, plus a minced clove or two of garlic.

·   **Make** a béchamel (white) sauce and then add a mild cheese, crab meat and cooked asparagus.

·   **Add** to your favorite soup, or, make an asparagus soup using the saved tough ends for stock...what color!

·   **Whip** up a mayonnaise-based sauce by adding herbs such as tarragon or dill, or mixing in Dijon mustard or relish.

·   **Use** sprinkled sesame seeds, slivered almonds or pine nuts for garnishing.

Bay Style French Fries

Serves four

Delaware Bay crabs are often seasoned with crab boil seasoning blends, and that has carried over toward flavoring other foods with their aroma. Note that these spices, formulated for crab boils, are notoriously salty, some more so than others. Their aroma, however, is sure to wet anyone's appetite. Also, this two-stage cooking step is worthwhile to bring out the crispest fries. Pass on the cold water soaking if you don't have the time.

    4   large baking potatoes, Russet Burbank preferred,
            peeled and cut into 3/8-inch square pieces.
        Vegetable oil as needed
    1   teaspoon crab boil seasoning

If time permits, rinse the cut fries in cold water and allow to rest in the refrigerator for about a half hour. **Drain** and pat dry well. **Meanwhile,** in an electric fryer or deep, heavy pot suitable for frying, add sufficient vegetable oil to cover a cup-size batch of potatoes. **Relying** on a clip-on thermometer, bring oil temperature up to 350 degrees F. **Dropping** in carefully about a cup at a time, fry each batch until the bubbling ceases. Set aside to drain on paper towels or on a brown bag. **Allow** fried potatoes to cool for at least 5 minutes. Bring the oil temperature up to 350 degrees F. Fry again in batches until the fries are golden brown, about 2 minutes. **Before** they cool, toss in the crab boil seasoning, adjusting if needed. Drain again. **Serve** immediately. The crab boil seasonings should impart sufficient saltiness.

Delaware Bay Estuary

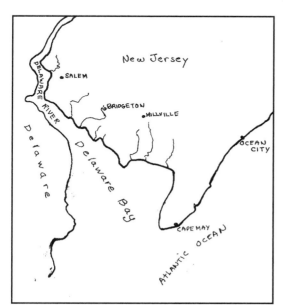

Defined as the region where fresh water from the Delaware River and its contributing streams drains and mixes with salty ocean water, it's an exceedingly rich biological area.

Before the Europeans arrived, native Lenni Lenape fished the estuary with spears and nets. The new immigrants soon discovered the bounty of the Bay and continued to harvest fish and shellfish. In more recent times, after years of pollution abuse, the Bay water has vastly improved in quality during the last few decades.

American shad, weakfish, stripped bass, blue crab and oysters are among the most harvested species.

Sautéed Green Beans with Soy Sauce

Serves four

My friend Jim Lui from Pine Hill passed this recipe along to me. As green beans in Down Jersey can be had fresh at local markets from mid-June through October, it's a recipe that can be repeated often. Frozen green beans are an acceptable, though a less desirable option. Use of a wok allows easier tossing without a mess around the stove. However, if you use a large sauté pan, you will do fine. By adding the mixture of cornstarch and chicken stock or water at the end of the cooking, the beans are filmed with a delicious coating. The reason that this coating helps is that green beans, unlike other vegetables, don't absorb flavors easily. Even if you use too much cornstarch coating and it gets clumpy, it's still delicious.

3/4 pound green beans, washed
and cut into 1-1/2-inch lengths
2 tablespoons vegetable oil
2 scant tablespoons soy sauce
Mixture of 1 tablespoon cornstarch
and 2 tablespoons chicken
stock or water

Dutch Skillet

Heat a pan over medium high heat, add the oil, then add and toss the green beans to coat evenly with the oil.

Lower the heat to medium, cover and cook for 3 minutes.

Remove cover, raise heat to medium-high, add soy sauce and stir frequently for 2 more minutes.

Give corn starch/chicken stock mixture one last stir, add to the pan and stir for another minute, then serve. If you like, serve with a sprinkle of sesame seeds on top.

Variation: For a spicier version, add a 1/4 teaspoon of Oriental chili hot sauce (sometimes sold as chili garlic sauce) or a dash of cayenne to the pan with the oil. Or, use 1 teaspoon of soy sauce with 1 teaspoon oyster sauce. For vegans, be mindful that vegetarian oyster sauce is available at many Asian markets.

Shopper's Tip: Select beans that don't show the prominent bean seeds, are relatively free of blemishes and are firm and waxy to the feel. Opt for hand-picked when available. The farmer's extra expense of hand picking the beans yields beans with fewer blemishes and they have a longer shelf life. Yellow, or "wax" beans are seldom machine picked because the machine injury causing brown scars is too obvious. Don't wash the beans until just prior to use as they have a natural protective wax coating.

Boxty
(Potato Griddle Cakes)

Serves four

This is another recipe passed along from Donna Robinson, owner of the Green Dragon Irish Imports store in Salem. She tells us that it is a great way to serve potatoes, an Irish mainstay, of course. She also tells us that this preparation is found mainly in the northern counties of Cavan, Donegal and Leitrim. Here in Down Jersey, potatoes, which thrive in the cool growing conditions, will grow well for local farmers and gardeners as spring and fall crops.

```
 1   pound all-purpose potatoes, peeled
 2   tablespoons flour
 1   egg, beaten
1/2  grated onion
 1   teaspoon baking powder
3/4  teaspoon salt and pepper to taste
2/3  cup milk
     Vegetable oil or lard for frying
```

Grate potatoes into a large bowl, add flour, baking powder, egg, onion, salt and pepper and mix. **Add** the milk and mix well.

Bring a heavy pan filled with oil, sufficient for deep frying, up to frying temperature. Test by dropping in a small pinch of bread. When it bubbles, the oil is ready for frying.

Using a large spoon, carefully drop several spoonfuls of the potato mixture into the hot oil. **Cook** for 4 to 5 minutes until golden.

Serve hot. Variation: Mix grated raw potato with mashed potatoes, it's quite popular.

An old Irish poem: *Boxty on the griddle,*
Boxty in the pan,
If you can't make boxty,
You'll never get a man.

Potato Varieties in 1886: In 1886, the Honorable Thomas H. Dudley reported at the New Jersey State Board of Agriculture that the most popular varieties of potatoes for the market were:
Early Ohio, Early Vermont, Lee's Favorite, Early Rose, Queen of the Valley, Burbank, White Elephant, Rosy Morn, American Magnum and Bonum.

*P**ray for peace and grace and spiritual food,*
For wisdom and guidance, for all these are good,
But don't forget the potatoes.

John Tyler Pette

Anytime Broccoli Pancake

Serves four

Originally, this pancake was created to make use of the abundance of broccoli coming from our farmers in the fall. Because broccoli topped the pancake, it was at first called Breakfast Broccoli, but in our family we soon learned that it's an anytime dish. Simple meat additions add the extra protein that elevates the dish to a light lunch or full dinner.

Pancake batter for approximately 6 pancakes
- 3 tablespoons olive oil
- 1/2 medium onion, diced
- 3 garlic cloves, sliced thinly
- 3/4 pound broccoli
- Salt and pepper
- 1/4 pound Mozzarella cheese
- 3 tablespoons grated Parmesan or Romano cheese

Cut and trim the broccoli florets, discarding all but the tender floret buds.

In a heavy pan, preferably cast iron, approximately 10 inches in diameter with an oven proof handle, cook the onions with 2 tablespoons of the olive oil over medium heat for two minutes.

Add the garlic, stir in and cook for 30 seconds.

Reduce the heat to medium-low, add the broccoli, stir in to mix and cook for 4 minutes, covered.

Remove the broccoli mixture to a separate platter.

Preheat the broiler.

Continuing at medium-low heat, add 1 more tablespoon of olive oil and pour the pancake batter in the pan. As soon as the batter begins to bubble indicating that it would be time to turn the pancake, add the broccoli mixture to the top.

Top off the broccoli mixture with the mozzarella and Parmesan cheese.

Place in the preheated broiler about 6 to 8 inches from the heating element. Broil until the cheese begins to brown slightly. Remove and serve straight from the broiling pan.

Note: We have found that maple syrup, applesauce or plum sauce are excellent served as optional sauces. For a heartier meal, add diced ham, bacon or sausage. It would be best to sauté them separately and add back to the broccoli mixture when it is added back to top the pancake batter.

Sautéed Broccoli

Serves six to eight

This straight-forward preparation can be taken many ways, all of them delightful. The starting recipe has a small amount of soy sauce to flavor a sauce wonderful as a topping over rice or pasta. To that, you can add slices of meat, perhaps beef, or other ingredients. The other version takes you to the Mediterranean with a final touch of Parmesan cheese, and it's just as versatile. If it's a side dish you want, reduce the amount of chicken stock.

1-1/2	pounds broccoli, about one bunch
2	tablespoons vegetable oil
1	medium onion, sliced lengthwise
2	cloves garlic, minced
1	(13-ounce) can chicken broth
2	tablespoons soy sauce
2	tablespoons cornstarch
3	tablespoons water

Peel outer stems and slice into 1/4-inch slices. **Cut** florets into 1-inch pieces. **In a** sauté pan over medium heat, cook onions in oil for 2 minutes; add garlic; stir. **Sauté** garlic for 30 seconds; add chicken stock, soy sauce and broccoli stems, and stir. **After** 1 minute, add florets and simmer for 2 minutes. **Mix** the cornstarch and water, give it a stir, and add to pan. **Stir** for another 1/2 minute and serve. **With** use of soy sauce, no additional salting is needed. **For a variation**, 2 teaspoons of oyster sauce can be added or a dash of cayenne. Julienned meats would add enough body to make this a complete meal over rice or pasta. **Note:** Reduce amount of chicken stock if this is to be a side dish. **Italian Version:** Replace the soy sauce with Parmesan cheese, which is added at the end of simmering. Add salt and pepper to taste.

Oriental Sweet and Sour cabbage

Serves four to six

A wok works best, but a large sauté pan will do. Billed as a cabbage dish, do consider the original and Jersey available Chinese cabbage or pak choi. I like it spicy hot.

1/2	green, red or savoy cabbage, chopped
2	tablespoons vegetable oil
	Pinch of cayenne or dash of Chinese chile garlic sauce
	Mix of 2 tablespoons rice wine vinegar or cider vinegar
	and 2 tablespoons sugar

Heat oil in pan, add hot sauce and stir in for 30 seconds. **Add** cabbage and over medium high heat, stir or toss cabbage until almost cooked. **Add** vinegar/sugar mix; stir to cook 1 minute more. **Salt** to taste and serve as a vegetable side.

Lemon Dill Broccoli

Serves four to six

This broccoli prep borrows on the Greek penchant for lemons. It celebrates the freshness of homegrown or local market broccoli as well as keeping its lightness without relying on heavy creams.

Steaming, the method suggested here, retains the most flavor while minimizing vitamin loss. Note that steaming time might be as quick as seven minutes, because when it's hours rather than days from the field, it's so much more delicate. Figure on local broccoli being available fresh from the fields from June through November, although mid-summer is a slack season for cool-weather broccoli.

Whereas most of us may use a collapsible steamer basket, other steamers or improvised arrangements may be used as well. Then again, boiling, though a lesser choice, will suffice.

> 3/4 pound broccoli, washed, and cut into tiny florets
> see note below on stems)
> 3 tablespoons extra-virgin olive oil
> Juice of one large lemon
> 1/4 cup fresh chopped dill weed, or 2 tablespoons dried
> Salt and fresh ground black pepper to taste

Bring the water in the base of the steamer to a boil, reduce to a brisk simmer, add the broccoli, salt and cover.

Steam the broccoli for 5 minutes, then insert a knife into the stalk to check for doneness. The broccoli should be tender after no more than 5 minutes of further steaming. It needn't be stirred during steaming.

Meanwhile, in a small bowl, mix the olive oil, lemon juice, dill weed, salt and pepper.

Remove broccoli from steamer and allow to cool.

Add the sauce and toss with the broccoli. Permitting the broccoli to cool before adding the lemon juice prevents the color from turning muddy green.

Note On Broccoli Stems: By cutting the tender portion of the stems into 1/4-inch-thick rounds, they will cook at the same rate as the florets. When more of the stem is desired for use, or if the stems are not as fresh, the outer skin may need peeling. Using a peeler, start from the cut end and peel toward the florets. Don't worry if it doesn't peel all the way, that's the tender portion. Because tough stems take longer to cook, add them to the steamer first, about two minutes earlier. Sometimes the stems can be set aside for stir-frying where the added crunch is a most desirable part of Asian food enjoyment.

Bright and Best
Brussels Sprouts

It's no wonder many avoid Brussels sprouts. Unless frost-sweetened and quickly cooked, they will be lacking in sweetness and drab looking. Gardeners know this. Others should head for the nearest farm market to select them after the chill of fall and when they have not been in storage for any length of time. This recipe makes good use of the cooking-chemistry principle that the green color of a vegetable is lost after seven minutes of cooking. By taking the time to separate the tiny leaves, they cook quickly, thus keeping their bright color.

```
1   pound Brussels sprouts
2   tablespoons vegetable oil
Salt and pepper to taste
1   tablespoon soy sauce
1   tablespoon oyster sauce, optional (Asian store
ingredient)
Leftover rice, small pasta cuts, or potatoes
```

Trim sprouts and either pull away the little leaves or cut thinly across the sprouts. **Heat** oil in a large pan or wok over medium heat. Cover and cook for two minutes. **Uncover**, raise heat, add soy sauce and oyster sauce if used, and stir regularly until done, about two more minutes. **Adjust** for salt and pepper seasoning.
Since these sprouts blend well with leftover rice, pasta or potatoes, add an equal amount of one of them when the pan is still warm enough to warm through, and serve.

Brussels Sprouts with Mustard Butter

The assertive punch of mustard butter takes on the challenge of flavoring the fullness of Brussels Sprouts. By slicing them in quarters, the Brussels sprouts should be done in time to keep their color.

```
1   pound Brussels sprouts, cut in quarters
Salt and pepper to taste
2   tablespoons each of softened butter and prepared
        mustard, mixed together
1/2 teaspoon caraway or celery seeds,
        bruised in a mortar
```

Bring a large pot of water to a boil, add the salt; cook the sprouts in a strainer at a medium boil until tender, about 5 minutes. **By cooking** in a strainer, removal and cooling will be easier. **Meanwhile,** mix butter, mustard and celery seeds together. **Remove,** drain, cool with water, toss with mustard sauce; adjust seasonings and serve.

Cheesy German Cabbage

Serves four

For being so easy to prepare, it's a very satisfying dish. German cooks put this together whenever they have cabbage, onions and cheese handy. Only attempt this dish when you have access to fresh cabbage, or cabbage that has been stored properly for only a short period.

> 1/2 small to medium green cabbage
> 1/2 medium onion, sliced
> Salt and generous black pepper to taste
> 5 thick slices of American cheese
> Rye bread as a side

Select an attractive, large cooking and serving pan.

Wash the cabbage, removing any damaged or wilted outer leaves. Carefully, with a sturdy knife, cut the head in half from pole to pole; put aside one half and cut the other in half again. **Remove** the core sections, use them for pepper hash or discard. **Thinly** slice the two quarters into shreds.

In a large sauté pan over medium-low heat filmed with vegetable oil, sauté the onions for one minute. **Add** the cabbage shreds, stir in to mix. **Add** salt and pepper and stir occasionally for 5 to 7 minutes until the cabbage is tender.

Turn off the heat and immediately layer the cheese slices over nearly all of the warm cabbage and allow to melt.

Serve directly from the pan with rye bread as a side.

Author's note: When this recipe was shown to a friend, she said this is how she would cook cauliflower, hot with melted cheese on it.

Parsnip Fritters

In 1889 Caroline Hartmeter wrote this recipe in her notebook:

Boil four or five parsnips. When tender, peel, mash and then add a teaspoonful of flour and a beaten egg. Make into small cakes and fry in salted lard till nicely brown on both sides.

Growing parsnips in Down Jersey: Parsnips, a close cousin of the carrot, thrives in the deep sandy soils in southern New Jersey. Sow in early to mid-spring as they need a long season to grow. Their sweet flavor is deepened after one or two hard frosts, so they are best harvested in late fall. Their taste continues to improve throughout winter, and in fact, they should remain in the ground for continued harvesting. It's a good idea to place sticks in the parsnip bed to pinpoint their location for digging later when snow covered. Though planting instructions are usually sufficient on seed packets, be aware that parsnip seed, if stored cold and dry, will survive a maximum of two years at best.

Polish Panned Cabbage

Serves four to six

While the Dutch were the first immigrants to find Jersey's climate and soil hospitable for growing cabbage, later arriving Polish found them to their liking as well. Primarily a late spring and fall crop due to our warm summers, cabbage fares better in the fall where it easily sloughs off early light frosts and holds on to become sweeter. Try, if you can, to select cabbage that hasn't been in storage for any length of time.

AL FOSTER

This recipe was first encountered at my Cioci (Polish for Aunt) Jennie's house where I found it amazingly tasty, yet it has only two main ingredients. "I like to enjoy cabbage with a tender bite, so I steam it (covered in the pan) and I am careful not to overcook it. I don't use any seasonings other than black pepper, but use caraway or bacon if you like," Cioci Jennie told me.

> 2 tablespoons vegetable oil
> 1/2 medium onion, diced
> 1/2 head fresh green cabbage, washed, shredded and diced
> Freshly ground black pepper to taste
> Salt to taste

In a large non-stick skillet, sauté the onions over medium heat until barely clear; remove and set aside.

In the same pan, add 2 tablespoons of water, the cabbage with its wash water still clinging to it, and the pepper and a light amount of salt. **Steam**, covered, until just tender, about 15 minutes, stirring occasionally.

If any noticeable liquid remains in the pan, tilt pan to remove excess water.

Add the onions back to the pan with the cabbage, taste and adjust for seasoning, and serve, preferably with rye bread.

Variations: Sauté two slices of bacon, diced, with the onions, or add 1 tablespoon of caraway seeds with the cabbage during the steaming.

> **Fresh Green Cabbage** should have a sweet, spicy aroma that is dramatically revealed when cut in half. At the market, look for cabbage whose cut end doesn't show excessive browning and whose leaves are tender and bright green rather than lighter green interior leaves, which indicates wilting and removal of outer leaves. Grasp the head and firmly twist, it should almost feel and sound squeaky.

Prussian-Style Red Cabbage

Serves six

Mrs. Santaniello, who emigrated from the Prussian section of Germany following WWII, farmed dairy and vegetables with her husband in Vineland. Many of the dishes she prepares today are those brought from her homeland. She says that since her grandchildren like this red cabbage dish so much, that is probably how she will be remembered. I think you will agree.

1/2	medium red cabbage
2	tart apples, peeled and sliced
3	slices bacon, or 4 ounces of salt pork
2-3	slices lemon, with peel
	Pinch of cloves
	Salt and pepper to taste
2	tablespoons cider or other mild vinegar

Slice the cabbage in half carefully, set one half aside and cut the remaining half in half again. Remove the core and discard.

In a large sauté pan over medium heat, add cabbage, apples, bacon, lemon and cloves, plus 1/4 cup of water. **Reduce** heat to medium-low and cook for 15 minutes, uncovered.

Add vinegar, correct for seasonings, and serve.

Note: Mrs. Santaniello remembers that in Prussia they used goose grease and as she said, "You want the good taste of grease, but it shouldn't taste greasy."

What's with red cabbage? Along with green cabbage that stores so well that they sustained our ancestors for ages, red cabbage has it's own distinct qualities. Generally, red cabbage leaves are sturdier, making it more suitable for dishes where more crunch is desired, either before or after cooking.. Farmers, however, find it more fickle to grow than green and the market demands are more uncertain as well. Hence, the price at the market is likely to be higher.

Though cabbage is found at local markets from June onwards, the best season for the tastiest cabbage is during the cooler months of fall well into November or beyond, if the weather permits.

Farm Market Baked Cauliflower

Serves six

From the Duffield family, well known for their quality vegetables, bakery and deli departments at their Sewell farm market, we have this excellent recipe for cauliflower. In our southern New Jersey area, cauliflower is at its prime in the fall season when it arrives from local fields. They suggest steaming as a first choice since boiling can leave it waterlogged.

1	large head cauliflower, trimmed
1/2	cup sour cream
1/2	cup mayonnaise
1	tablespoon parsley
1/2	tablespoon dried onion, optional
1	tablespoon dill weed
1/2	tablespoon seasoned salt, or salt mixed with paprika

Logo of the New Jersey Farmers' Direct Marketing Association

Preheat oven to 375 degrees F.

Cut cauliflower into small, bite-size florets and place in a steamer with 1 inch of water.

Cover, bring water to a boil and steam for 15 minutes, or until tender.

Alternately, place florets in water to cover, bring to a boil, reduce to a simmer and cook for 10 minutes or until tender.

Remove florets and toss with remaining ingredients.

Place the florets with mix in a baking dish and bake for 10 to 15 minutes, or until surface is lightly golden.

Old Bay Cauliflower

Serves six

In Down Jersey, everyone takes to the aroma of Old Bay, yet we often use other crab boil seasonings. Some of them, such as J.O. or Baltimore Spice might be more to our liking.

1	head cauliflower, trimmed
2	tablespoons butter
1	tablespoon crab boil seasoning

Cut cauliflower into small, bite-size florets and place in a steamer with 1 inch of water. **Cover,** bring water to a boil and steam for 15 minutes, or until tender. **Remove** florets, toss with butter until it melts and toss and mix in crab boil seasoning. **Note:** Crab boil seasonings are heavy on salt, so proceed cautiously.

Paprika or Curried Corn & Red Peppers

Serves four

When fresh, sweet corn is in season, mature red bell peppers are close behind in availability. When the kernels are cut directly from the cob, the simple addition of the peppers and a bit of curry seasoning delights the eye as well as bringing a truly summertime-only flavor. Cooking time is quick, actually.

    Stripped kernels from 6 ears of corn
    2   tablespoons vegetable oil
    1   teaspoon curry powder, or 1 Tablespoon paprika
    1/2 red bell pepper, diced same size as corn kernels
    Salt to taste

Add corn kernels, red pepper and salt, sautéing for about 3 to 5 minutes, according to degree of caramelization desired, stirring frequently. **Move** a baseball size portion of the corn and peppers aside, add the curry or paprika, and stir for 10 seconds in the hot oil. If no oil is in the cleared area, add a tablespoon. **Toss** seasoning in with mix; cook for another minute. **Check** for seasoning and serve. **Note:** If red peppers are not handy, use other colorful vegetable, such as carrots, radishes or tomatoes.

Cook's Comment: Among the newer varieties of corn, the supersweet or, sH types, have a tough outer skin, or pericarp, that takes forever to tenderize in cooking. For corn-on-the-cob enjoyment use supersweet corn. For cooking, use either the standard sugary kinds such as Silver Queen, or the sugary enhanced types like Argent or Silver King found at local stands.

To add confusion, newer breeds of corn are being introduced that combine elements of all three types. They are being called synergistic and we, as cooks, have to experiment to learn how they fare in cooking.

Sweet Corn Guide:

Normal Sugary (su). Traditional corn flavor and tenderness with moderate but varying degrees of sugar, depending on variety. This is the corn that loses its sugar rapidly after harvesting and is the reason for the old adage "Pick the corn after the water comes to a boil."

Sugary Enhanced (se). Sometimes called supersweet, it contains a gene that increases the sugar levels, but retains tenderness and creaminess. Slower to lose its sweetness, this type is great on the cob and keeps its tenderness when cooked. They are a choice buy at local farm markets.

Shrunken (sh2). Perhaps most often thought of when the name supersweet is used, this type has the highest levels of sugar and is the slowest to convert its sugar to starch, so it is popular at the major food chains. It has, however a tough outer skin and is slow to tenderize in cooking.

New releases of varieties that try to combine the best of all three above types are in the works. Fresh, off-the-cob eating no doubt is great with supersweet corn. Cooking them is another matter.

Crispy Cinnamon Cucumbers

Serves four

Itinerant Pakistani farm field workers found a treasury in the bountiful crops of Jersey cucumbers for their homeland's practice of cooking cukes.

Odd as this recipe may seem to us, by sautéing cucumbers coated with flour and seasoned with cinnamon, a whole new delight comes about when you thought there would be no more ways to do cucumbers. This recipe deserves use of those crispy, sweet Oriental types that are slim, long and rarely waxed. A closely related type, also not waxed, the burpless cuke, is often found shrink-wrapped at greengrocers. Or, grow your own.

        3/4 pound Oriental cucumbers, more or less
             Flour for dredging, about 1/4 cup
        1/2 teaspoon cinnamon
             Salt and pepper to taste
          1 tablespoon butter
          1 tablespoon olive or vegetable oil
        1/2- teaspoon lemon zest, optional

Wash and remove the stem and blossom end of the cucumbers. **Cut** crosswise into 3/8-inch slices.

Mix flour, cinnamon and salt and pepper; dredge slices in flour mix, shake off the excess. **In a large** sauté pan over medium-high heat, add cucumbers in a single layer. **Sauté** for about 5 minutes or until lightly browned, and flip over to repeat for about another four minutes. If they clump, it's no matter. These cucumbers go well with spicy foods.

Socketed Pots

Remove from heat, optionally lightly toss with lemon zest while still warm and serve hot or cold.

Variation: Instead of slicing, coarsely grate, squeeze out as much water as you can, and form a patty that is then dredged in the flour mixture and sautéed.

Collard Greens

When Elnora Gardenhire, from Piney Hollow near Newfield, makes collard greens, she makes it for all her children and grandchildren. She prefers to stay with just collards and not mix in other greens.

8-10	(10-ounce) frozen packages collard greens, thawed
1	pound smoked turkey meat, or 3/4 pound smoked pork neck bones
4	cloves garlic, minced
1	onion, diced
1	teaspoon salt, or to taste
1/2	teaspoon sugar

In a large soup pot, add the turkey and garlic, and barely cover with water. **Bring** to a boil, reduce to simmer and cook until turkey meat is tender, about 20 minutes.
Add the onions and salt; simmer for 5 more minutes.
Add the collard greens and sugar, stir in and simmer until cooked, about 5 more minutes.
Serve with cornbread and add a dash of cayenne if desired.

Pole lima beans.....like no other

A traveler along Down Jersey roads observing vegetable gardens might catch sight of gardens with rows of wire-trellised poles about six feet in height. Locally known

simply as "bean poles," they are sure signs that pole limas are grown, a favorite specialty crop. Anyone who has tasted fresh-cooked pole lima beans and compares them to the more common bush-type lima bean would say, "Can't go back."

The special flavor of the large pole lima bean has eased them into many soups and stews, and because of their abundance, into casseroles that call for heaps of beans. It is quite common for the Polish to include pole limas in their soup mainstay, borscht. In our household, we serve limas straight up with butter and generous black pepper, tossed in with rice, and as a side dish for seafood.

What many don't realize is that pole limas need a relatively warm and long growing season, and yet, they resent it when it's too hot. The southwest breeze flowing across the nearby Chesapeake region and our own Delaware Bay provides an extended late summer warmth that helps the lima beans develop reasonable yields of tasty bean-laden pods. On the other hand, should there be too many summer days where temperatures reach into the high 90's, the stress would cause the flower to abort, resulting in loss of emerging pods. So, only a few hundred mile south, gardeners will resort to the more heat tolerant pole lima beans, such as the Henderson bean, although a good bean, it is not a Down Jersey pole lima bean. Travel fifty miles west into Pennsylvania, or 50 miles northwards, and few gardeners there would bother to grow pole limas as their season would be so short for the beans to mature, and thus reap a meager harvest.

Since picking the beans can't be mechanized for farms on a small scale with current technology, few farmers in Jersey venture into growing them. Those that do will sell their excess crop to nearby farm markets. A basket of limas in the shell can fetch 15 to 20 dollars at farm markets.

So strong is the tradition for pole limas that most gardeners save their own seeds from year to year. Some go to the extent of examining each bean under a magnifying glasse so as to save only the best.

Most seed savers can't remember the origins or the names of the parent varieties that they now save. Among the most popular heirloom varieties found at garden marts that sell local lima bean seeds are Cape May Giant, Garwood and Big Six.

Should you find them at a farm market during their high season of August and September, select lima beans whose pods are light green with no sign of yellowing or shriveling. Treat them as you would fresh corn, keep as cool as possible until they are used or put up. They will keep in the freezer, after blanching, for about six months.

A lesson learned. Recently, I chose to cook dried lima beans from an uncovered jar that had been in storage for unknown years under our basement steps.
What a disaster! The resulting soup tasted like essence of cellar steps.
The moral of this story is to cover even dried beans, or else they will pick up aromas from the environment they are stored.

Vegetables..... 81

Tuscan-Style Lima Beans
with Campbell's V8

Serves four

This is another example of a preparation that uses a popular, locally produced item from the Campbell Soup Company's plant in Camden. As the name implies, V8 contains the flavoring of eight vegetables that, besides the wholesome drink it provides, is a terrific flavor enhancing sauce for our Jersey garden vegetables. This is one of our family favorites. Please be mindful that this recipe works equally well with green snap beans.

3	tablespoons extra-virgin olive oil
1	tablespoon dried sage leaves
1	(5.5-ounce can) V8 Juice, use 11.5-ounce size can if more sauce is desired
10-12	ounces lima beans, pole limas preferred, or green beans, cut in bite-size pieces

Heat olive oil in a saucepan over medium low heat and add the sage, stirring for about 30 seconds. **Lower** the heat and add the V8 cautiously as it may splatter. Use of a splatter screen or pot lid may be warranted. **Stir** for about 2 minutes
Add the lima or green beans and simmer 15 minutes for limas, about 10 minutes for green beans. **Add** more water if you want more sauce. Salting shouldn't be necessary.
Variations: Use other beans and other seasoning choices, such as black beans and cumin, kidney beans and chile powder and so on, but maintain the generous olive oil and V-8 flavor base. Or, give it a German flair by using summer or winter savory and use vegetable oil instead of olive oil.

    A friend once announced to me that she had purchased a house in Camden, that, to her good fortune, included a basement kitchen. My immediate response was, "Oh, you bought a house that was occupied previously by an Italian family." Now that she owned the house, it was something strange but welcome.

    To me, having a downstairs kitchen seemed so sensible since that's what my Mother had arranged when a kitchen extension was added to our house immediately after WWII. In the basement below the upstairs kitchen, she bought a Sears three-burner kerosene stove to begin its duty in a second kitchen. In time, the old electric stove found another home down there, along with a laundry sink and our old enameled dining table.

    That downstairs kitchen came into use for doing the "dirty" cooking chores such as when someone brought home crabs from the Delaware Bay, for soaking the odiferous bacala (dried cod) away from the main household, making pizzeles or drying homemade pasta, and of course, tomato canning.

    Before the days of air conditioning, that retreat kitchen sure was a relief in the hot, dog days of summer. As the cool days returned, we would return to our upstairs kitchen again.

    We seem to have come full circle again, as messy cooking gets relegated to the outdoor barbecue on the deck so as to not infringe on the clean kitchen.

Hackett's Fried Tomatoes

Serves four to six

Sometimes the easiest way is the best way. In this version, Hackett's Farm Market in Bargaintown, near Northfield, has found that the use of a crab boil seasoning mixed with cornmeal drew the most raves from their customers. More elaborate coatings and seasonings lost out to this easy way.

Despite the common perception of use of round slicing tomatoes, the Hackett's have learned that ripe Jersey plum tomatoes hold up quite well during the sautéing, even when ripe, and don't require sugar to balance acidity as round tomatoes might.

> 6   large, ripe plum tomatoes
> 1/4   cup corn meal
> 1   heaping tablespoon crab boil seasoning such as Old Bay, Baltimore Spice, or J.O. Crab Seasoning
> 2   tablespoons vegetable oil

Wash and slice tomatoes into 1/2-inch thick rounds by slicing off the tip and using the stem end to hold the tomato securely for slicing the rounds. If the cuts close to the stem end show an area of firm greenness in the core, the tomatoes are not ideally ripe, but can be used by removing the green core.

Mix the corn meal and crab boil seasoning in a wide bowl for easier dredging later.

Add the vegetable oil to a large non-stick sauté pan over medium heat.

When the oil is hot, dip the tomato slices on each side in the cornmeal mix and carefully add to the pan.

Cook until golden brown on the underside, about 3 to 4 minutes, and repeat for the other side, about 3 minutes.

Carefully remove the tomato slices from the pan to a serving dish by either easing them out of the pan by tilting it, or by the gentle use of a large spatula.

Notes: Flour or breadcrumbs can be substituted with a corresponding change in texture. Use of round slicing tomatoes may call for addition of sugar to balance their increased tanginess. Green tomatoes will need sugar added to the coating mixture.

Okra and Tomatoes

Serves six to eight

Here is yet another example of southern foodways that found acceptance in Down Jersey as the soil and weather are favorable to growing heat-loving okra plants. This recipe, shared by Elnora Gardenhire, combines the special taste of okra and the famous Jersey tomatoes while bringing in the local abundance of peppers. In the southern tradition, it is served over rice.

3   tablespoons butter
1   medium onion, chopped
1   pound fresh okra, trimmed both ends, cut in 3 pieces
6   vine ripened Jersey tomatoes, peeled and diced
1   bell pepper, green or red, chopped
Salt to taste
Dash of cayenne, optional

In a cast iron pan over medium heat, sauté the okra in butter for 3 minutes; add the rest of the ingredients and cook for 5 minutes more. **Do not** over cook as the okra will lose its crunchiness.

On November 30, 1858 Vineland area native, **John Landis Mason** patented a shoulder seal jar with a screw cap at a time when canning was important to the home economy. By 1874, Mason's patent was in the public domain, enabling other manufacturers to use the Mason name. The first production of Mason jars has been attributed to the Crowleytown Glass Works in Crowleytown, NJ.   Made with heavier glass to withstand higher sterilizing temperatures, the "Mason Jar" is still in use today, although the zinc lids are no longer recommended for home canning. The two-piece metal top is the healthiest choice today.

The jar in the exhibit at the Museum of American Glass at Wheaton Village in Millville is one of the original Mason patents and the first example acquired by the museum. (Not the jar shown here)

Cumberland County Pickled Peppers

This recipe appeared in a pamphlet published by Cumberland County Freeholders Ed Salmon and Jim Quinn, titled "A Treasury of Cumberland County Recipes" and was developed by late Mayor Patrick Fiorilli, author of the Pat's Pantry food column that appeared in The Press newspaper regularly. Though not dated, the pamphlet appears to have been published around 1985.

As you can see in the recipe, it suggests using sweet cheese or white cap peppers. They are unique old varieties found in the Cumberland county area where pepper production, both on commercial farms and in home gardens, excels.

Any variety of sweet peppers can be used in this recipe, but sweet cheese, or white caps, seem to be best. You must have pickling quality vinegar of 40 to 50 grain, or percent acidity, for proper fermentation. Some stores carry pickling quality vinegar, but you may have to buy it at a pickling factory. If the vinegar is 100 grain, mix it with equal parts of water and you will have 50-grain vinegar.

Next select the container you will use for pickling. *Do not use a metal container.* Wood, plastic or glass is best. Make a wooden plate that will fit inside the top of the container to hold the peppers submerged; this is important. Wash the peppers with cold water and stack them in the container whole, with their cores. Do not cut the peppers to pickle them. With the peppers in the container, add 1 tablespoon of salt for each gallon.

Place the wooden plate on top of the peppers and secure it so it holds the peppers at least 2 inches below the top of the container. Now add the vinegar, filling the container to 1 inch from the top, or 1 inch over the peppers. Cover the container with a cloth and store in a dark, cool place. Check the vinegar level each day for the first week. As the peppers absorb vinegar, the level will go down and you will have to add more. After the first week, check the vinegar level once a week. Never seal the container. There must be a free oxygen supply for proper fermentation. If a white mold appears on top, it is merely spent yeast spores. Remove them with a spoon and add more vinegar if needed. It will take 8 weeks for proper fermentation.

At the end of 8 weeks, your peppers are ready to use. Remove only as many peppers as you need at one time. Leave the rest submerged in the vinegar until you are ready to use them. Remove the pepper cores and seeds and cut skins into 3/4-inch wide strips.

Put 8 ounces of your favorite salad oil in a blender and add 4 cloves of garlic and 1/2 of a large onion along with 1 teaspoon of salt and 1/2 teaspoon of black pepper and blend well. Pour this mix in a bowl and mix in the pepper strips. Stir them so that each is coated with the mix and your peppers are ready to use. The peppers can be stored in your refrigerator in a covered container for several weeks.

Pepper Hash

Perhaps most popularized here by Germans, Dutch, Jewish, and other northern European immigrants, pepper hash takes a European native, cabbage, and combines it with American peppers. Germans from New Jersey and Pennsylvania were among the first to make vats of pickled cabbage. Following the German trait of thrift, pepper hash came to be a frugal use of its two main ingredients, cabbage and peppers, especially since more of the tougher cabbage core can be used to full benefit.

Now popular in other parts of the U.S., pepper hash has held on strong here as it's a great condiment with our seafood. It has also been a favorite topping for hot dogs. We have halved the old time recipe to better suit today's smaller families, but it surely can be doubled if you like.

We suggest that you be very selective in purchasing the cabbage. It must be fresh or have undergone proper storage, leaving it with a fresh and spicy aroma. Ask your greengrocer or farm marketer when the primary ingredients, cabbage and peppers, will be in season, which is usually from mid-summer to early fall.

This hash will keep for several weeks in the refrigerator.

1/2	head cabbage, green or Savoy
1	green or red bell pepper, minced
1	carrot, organic preferred, minced
1/2	cup cider vinegar
1/2	cup water
1/4	cup sugar

If you start with a whole head of cabbage, carefully cut it in half and the half to be used in half again. **Remove** the core with a diagonal cut and discard.

With a chef's knife, if you have one, or a large sturdy knife, carefully shred the cabbage quarters into thin ribbons or pulse in a food processor until approximately 1/4-inch pieces or less.

Continuing by hand, mound the ribbons in a pile and dice into approximate 1/4-inch pieces or less.

Core and mince the pepper into 1/4-inch pieces or less. After peeling the carrots, do the same. **Mix** the cabbage, peppers and carrots together.

In a separate bowl, stir the vinegar, water and sugar together until the sugar is dissolved. **Combine** the vinegar mix with the cabbage and allow to rest in the refrigerator for one day before use.

Variation: Some may prefer to add a teaspoon of celery seed and/or a dash of hot red pepper flakes. **Note:** When prepared expressly as a condiment for fish, you may want to moderate the sugar.

Red Pepper Panned Potatoes

Serves four to six

Out-of-state travellers have said that they could only find "sweet frying" peppers at Down Jersey farm markets, so here's a super prep for panned potatoes that, by just adding a few red frying peppers, a whole new dish arises. Adding a small amount of meat, such as ham, carries this light dish to a main meal event. It's one of our family's favorites.

8 medium baking or all-purpose potatoes, washed
3 tablespoons olive or vegetable oil
1 clove garlic, sliced in half lengthwise
1/4 medium onion, diced
4 sweet red frying peppers, or 1-1/2 red bell pepper,
     diced
Salt and pepper to taste, plus cayenne if desired

Partially cook potatoes in a 1,000 watt microwave for 8 minutes, or boil for 12 minutes. **Cool**, peel and cube. **In a large** skillet pan over medium heat, add oil and sauté garlic till golden. **Remove** and discard..

Add onions and peppers and sauté, uncovered, slowly over low heat until very slightly browned, about 3 to 5 minutes. **Remove** with a slotted spoon, set aside, keeping as much flavored oil in the pan as you can.

Add the potatoes to the pan, raise heat to medium, add more oil if needed, add salt and pepper and sauté potatoes until browned on most sides, turning occasionally.

Return onion and pepper mix, adjust salt and pepper, and cook for 1 minute more.

Pan-browned Potatoes with Paprika

Serves four to six

Southern New Jersey farmers grow a lot of peppers. At farmers markets, one can find great bargains on sweet bell peppers in late August through September when green bell peppers have matured to red. Red bell peppers, you see, are the ingredient for paprika, with perhaps a few hot peppers thrown in the batch to provide more interest. See page on making paprika.

8 medium baking or all-purpose potatoes, washed
2 tablespoons vegetable oil, or olive oil
2 cloves of garlic, smashed
Salt to taste
1 heaping tablespoon of quality, fresh paprika

Partially cook potatoes in a microwave oven for 8 minutes. **Cool**, peel and cube. **In a large**. sauté pan, over medium heat, sauté garlic in oil until lightly browned. **Remove** garlic and discard. **Add** the potatoes to the pan, raise heat to medium, add more oil if necessary, add salt and pepper and sauté potatoes until browned, turning occasionally. **Turn** off heat and mix in paprika, and serve.

Easy Curried Spinach

Serves six

Spinach finds its way into many of our dishes as our climate and soil are friendly to its growth. Our winters are often sufficiently mild to allow extended cuttings from the fields. In four winters out of five, spinach will over winter, allowing for a late winter cut. With the benefit of repeated cuts and nearby local processing plants, spinach is a major crop for farmers. For us, we find heaps of this wholesome green in the bins at local farm markets in all but the coldest and hottest of months.

If there is a trick to this recipe, it is to use a fresh batch of curry (too often we use spices that should have been tossed long ago) and use it at a level below what would be overpowering for the diner. Tip: Many spinach dishes can easily be too watery if sufficient water is not squeezed out after washing.

2 tablespoons vegetable oil
1 medium onion, sliced
Salt to taste
2 teaspoons curry powder
1 pound fresh spinach, chopped

Test spinach stem tenderness by taking a small bite, if it is mild and tender, don't take the extra time and effort to cut and discard a very usable stem that adds welcome texture and volume to the dish.

Wash the spinach by filling a large pot with tepid water, which allows the leaves to relax and release any grit, but not so hot as to have the leaves wilt and cling to each other. **Place** the spinach in the water, in batches if the pot isn't quite large, and gently swish and lift out with your hands. **Give** them a firm hand squeeze.

In a large saute pan that can be covered, add oil and onions over medium heat.

When onions are golden, add curry, stirring around in the oil for a moment until the aroma is released.

Add spinach that's still moist but with excess water squeezed out, salt to taste, and cover. **Reduce** heat to medium-low, and steam until barely wilted, about one minute.

Uncover, stir and cook for another minute to allow some moisture to escape. **If** too much water remains, better to remove from the stove and tilt the pan to drain off the water than to overcook the spinach.

Remove spinach from pan and serve as a side or tossed with rice.

Variations: Mild melting cheeses, such as Muenster or Mozzarella would add body to this dish for a light luncheon when served with a crusty peasant bread or pita bread. Firm crumbled or mashed tofu also partners well. Add either of them after the process of uncovering to allow warming and marrying of flavors. Between the saffron-yellow look from the curry and the cream-colored cheese or tofu, the dish isquite inviting to the eye, the first judge.

Fried Sweet Potatoes

Serves four

Fried sweet potatoes are overlooked too often, yet they shouldn't be. Even for first-timers, they are instantly likeable.

> 3 sweet potatoes or yams, sliced into matchsticks or
>   potato-chip thick.
> Vegetable oil for frying
> Salt to taste
> Dash of cayenne pepper, optional

In a heavy pan, pour in enough oil to cover pan 1/2 inch and heat to frying temperature, somewhat below the smoking point.

Fry in small batches, drain on paper towels, and sprinkle with salt and pepper to taste.

Variation: Serve with a dusting of powdered sugar instead of cayenne.

What is paprika? Paprika is nothing more than dried red peppers. As simple as the source is, it can vary widely in quality, so much so that much of the paprika bought from supermarkets and used today has gotten the reputation of only being useful as a coloring agent. True, it does add a touch of color, but when quality paprika is used, it brings an aromatic pepperish sweetness as well. Some of the factors in arriving at high quality paprika are the speed at which the peppers are dried, the removal of stems, veins and seeds, and freshness, as paprika has a relatively short shelf life as dried spices go. Incidentally, the thick outer skin on bell peppers that is a nuisance when cooked, is of no matter when drying peppers for paprika.

While paprika can be made from thin-walled peppers, the practice of processors is to use thick-walled, fleshy peppers to extract a higher yield. The major paprika growing regions, notably Hungary and Spain, have their favorite varieties that they often refer to as their "paprika" peppers; many of them are triangular in shape. The variety of pepper used is more important to commercial growers than it is to home gardeners who dry their own.

Making your own paprika In southern New Jersey, we can arrive at high quality home dried paprika by using red bell peppers, which are green bell peppers that have matured to red, and preferably those that are not waxed. Wash, trim off stems, veins and seeds and cut in thin strips to promote faster drying. Place on a cookie tray and set in the oven at its lowest warming temperature. Stir occasionally until crisp and brittle. Remove and blend in a coffee or spice grinder. Add a bit of cayenne to your sweet paprika to give a bit of a snap. Seal in the smallest jars you have and use quickly or share them as it's best used within six months, twelve at the most. Store in a cool location out of sunlight.

Hunter's Sweet Potato Casserole

Serves six to eight

A third generation farm family in Burlington County, the Hunter's commit considerable acreage to growing sweet potatoes. Local customers especially appreciate their continued availability of heirloom varieties such as Jersey Red (a dry sweet potato) and Jersey White, a moist sweet potato. Neither of these can be found at area supermarkets.

2	eggs, beaten
1	teaspoon vanilla extract
1/2	cup melted butter
1/3	cup milk
3	cups cooked and mashed sweet potatoes

Mix together all ingredients together and pour into a buttered 8x8-inch baking dish and add topping of:

1	cup brown sugar
1	cup chopped walnuts
1/3	cup flour
1/3	cup butter, melted

Mix together above ingredients and add on top of sweet potato mixture and bake at 350 degrees F. for 25 minutes.

Mary Brown's Sweet Potato Casserole

Serves six to eight

This recipe, contributed by Mary Brown from Sicklerville, came from her grandmother, Rose. It was often prepared for church suppers where its homey goodness would always be appreciated. Surely, there would be a lively discussion as to the most suitable variety to use.

3	pounds sweet potatoes, peeled, coarsely cut and boiled until tender, and mashed
1/4	pound butter (1 stick), melted
1	teaspoon. cinnamon and 1 tsp. nutmeg
1	teaspoon. vanilla extract or 1-1/2 tsp. lemon juice
2	tablespoons frozen orange juice concentrate and 2 tablespoons honey or sugar, or 2 tablespoons orange marmalade, plus 2 tablespoons of water

Preheat oven at 350 degrees F. **Mash** sweet potatoes and mix in all other ingredients. **Place** sweet potato mix in a buttered casserole. **Top** with chopped pecans if you prefer. **Bake** at 350 degrees F. for 30 minutes. **Cool** slightly and serve.

Stewed Tomatoes

Serves four to six

It is easy to understand why our early German immigrants' contributions to our cuisine blended into the background as unremarkable American food. One of them, stewed tomatoes, deserves warming up again at our tables.

With our bounty of tomatoes, it's safe to assume that stewed tomatoes were common table fare here during the summer months. The tanginess of our round tomatoes would have begged for a touch of sugar to offset the sourness, but not if old heirloom varieties were used, such as the German Paste Tomato chosen for sauces due to its sweetness and high solids content.

Below is a recipe for stewed tomatoes alone or with pole lima beans, a natural combo any cook would have tossed together when both were in season. For today's preferences, cooking time has been shortened.

2	tablespoons butter
6	large round tomatoes, washed and peeled
1/2	small onion, minced
2 or 3	cloves
1/2	teaspoon salt, plus black pepper to taste
2	teaspoons white or brown sugar
1/2	cup plain breadcrumbs, optional, or 1 teaspoon flour mixed with 2 teaspoons of water for thickening

Place a heavy bottomed pan over medium heat; add butter to melt.

Add the peeled tomatoes, onions, cloves, salt and pepper, and sugar.

Adjust heat to a light simmer. **Cook** for 15 minutes, uncovered, stirring occasionally.

If thickening is preferred, add breadcrumbs or flour/water mixture and cook for 2 minutes more.

Variations: A half-cup of chopped celery can be added with the tomatoes at the beginning. Other spices such as paprika or curry can be added. Chopped parsley adds a nice garnish touch.

Stewed Tomatoes with Lima Beans

It is suggested to cook the lima beans separately as their tenderness varies according to freshness and size, and so does cooking time.

1	recipe stewed tomatoes, above
3/4	pound fresh lima beans, pole limas preferred

Boil or steam lima beans, until tender, about 15 minutes when boiled in salted water, 20 minutes for steaming. **Add** to stewed tomatoes and serve.

Mashed potatoes are a favorite pairing.

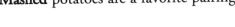

Salem Fried Tomatoes

Serves six to eight

This is another recipe excerpted from Francis Blackwood's "Once Upon a Time" cookbook that also appears in "Alloway Remembers." a publication of the Alloway Township Bicentennial of the Constitution Committee, second edition, 1988.

> 5 or 6 firm ripe tomatoes
> 1-1/2 tablespoons chicken fat or butter
> 6 tablespoons flour
> 1 teaspoon salt
> 1/2 teaspoon sugar
> 1/8 teaspoon pepper
> 2 cups milk

Wash tomatoes, wipe dry and cut thin slices from each end. **Discard** these. **The** number of tomatoes to be used must depend on their size and the family appetite. **Cut** the remaining tomatoes into 2 to 4 slices of equal thickness and allow 3 or 4 slices per person. **In** a soup plate or other saucer mix the flour, salt, sugar and pepper. **One** at a time, while butter melts in a large heavy skillet, coat each tomato slice in flour mixture. **Shake** off excess. **Place** floured slices side by side in the hot fat. **Fat** must be hot when slices go into it. **When** all are in, reduce heat somewhat and let tomatoes fry over moderately hot heat until browned on one side. **Turn** and brown on the other side. **Some** of the slices may seem to melt and break up during this frying; never mind. **As** the others brown, lift to a hot meat platter. **When** all are done, sprinkle 2 tablespoons of the remaining flour used for coating the tomatoes, into fat and broken slices in the pan, stir and scrape all possible brown bits from the pan into the gravy, add milk and cook until gravy is as thick as rich cream. **Pour** gravy boiling hot over the tomatoes on the platter and serve.

The cover of **Leddens' Seeds and Plants Price List** (now out of business), 35 pages, for the spring of 1933 shows interesting assertions. It states, "For the Farmer, Gardener, Canner and Kraut Packer....Store opposite Penna. Railroad Station...Western Union Telegraph at Sewell Station...Bell Phone, Wenonah 400."

The catalog shows the plants in demand at that time. There were listed seven varieties of celery and only one variety of eggplant, hardly a mix that would be offered today. It's also comforting to know that some of the varieties offered then are still in circulation today: Early Jersey Wakefield Cabbage, Marglobe and Ponderosa tomatoes, King of the Garden pole lima and others.

Chapter 4

All Together at Main Family Courses

When I think of main dishes, the aromas that drifted out from kitchens in earlier days come to mind. When more of us lived in towns and villages where walking by front porches took in heady fragrances, sometimes a bit foreign to our senses, we knew suppertime was approaching for those fortunate families. These drifts of diversity still linger, but we are less aware as we speed through neighborhoods in closed-window autos.

Capturing and recording that ethnic diversity from our own region is at the heart of this work. It would make all the research worthwhile to learn that just one person would later say, "That's a dish my grandparents used to make, and now I have the recipe to prepared to pass on to my children."

While respecting our roots, I haven't stopped at the recipes that our ancestors adapted to local food supplies when they settled in Down Jersey. As more speeialty items become accessible at our local markets, we have been broadening our cooking styles. And today's busier lifestyles have us keen on recipes that make the best use of our time, so we have updated recipes as well.

That said, we all look forward to making time now and again to prepare one of those time consuming main courses that bring us back to our past. It also happens to be an ideal time for the family to work together again, especially with our children. Nevertheless, I have worked to update and trim the time required, while aiming to retain the intregity for the recipes whose aromas send us back to instantly remembered memories.

Ritter's Farm Field Stew
with Lima Beans and Wedding Soup Meatballs

Serves six to eight

This stew calls up the fondest memories from Paul J. Ritter, whose mother Virginia Sorantino, would prepare this for the crews working on the farm. She would make big pots and carry it out to the fields or the packing sheds where the workers took their lunch breaks. Ritter said that by far this is still his favorite dish. He recommends that it be served with a loaf of Italian bread. Like many others, they favored use of the smaller pole lima beans.

I have taken the liberty of offering also an alternative method to the use of the small meatballs we find in Italian wedding soup. In a bow to expedience, we suggest a way I learned from a waterman, Steve Crane. Instead of making the small meatballs that seem to take forever, ground meant is browned in the pan and broken into bite-size chunks.

Meatball mixture:

- 3/4 pound ground beef, chuck preferred, or a mixture of beef, pork, and veal
- 1 egg, beaten
- 1 teaspoon black pepper and pinch of salt
- 2 cloves garlic, minced
- 8-10 fresh basil leaves, or 1 tablespoon dried crushed
- 1/4 cup grated Romano cheese
- 1/2 cup bread crumbs
- Olive oil for frying

For the stew:

- 1 quart marinara sauce
- 1 (16-ounce) can chicken broth, low salt preferred
- 1/2 cup dry red wine
- 1 pound fresh or frozen lima beans, small pole lima beans preferred
- Salt and pepper to taste
- Cooked pasta, such a rigatoni or penne

Mix all meatball ingredients. **Sauté** a small meatball to test for seasoning adjustment. **Either** hand roll into marble sized meatballs or break into similar size with a spatula when sautéing meatball mixture with olive oil. **Proceed** to sauté in olive oil in the stewing pot until browned; set meatballs or broken browned mixture aside. **In** the same pot, heat marinara sauce and chicken broth. **Bring** to a boil, reduce to simmer and add the wine, stirring occasionally. **Simmer** for 5 minutes; add the lima beans and the meatballs. **Simmer**, stirring occasionally until limas are tender, about 15 minutes. **Serve** with cooked pasta or Italian or French bread.

Ritter Labels were revised in 1917 to red, white and blue in the spirit of patriotism during the time of WWI.
Note the spelling of catsup.

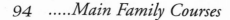

Swedish Meatballs

Makes about 48 to 50 small meat balls

If there were a lingering link to a popular Swedish dish, Swedish meatballs would be one of them. At church suppers at the Trinity Episcopal Church in Swedesboro meatballs have been served from the earliest of times. The recipe presented here is from the late Alice D. Jess, whose recipe appeared in "Historic 'Old Swedes' Trinity Episcopal Church Recipes" Anniversary Edition 1784-1984. Written at church-supper size, you might want to cut the recipe in half.

2 pounds finely ground beef	1/4 teaspoon allspice
4 tablespoons onions, finely chopped	1/2 teaspoon nutmeg
2 beaten eggs	2 tablespoons caraway seeds
1 cup fine dry bread crumbs	3 tablespoons flour
1-1/2 cups milk	1/2 cup butter
1 teaspoon salt	2 cups beef buillion or broth
1/2 teaspoon pepper	

In a large bowl, combine all ingredients, except the flour, butter and bouillon. **Mix** ingredients well. **Use** a teaspoon to form balls.

In a frying pan over medium heat, cook balls in butter until evenly brown; remove from pan. **Add** bouillon to pan. **Combine** flour with 1/3-cup water; add to pan, stirring constantly until thick. **Return** meatballs to pan; cover and cook slowly for 20 minutes. **Serve** immediately.

TRINITY EPISCOPAL "OLD SWEDES" CHURCH
A Brief History

Two hundred years ago, the small Swedish Evangelical Lutheran Church on the hill above Raccoon Creek fell into a sad state of disrepair. It had fulfilled its purpose. The Swedes at Raccoon (town) had need of a Church of their own. The tiresome and sometimes dangerous trip down the creek and across the Delaware to Old Christina, Wilmington, Delaware or Gloria Dei, Philadelphia, was a weekend journey.

Nine Swedish Pastors had come and gone. The tenth and last of the Swedes was Nicholas Collin. Pastor Collin was a learned and wise man. He recognized the time for expansion had arrived. The project was a daring one; money was a definite problem.

Collin's "Journal" tells the trials, the sweat, blood and tears far better than any other account. The Church, a living monument to Nicholas Collin, stands today where he planned. There have been changes and additions, but the basic plan still survives to give glory to God.

May Pastor Collin know that his Church is one of the architectural beauties of our State.

Trinity Episcopal (Old Swedes) Church
Swedesboro, New Jersey

Mildred S. Auten, wife of
Rev. Parker F. Auten, Ret.
(Rector of 40 years)

Sukiyaki

Perhaps better known for her teaching of Japanese origami, Fusaye Kazoaka, who resides in Seabrook, is eager to share knowledge of her homeland's cuisine. She has found the variety of locally grown produce excellent for sukiyaki, although a few Japanese speciality ingredients are still desired. In Kazoaka's recipe, feel free to change the ingredients to the freshest of the season and to a mix you prefer. Many different cuts of beef can be used, but usually leans cuts such as top or bottom round are preferred.

Sukiyake is commonly served from a pan placed in the center of the table, so use either a heavy pan over a portable stove or an electric fry pan. This is the ultimate conversation dish, plus each diner gets to choose their particular favorites from a variety of ingredients.

Mix together:
- 1-1/2 cup chicken or beef broth
- 1/3 cup soy sauce
- 1/3 cup sugar
- 1/4 cup either sake or rice wine, or 2 tablespoons rice vinegar

Chop and place in bowls:
- 1 bunch green onions cut into 1 ½ inch pieces
- 1/2 pound mushrooms, whole, stems removed if tough
- 1 cup shiratake, (yam noodles) washed and drained, or cellophane noodles
- 1/2 Napa cabbage, shredded, or 1/2 pound spinach leaves
- 2 small fresh bamboo shoots, cooked until tender, or 1 small can bamboo shoots, drained, cut into bite-size pieces
- 1 tofu package (soy bean cake) drained, cut 1-1/2 square
- 1 large onion, sliced
- 1 pound top or bottom round, or rump roast, partially frozen and sliced thin

Heat the fry pan over medium heat with a small amount of stock mixture, then add meat and vegetables, keeping each ingredient separate. **Do not** stir together as you would want all items arranged attractively in the pan. **Pour** more of the liquid stock and continue cooking uncovered on a medium setting. **When** ingredients are cooked to satisfaction each diner selects their choice of the various selections. **Add** more ingredients to replace those that guests eat, adjusting heat as needed. A traditional, optional practice is for each diner to beat a raw egg with a teaspoon of soy sauce to dip the cooked meat and vegetables before eating. **Additional** vegetable choices are carrots, celery, frenched green beans and watercress. **Note:** If your butcher cannot offer sliced beef, partially freeze the beef at home and slice thinly across the grain with a sharp knife.

Captain Fenton Anderson's
Oyster Boat Beef Stew

Serves six

We have this special recipe, thanks to the efforts of Barbara Adams from Port Norris. Years ago, Adams had the opportunity to meet a retired and well-loved oyster boat captain by the name of Fenton Anderson. As he was advanced in years, Adams asked if he would share his recipe for his oyster boat stew, which until that time, he had not given out. He assented, and here it is. As you can imagine, after hauling, sorting and tossing oysters about all day, no waterman had an appetite for an oyster stew. They clamored for a beef stew!

Since Captain Anderson's stew was started in the early morning while sailing out to the oyster beds, his stew was meant to take its time, so take advantage of the tougher, but tastier cuts of beef such as chuck or brisket.

> 1-1/2 - 2 pounds beef cubes, fat trimmed, cut into bite size
> 1 medium yellow onion, chopped
> 2 cans Campbell's Tomato Soup
> 2 soup cans (14.5 ounce, each) of water
> Black pepper to taste
> 1 teaspoon oregano
> Two shakes of thyme (about1/2 teaspoon)
> 1 (16-ounce) can green beans
> 1 large handfull broad noodles
> 3 medium-large potatoes, diced into bite size
> 1 (8-ounce) can carrots

Combine beef, onion, soup and water. **Bring** to a boil, reduce to a simmer and cook for 3 to 4 hours, stirring occasionally. **Add** the pepper (shouldn't need salting), oregano and thyme; give a good stir. **Add** the potatoes and cook 15 minutes. **Add** the beans and carrots with can juice, and noodles; boil 7 minutes more. **Captain** Anderson instructed us to leave the stew on the burner after the heat has been turned off, and add more water if the stew is too thick.

A series of **shipping sheds,** built by the railroad company and leased by individual oystermen (planters and packers) served to centralize the oyster industry in Bivalve. Everything needed to run the industry efficiently was housed in these segmented sheds along the Maurice River wharves. Included in the buildings were chandleries, meat markets, a post office, living quarters and office space. A smaller yet similar wharf was constructed on the Cohansey River-Greenwich Piers.

Old Original Mincemeat Pie Filling

Makes filling for four nine-inch pies

Mincemeat pies have such a strong tradition, having been brought to the colonies from England and northern Europe, that we will share a recipe even though few would be inclined to prepare it today. But it's well worth the effort.

The use of citrus, sweeteners, beef fat and brandy all had their basis in helping the keeping qualities of cooked beef. Yes, in the original versions beef and suet were essential ingredients, though recent adaptations have omitted meat.

It's interesting, too, that most of our canning factories, including Campbell's Soup and Ritter, had tinned mincemeat in their product lineup.

Our recipe has been shared by Noel Margarum, whose grandmother passed down the recipe to her. Although the written instructions call for canning and processing, we believe today's cook would more likely consider using the cooked mincemeat as a pie filling.

This recipe may be easily halved. Also, reduce the sugar as much as desired if your intentions are not to have the mincemeat stored for any length of time as was originally intended.

2	pounds beef, chuck cut suggested
1	pound beef suet, finely minced
4	pounds tart apples, peeled, cored and chopped
6	cups sugar
3	pounds currants
2	pounds dark raisins
1	whole nutmeg, grated
1/2	teaspoon mace, grated
2	oranges, juiced, and rinds grated
2	lemons, juiced, and rinds grated
1/2	pound citron, chopped
1	tablespoon salt
1/2	cup brandy
	Crusts for 4 pies

In a stewing pot, add beef and water to cover. **Bring** to a boil, reduce heat, and slowly simmer beef until tender, about 2-1/2 to 3 hours. Replenish water as needed. **Remove** beef from broth, allow to cool and chop into minced pieces; return to the broth. **To the simmering broth,** add the beef suet, apples, currants, raisins, spices, orange and lemon juice and their grated rinds, citron and salt. **If** not prepared for storage, add the sugar in increasing amounts until desired sweetness is achieved. **Simmer** slowly, stirring often, for another 30 minutes. **Remove** from heat. **Mix** well in a large non-reactive bowl; keep covered in a cool location until ready for use, often months later. **To make the pies:** Make pastry for 4 pies. **Put** the crust in place and fill with mincemeat. **Bake** pies at 350 degrees F. until crust turns golden. Noel Margarum said her grandmother would grate a raw apple over the filling and drizzle on a bit more brandy.

Pennsgrove Roast Beef Sandwiches

Makes about two dozen sandwiches

The Washington Club in Pennsgrove, an Italian-American social association, continues to serve their version of the ultimate home-cooked food, a pot roast of beef. They believe that serving thinly sliced pot-roasted beef served in crusty-roll sandwiches soaked in a tomato, cooking pepper and celery sauce is a worthy salute to beef. In fact, while once found at Italian weddings, it is now served at numerous festivals as walk-away food. Surely, other notable uses can be called up for this pot roast and sauce.

While chuck roast makes a great cut for pot roast with its juiciness, it suffers when one tries to slice it thinly for sandwiches. Top round can be too dry. An ideal cut for this recipe is bottom round rump roast. Secret: Use sweet frying peppers if you can!

1	(3- to 4-pound) beef rump roast, tied if not boneless	
3	tablespoons olive oil	
Salt and pepper		
4-5 cloves garlic, minced		
1	bay leaf	
1/2	cup red wine	
1	(14-ounce) can chicken broth	

Sauce:
2	tablespoons olive oil
4-5	celery stalks, chopped
2	medium onions, chopped
10 -12	long, sweet cooking peppers, red and green mixed, or 8 -10 Cubanelles
1-2	long, thin hot cooking peppers, chopped, optional
	Stock from roasting beef
1	(28-ounce) can crushed tomatoes
2	ounces tomato paste

Long hard rolls for the sandwiches

Heat the oil over medium low heat in a large, heavy Dutch oven. **Add** the roast beef, salt, and slowly brown beef all around, being careful not to burn. **Remove** roast to a platter. **Pour** off all but 2 tablespoons of the oil, return to heat; cook garlic for 30 seconds and add the wine. **Scrape** bottom of pot with a wooden spoon to release caramelized drippings; simmer 5 minutes. **Return** beef roast to pan, add chicken stock, crushed tomatoes, tomato paste, and sufficient water to cover 1/2 way up the roast. **Bring** liquid to a boil, reduce to a low simmer, and cook, covered, turning every 1/2 hour. **Cook** until tender, about 1-1/2 to 2 hours. **Remove** roast, slice thinly when cool; return beef to Dutch oven. **In** a separate, large sauté pan over medium heat, add 2 tablespoons olive oil and sauté celery, onions and peppers, lightly salted and peppered, turning occasionally. **Cook** until they release their liquid and are lightly browned. **Combine** cooked peppers, celery and onions to the beef in the Dutch oven and simmer 5 minutes more. **Check** for seasoning adjustment. **Serve** sliced roast beef in crusty rolls with sauce poured on the roll.

Pan-grilled Steak
with Portabella au Poivre

Serves two

Few joys jump to the height of a seared steak cooked well with an accompanying sauce of thickly sliced portabella in an au poivre (pepper) sauce. Ah, but getting there takes a bit of technique, and here we will attempt to guide you through it all. A main ingredient for au poivre sauce is a beef flavor, so the pan juices give you that, as many of us don't have a good beef base at hand. If you do, do make the mushrooms on their own if you wish.

2   beef steaks, rib, strip or sirloin, 3/4 to 1-1/4-inch
         thick
1   tablespoon vegetable or olive oil
Salt and 2 tablespoons cracked or coarse-ground black
         pepper

For the Portabella au poivre:

2   tablespoons shallots, scallions (white part), or
         onions, minced
1/4 cup brandy, bourbon or red wine
2   portabella mushrooms, stems removed, caps sliced
         1/2-inch thick
2   tablespoons chopped fresh parsley
1   tablespoon butter, preferably unsalted, optional

Trim steaks, pat dry. Add the oil to a heavy, sturdy pan over high heat until the oil begins to smoke, about 5 minutes.

Keeping the heat high, salt one side of the steak and immediately lay in the pan. Sear for 5 minutes, more for steaks thicker than 1 inch, less for thinner steaks.

Sprinkle the salt and cracked or coarse pepper on top of the steaks, pressing in with a spatula. Turn over and cook for 4 minutes for medium rare.

Remove steaks from pan, keep warm.

Reduce heat and add shallots, stirring and scrapping to bring up the "fond" in the pan from the steaks.

Sauté briefly, standing away from the stove, add the brandy and simmer for 3 minutes. At this point, add the sliced portabella mushrooms.

Simmer the mushrooms and the sauce for another 8 minutes at which time the mushrooms will be cooked and the sauce thickened.

Taste and adjust the sauce, add the parsley.

Finally, swirl in the butter, moving the pan to incorporate it into the sauce.

With a slotted spoon, lift out the mushrooms and plate. Pour the sauce over the steaks and serve.

Variations: Some may prefer to add a tablespoon of mustard to the sauce, or mix the black pepper with green peppercorns.

Steak & Kidney Pie

Makes one pie to serve four to six

Before you pass this so-English pie by, you will be surprised to discover that it has an intensely beefy taste, not at all what you might contemplate. True, it is rarely made in Down Jersey these days, but should be. In respect to the early English settlers, we offer this hearty pie for you to consider. Naturally, it accommodates an English ale quite well.

We thank Clay Cary, whose family traces back to the shires of England, for this recipe.

- 2 tablespoons vegetable oil
- 3/4 pound beef, chuck preferred, cut in 1/2-inch cubes, well trimmed
- 3/4 pound beef kidneys, veal preferred, duct removed and cut in 1/2-inch cubes
- 1 large onion, diced
- 6 ounces button mushrooms, sliced
- Pinch of thyme
- 1 bay leaf
- 1 tablespoon parsley, chopped
- 1-1/2 teaspoon salt, 1/2 teaspoon pepper
- 3 tablespoons all-purpose flour
- 22 ounces beef broth or stock
- 1 recipe for suet dough (enough for 2 pies) see next page

Add vegetable oil to a heavy skillet, preferably cast iron. Over medium heat sear the beef until lightly browned. **Remove** and set aside. **Repeat** for the kidneys.

In the same skillet, add the onions and sauté for 1/2 minute.

Add the mushrooms and seasonings of thyme, bay leaf, parsley, salt and pepper.

Stir in flour, cooking for 2 minutes with continuous stirring. **Return** the beef and kidneys to the skillet. **Allow** to cool; set aside.

Line a deep fireproof baking pan, 10-inch pie pan, ceramic crock or glassware with the suet dough.

Add the meat and seasoning mixture to the suet dough. **Remove** bay leaf.

Add beef stock.

Cover with top crust, pinching edges and cut out a 3-inch vent hole.

For a glaze, brush with a wash of 1 whole egg beaten with 1 tablespoon water.

Bake, uncovered, at 400 degrees F. for 10 minutes, then reduce to 325 degrees F. and bake for 45 minutes or until bubbly.

Suet Crust

Makes two pies

While this suet crust accommodates the preceding steak and kidney pie, it is ideal for most other English pies. The English have a fascination for putting many wonderful ingredients in pies. As an Englishwoman once said the me, "And where do you think American apple pie came from?" Enough said.

As you know, working in a cool room and working fast as to not melt the butter or warm the other ingredients is the secret of a flaky dough, along with the lard or suet, of course.

1	pound, 4 ounces all purpose flour
12	ounces cold suet or lard, cut into 1/4-inch dice
4	ounces cold butter, cut into 1/4-inch pieces with dough cutter
1	ounce sugar
5-6	ounces water
1-1/2	teaspoons salt

In a large bowl, cut fats into the flour the size of hazelnuts.

Blend sugar and salt into water and dissolve.

Combine liquid with flour until it forms a ball.

Quickly work the dough to a maximum of 5 minutes on a lightly floured surface until all the liquid is absorbed.

If dough crumbles, add water cautiously.

Wrap dough in plastic wrap and refrigerate for 1 hour minimum.

Cut dough into 4 equal sections and, on a floured surface, roll into 1/8-inch thickness. **Dust** with flour as needed, brush off excess.

Use as directed in the recipe. This dough will store in the refrigerator for up to one week.

Muskrat board used to stretch and dry the fur.

The English were among the early settlers that relied on muskrat trapping for a livelihood. Until recent times when leg hold traps were banned, schoolchildren living near the marshes where the muskrat habituated would go "ratting" to earn money for school clothing and books.

Muskrat meat, appreciated by some toady, still draws a sell-out affair at annual muskrat dinners in Salem County.

Irish Beef and Guinness Stew

Serves six to eight

We thank Donna Robinson at Green Dragon Irish Imports, Salem for this recipe. In our taste trials, it has been extremely well received.

Cattle, though kept for their milk, were also used for their beef. Beef was prepared as a special dish and to be regarded as a meal of great importance. Lamb was used more often in Ireland because beef derived from their cattle was used for milk, cream and cheese. Here in America the Irish came to prefer the relatively inexpensive beef that is available here.

2 pounds lean stewing beef
3 tablespoons vegetable oil
2 tablespoons flour
Salt and freshly ground pepper,
     and a pinch of cayenne,
     if desired ·
2 large onions, coarsely
     chopped
1 large clove garlic, crushed
     (optional)
2 tablespoons tomato puree,
     dissolved in 4 tablespoons
     water
1-1/4 cups Guinness stout
2 cups carrots, cut into chunks
Sprig of thyme
Parsley, chopped, for garnish

Until the mass marketers prevailed, local brews were more common. This is Patti Brown's rendering of a can of Camden Lager Beer, which ceased brewing in the early 1960's. Its slogan was "None Better." and on the label proclaimed "Brewed with crystal clear water from our own artesian wells."

Trim the meat of any fat or gristle, cut into cubes of 2 inches and toss them in a bowl with 1 tablespoon oil. **Season** the flour with salt, freshly ground pepper and a pinch or two of cayenne.
Dredge the meat in the mixture to coat with flour.
Heat the remaining oil in a wide frying pan over a high heat.
Brown the meat on all sides.
Add the onions, crushed garlic and tomato puree to the pan, cover and cook gently for about 5 minutes. **Transfer** the contents of the pan to a casserole, and pour half of the Guinness into the frying pan. **Bring** to a boil and stir to dissolve the caramelized meat juices on the pan. **Pour** pan juices onto the meat with the remaining Guinness; add the carrots and the thyme. **Stir**, taste, and add a little more salt, if necessary.
Cover with the lid of the casserole and simmer very gently until the meat is tender, 2 to 3 hours. **The** stew may be cooked on top of the stove or in a low oven at 300 degrees F. **Taste** and correct the seasoning. **Scatter** generously with chopped parsley.

Salem County Pork Ribs

Serves four, more as appetizer

Yes, Down Jersey does have a style of ribs that's unique to us. Not as sweet as New England's, not as fiery hot as Texas, and when finished outdoors on the barbecue, we prefer the infusion of hickory or oak wood smoke.

Anyone who has searched for a rib recipe knows that they are either a rib seller's proprietary recipe or a family secret. Thanks to Moyo "Mo" Nessor, the chef at Isabela's Cafe in Woodstown, he graciously shares his family recipe for the first time. His uncle, John Leake, who came up from Waynsboro, NC in the 60's, originally created this recipe.

The closest spice blend to Leake's spices would be Jerk seasoning, but it's worth the extra effort to blend your own, especially when all of your spice supplies are fresh. And in keeping with a Down Jersey style, there is a decided preference for Crystal Brand Hot Sauce, as it has a milder controlled heat than Tobasco Sauce.

Please note that Moyo's dry rub is given an overnight absorption time. Also either have your butcher "crack"(for more even cooking and easier eating) the ribs with a butcher's knife, or do it carefully at home with a heavy knife.

3-1/2 to 4 lbs. pork ribs, full rack
Extra-virgin olive oil for rubbing
Dry Rub Blend: (makes 1/2 cup)
2 tablespoon paprika
1 tablespoon allspice
1 teaspoon ginger powder
1 tablespoon red pepper flakes
1 tablespoon sugar
1/2 teaspoon nutmeg
1 teaspoon salt
2 tablespoons black pepper
3 cloves garlic, minced
1/2 teaspoon thyme

1 teaspoon lemon zest
1/2 teaspoon cinnamon
1/2 teaspoon star anise, ground,
     or anise seed
1/4 teaspoon cloves, ground
Barbecue Sauce:
1-1/2 cups brown sugar
1 cup orange juice
Crystal Hot Sauce to taste
1 tablespoon black pepper
1/2 teaspoon salt
2 cloves garlic, minced

Wash and pat dry the rib rack. **Hand** rub the ribs with a light coating of olive oil, then thoroughly rub on the spice blend. **Place** the ribs in a baking type pan and place in the refrigerator, covered, overnight. **The following day**, remove the ribs from the refrigeratorbefore making the barbecue sauce. **In a saucepan,** add and mix the brown sugar and orange juice. **Bring** to a boil, reduce to a simmer, and add the hot sauce, black pepper, salt and garlic. **Stir** occasionally; simmer for 25 to 30 minutes. **Preheat** oven to 400 degrees F. **Place** ribs in an oven baking pan and bake for 45 minutes or until lightly browned and cooked inside. **Remove** pan, pour the barbecue sauce over the ribs, cover the pan with foil, and bake for 20 to 25 minutes. **Remove** foil to check for doneness, remove ribs and cool somewhat. **Cut rack** into individual ribs, spoon sauce over sauce. **Serve** ribs with warm undiluted sauce on the side.Besides spooning over ribs, the sauce is excellent over vegetables.

Sunday Meatballs

In our family, when we smelled the intense aroma of meatballs frying in a cast iron pan, it meant it was Sunday, the traditional day when they were made to accompany homemade pasta, or "homemades" as we called them. Before they found a home alongside pasta, the meatballs were served hot from the pan without gravy, on a fork with a cup of hot coffee. What memories!

Today, the quality of fresh pasta from a number of purveyors is such that we now lean on them, but in no way do we opt for store-bought meatballs when we can make our own exactly the way our family likes them.

If you disregard the usual spices, the meatballs taste strikingly like round hamburgers, and if you try to make them too healthily lean they become too tough. Better to use a medium-lean ground beef and serve fewer than to have them become disagreeably dry.

Do consider use of meatballs beyond the icon of spaghetti and meatballs. They freeze well and they fill the need for an Italian-flavored meat compliment to many other dishes.

Each meatball fancier will have to find their own balance of meat fat and milk-soaked breadcrumbs to arrive at desired levels of tenderness and juiciness.

1	pound ground beef, medium leanness or a combination of beef, pork and veal
1	egg, beaten
2	cloves garlic, minced
2	tablespoons grated Romano cheese
1/4	cup fresh chopped basil, or 2 tablespoons dried
1/3	cup fresh parsley, chopped
1/2	cup fresh dried bread crumbs, lightly soaked in milk
1/2	teaspoon salt
	Olive oil for frying, preferably extra-virgin

Combine all of the above ingredients, except the oil, in a sufficiently large bowl.

Knead the mixture with your hands until smooth.

Form one small meatball for test frying and seasoning adjustment.

Film a frying pan, preferably cast iron, with a 1/4-inch of oil for "pan-frying." **Heat** oil up to frying temperature, about 350 degrees F.

Fry the test sample meatball, turning to brown around sides.

Adjust main meatball mix as needed and form into meatballs. Be mindful that meatballs made too large may not cook sufficiently in the center, but will finish cooking when placed in gravy (sauce) and heated through.

Treat yourself and your family with hot, fresh fried meatballs before they reach their main destiny in the gravy for spaghetti. **Don't** forget the coffee!

Note: Creative cooks might want to use the remaining frying oil for variations on pasta with garlic-oil sauce.

Delaware Bay Style Chile

Serves eight

This recipe for chile goes beyond a spicy hot beef and beans pot to a calculated list of ingredients. Developed by my friend Steve Crane, it has all the style and impact of a recipe that you would find back in the bayous of Louisiana. That's not surprising as the watermen of the Delaware Bay, often fashion their ways much as their counterparts near New Orleans, or for that matter, our own Pineys. Crane simmers his chile on his wood burning stove, slow and lettin' in a bit of that extra smoky old-time goodness. The rest of us will have to simmer and stir.

2   pounds. ground or chopped beef
2   tablespoons vegetable oil
1   medium onion, diced
1/2   green or red bell pepper, diced
1/2   pound country ham, diced, optional
3/4   cup button mushrooms, 1/4 cup if using dry
3   tablespoons brown sugar
2   tablespoons chili powder
1   tablespoon cumin powder
Salt to taste
1   quart cooked and strained tomato sauce
1   can light red kidney beans
4   drops hickory liquid smoke
10-12 drops bitters, preferably Peychaud's Aromatic
Cocktail Bitters, optional
Pinch of nutmeg
Cayenne powder to taste

Break apart ground beef, if using, into 1-inch or so chunks. **Bring** a large Dutch oven to a medium heat and add the oil and beef. **Cook**, stirring occasionally, until beef is lightly browned. **Break** beef into chunks somewhat larger than the kidney beans that you will add later, and add the onions, bell peppers, ham, and mushrooms. **Cook** until onions are golden and peppers are tender. **Add** the brown sugar, chile powder, cumin, and salt. **Stir** in and cook for 1 minute. **Add** the tomato sauce, kidney beans, hickory smoke, bitters and nutmeg. **Add** half of the cayenne you intend to use, making final adjustment at the end of the cooking. **Simmer** on a wood stove all afternoon, or in a 200 degree F. oven. **Add** water as necessary. **Otherwise**, reduce the heat to a simmer and cook for 1-1/2 to 2 hours, minimum, stirring frequently to avoid burning. **Adjust** seasonings and serve.

> **Steve Crane's mushroom tip:** When storing mushrooms, place them loosely on a paper towel, rolled up and placed in a paper bag in the refrigerator. In that way, the ones you don't get around to using in a few days will, in a frost-free refrigerator, begin to dry without getting moldy. Actually, dried mushrooms have a more intense flavor and a bit more of a pleasing bite.

Prussian Meatballs in Lemon-Cream Sauce

Serves four to six

Deep in Down Jersey, Vineland's Mrs Santaniello continues her Prussian heritage foodways by making this Prussian-style of meatballs (Koenigsburg Klope) that pleases her children and grandchildren. She remembers this preparation as popular in and around her home city of Koenigsberg, former capital of East Prussia, which is now called Kaliningrad. "Oh, what a beautiful city it was back then," Mrs. Santaniello laments. Her memories of that fair city may have faded, but not her practice of making these meatballs for her family.

For the meatballs:
- 1-1/2 pounds mixture of ground beef, pork and veal, or just beef
- 2 eggs, beaten
- 1 medium onion, diced fine
- 2 tablespoons brown mustard
- 1/2 cup breadcrumbs
- 1 teaspoon salt, plus pepper to taste

Poaching Liquid:
- 2 quarts water
- 1 medium onion, pierced with 1 whole clove
- 1 bay leaf
- 1/2 teaspoon salt

For the sauce:
- 1 bay leaf
- 3 lemon slices, 1/4-inch thick, with peel
- 1 scant teaspoon allspice powder
- 1 8-ounce cup sour cream
- 2 tablespoons flour mixed with 4 tablespoons water
- 2 tablespoons bacon, goose or pork fat, optional

Combine meat mixture with beaten eggs, onions, mustard, breadcrumbs, salt and pepper to taste. **Hand** roll mixture into meatballs 2 inches rounds, about 12. **In** a heavy 6- to 8-quart saucepan or soup pot, bring poaching liquid to a boil, reduce to a simmer, and drop in the meatballs. **Cook**, uncovered, until the meatballs are cooked through the center, about 20 minutes, or until the meatballs rise to the surface. **Remove** meatballs and keep warm. **Strain** poaching liquid; return to pot. **Add** the lemon slices, allspice, sour cream and, if using, the bacon fat. **Bring** to a low simmer. **Add** flour and water mixture, stir in, and cook for five minutes, stirring occasionally. **Return** meatballs to the pot, cook for two minutes more to thoroughly warm. **Serve** with the meatballs on a platter with sauce poured over them.

Notes: Mrs. Santaniello's family traditionally serves these meatballs with boiled and buttered potatoes, with pickles on each plate. Also, other versions call for 3 anchovy fillets, chopped, instead of the mustard in the meatball mix.

Braciole

(Stuffed, rolled steak)

Serves six to eight

After the first course of pasta, us six kids all eagerly searched for the braciole in the tomato sauce. For sure we knew there would be meatballs and sausage in the gravy, but braciole was a special treat. My mother's recipe can be made fancier, but there is no need to. If you are wondering about the number it serves, bear in mind that it is a second course and there are other meats to enjoy with the salad, served, of course, Italian style after the pasta course.

For today's cook, we suggest use of a good jarred marinara sauce as a base. If you like, you can add other meats as the sauce would be used for serving with the pasta course.

By the way, braciole means "arm" in Italian, which is what it appears to be.

1	pound top round steak
3	cloves garlic, minced
1/4	cup fresh parsley, chopped
	Salt and pepper to taste
6	hard-boiled eggs, peeled, see below
	Olive oil for sautéing
1/2	cup dry red wine
1	quart marinara sauce

Cut steak into to six pieces, place between heavy plastic and pound to flatten. **Try** to stretch a flattened piece about 4 inches by 7 inches to roll and stuff successfully. **On** the "inside" of each piece, spread an apportioned amount of minced garlic, chopped parsley, salt, and pepper. Keep the garlic in the center as escaping garlic may burn during sautéing. **Place** a boiled egg near the edge of each piece and roll up, tying each roll with butcher's twine. **Pat** each braciole dry with a paper towel. Place them in a sauté pan filmed with olive oil over medium heat; brown each piece on all sides. **Remove** the braciole and place in the pot of marinara sauce. **Pour** off all but 2 tablespoons of the oil in the sauté pan. **Add** the wine and return the pan to medium heat. **With** a wooden spoon, scrape the browned bits from the bottom of the pan, stir ocassionally; simmer the wine until it loses all alcohol aroma, about 3 minutes. **Pour** the wine sauce into marinara sauce ; stir in. **Simmer** for at least 1 hour. **Remove** braciole rolls from the sauce; cut and discard the strings and return them to the sauce. **Serve** after the pasta course and along with a salad and bread. **You** may prefer to carefully slice each roll with a serrated knife before placing on the serving plate.

Reminder on hard-boiled eggs: For this recipe, the eggs need only be boiled hard enough to handle as their time in the marinara sauce will finish their cooking. Place the uncooked eggs in a large pot of water, bring to a boil, and turn off the heatCover the pot and let it rest for 7 minutes. Remove, cool and peel.

Broccoli Rabe with or without Pasta

Serves four to six

Not that long ago, broccoli rabe (Brassica rapa) was known, and deeply venerated, mainly by the Italian community in southern New Jersey. No more. With rabe—it goes by so many spellings—you develop a liking to its slightly bitter taste that is a cross between broccoli and turnips, which it is, actually. Rabe, in Latin, means turnip.

The other side of our fascination with broccoli rabe is that it is in season precisely when we crave it the most, in the chilly months of autumn and spring.

Selecting the best broccoli rabe is the key, for it can be far too bitter if past its prime, or if the season has been unfavorable. Too much heat or moisture stress and rabe becomes unbearably bitter for most of us. The florets should be dark green without more than a hint of yellow, otherwise they will be too tough.

The recipe chosen is one that puts broccoli rabe for use as either a vegetable side, or it can be added to and tossed with pastas such a ziti, penne or rigatoni.

Broccoli Rabe

Serves four to six

1-1/2 pounds broccoli rabe, washed and trimmed to
        3 inch pieces after lower, tougher 1/3 of stems
        cut away
4 cups cold water
3 tablespoon olive oil
3 cloves garlic, peeled and cut in half
1 teaspoon salt
Cooked pasta, optional

In a large, deep sauté pan, add water, oil, and garlic; boil for 3 minutes.
Add rabe and cook over medium heat, covered, stirring to reduce mass of greens.
After 5 minutes, give the greens a good stir and add salt; cook for another 5 minutes.
Reserve a small amount of the boiling liquid if the greens will be served over pasta.
Remove from heat, drain, test for salt and serve.
Note: Some may prefer to add hot red pepper flakes when served, or with Parmesan or Romano cheese grated over the greens. Cooked sweet sausage, about 1/2 pound, can also be added to the pasta. Prior to serving, drizzle a bit more olive oil over the rabe.

Do you boil broccoli rabe first? Judging by colonial cookbooks, most greens, which were usually far more bitter than greens harvested today, were soaked in cold water for up to an hour before cooking. Boiling times were longer then as well, to reduce the bitterness, the compound of which is water soluble, and to insure killing of the germs. Today's improved varieties and cultivation methods simply renders long soaking times unnecessary.

Dodge's Extra Cheesy
Macaroni and Cheese

Serves six

If you read the recipe handout from Dodge's Market on Route 40 in Elmer, they implore you to try their extra-sharp cheese, which is available during Thanksgiving, Christmas, New Year's and Easter.

16 ounces cooked elbow macaroni
2 tablespoons butter
2 tablespoons all-purpose flour
1 teaspoon fresh ground black pepper
Dash of hot red pepper sauce
1 (12-ounce) can evaporated milk
1 teaspoon ground dry mustard
1-1/2 teaspoons Worcestershire sauce, optional
2-1/2 cups grated sharp cheddar or Monterey Jack
    Cheese, about 10 ounces
3/4 teaspoon salt

Preheat oven to 350 degrees F.

Cook macaroni, with a pinch of salt added, until almost tender. **Drain**, set aside and keep warm.

For the cheese sauce, melt the butter in saucepan, stir in flour, black pepper, hot pepper sauce, and milk together.

Cook over medium-low heat, stirring constantly, until smooth and slightly thickened.

Add the ground mustard, Worcestershire sauce, if using, grated sharp cheese and salt, stirring until melted.

Remove from heat.

Add the cooked macaroni and transfer to a 9-inch casserole dish (or another heatproof pan of similar surface area) and bake, uncovered, in a 350 degree F. oven for 25 to 30 minutes, or until bubbly.

Variation: For a crunchy topping to contrast with the melting silkiness of the cheese sauce, mix 1 cup of bread crumbs with 1-1/2 tablespoons melted butter. add to baked macaroni and return under the broiler until bread crumbs brown, about 1 to 2 minutes.

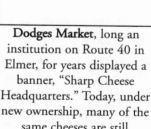

Dodges Market, long an institution on Route 40 in Elmer, for years displayed a banner, "Sharp Cheese Headquarters." Today, under new ownership, many of the same cheeses are still available.

German Lima Bean Pot Pie

Serves four to six

This is a wonderful adaptation the immigrant Germans have done with our immensely popular local bean, the pole lima. The famous German style chicken pot pie with its rolled noodles, rather than a crusted pie as in the English version, commendably salutes our pole lima beans.

For those too time-short to make bot boi noodles, egg-noodles may be substituted with a bit of bacon fat introduced to replicate the flavor that lard would have given.

Though this pie has no crust, it's still called a pot pie according to German tradition.

Bot Boi Noodles:
- 2 cups all-purpose flour
- 1/2 teaspoon salt
- 2 tablespoons lard or shortening
- 1 egg, well beaten
- 1/3 cup water

Combine flour and salt.

Cut lard or shortening in with one or two knives until the pieces are pea size. Lightly stir in beaten egg. When it reaches a dough consistency, remove from bowl and cut into quarters.

Roll out quarter until paper thin, using a sprinkle of flour if needed to keep it from sticking.

Cut into 2-inch squares and lay on a drying towel until ready for use.

Lima Bean Filling:
- 3/4 pound pole lima beans
- 1 (14.5-ounce) can chicken broth, plus water to cover
- 1 tablespoon dark mustard
- 1 teaspoon celery seeds
- 1 tablespoon sugar
- Salt and pepper to taste

In a large soup pot, add the lima beans, chicken stock and water to barely cover the beans. Bring to a boil and reduce to a simmer. **Add** the mustard, celery, sugar and a portion of salt and pepper to taste.

Gently fold in the bot boi noodles and continue simmering, occasionally stirring, for 20 minutes. **Give** a final taste for seasoning and serve.

Variation: Instead of homemade noodles, use prepared egg noodles and add according to cooking time. A tablespoon of bacon fat will steer this pot pie towards a more authentic German taste.

Chicken Parmesan

Serves four to six

As a classic, it's doubtless that it can be improved upon. Good chicken, good sauce and good cheese is all it takes, besides of course, family and friends at the table for sharing. No doubt it has earned its way into Down Jersey cooking due to our ever-appreciated tomatoes for the marinara sauce that is essential to the dish.

      4   eggs, beaten
      4   cups bread crumbs
      2   cups flour
      Salt and pepper to taste
      8   chicken breasts, boneless
      Olive or vegetable oil to film pan
      4   cups marinara sauce
      1/2 pound mozzarella cheese, shredded
      1/4 cup parmesan cheese, grated

Preheat oven to 375 degrees F.

Pour the bread crumbs and flour in separate bowls, large enough to dredge the chicken breasts. **Add** salt and pepper to the flour, stir in.

Dredge breasts in the flour, then the egg wash, then the bread crumbs and repeat.

In a large sauté pan filmed with oil over medium heat, sauté the cutlets until lightly golden, about 3 minutes on each side. **Remove** and place on paper towels to drain.

In a baking pan, pour in 3 of the 4 cups of marinara sauce. **Layer** the chicken in the sauce and place the mozzarella cheese on top, then the remaining cup of sauce and sprinkle the parmesan on the sauce. **Bake** at 375 degrees F. for 25 minutes, or until cheese is melted and the sauce bubbly.

When my grandfather came from the farm country of central Italy, he presumed his children and grandchildren would earn a living as farmers. He brought this grub hoe, also called an Italian vine hoe, with him across the Atlantic when he emigrated to the U.S..

For a long time we grandchildren thought of it as a family heirloom to be admired, but not used. In time, we learned that the grub hoe is a very practical tool to use today in our home gardens. It has the heft to do work that would be asking too much of a lighter weeding hoe. It is up to the task of hilling soil, grubbing out tough weeds, digging planting holes, and digging shallow trenches.

When I was researching the Native American method of planting the "Three Sisters" of corn, squash and beans in hills, the grub hoe was the ideal tool to use. Drawings of tools used by the Lenni Lenape show similar sized tools made from animal bones.

Grub Hoe, or Italian Vine Hoe
This is a very useful garden tool used in vine culture in Italy and brought to America

Before the Recipes, a Word about Chicken Pot Pies

What kind of chicken pot pie are you talking about? A waitress in Down Jersey would likely ask you, "Honey, do you want the crust pie or the one with the noodles?" That is, do you mean the pie that is full of chicken meat, vegetables in a white chicken-stock rich filling topped with a browned and crusty cover? Or, is it the old fashioned kind, with rolled noodles. No crust, but full of chicken, potatoes, vegetables and heaped with squarish, thick noodles swimming in a chicken stock thickened from the potatoes. The crust version can be linked back to English roots, the rolled noodle traces lineage to the Germans.

Both versions of chicken pot pie have a long history in the foodways of Down Jersey. Here, we will bring forward how German cooking left its mark on our cooking today.

The English, who settled in southern New Jersey shortly after the Swedes and who managed to reign over the Dutch presence, are known for making anything out of pies. Still today in England itself, pot pies of beef, steak and kidney and vension are the foundation of home cooking and pub grub. Among them, too, chicken is admirably suited as a filling within the layers of crust, sharing a usual partnership with English peas that grow favorably in their cool climate, and which they adore.

As to the German version, Carl Pancoast, my friend whose German-American family has roots deep in southern New Jersey, helped me demystify this pot boiler. Hearing that the noodle version was the "old-fashioned kind" wasn't good enough for me. How could a crustless dish be called a pie? Pies are baked, aren't they?

Pancoast unraveled the mystery: Many of the early settlers here were German, as was his family. They would prepare a boiled pot dish that was spelled, in German, bot boi. It literally means boiled pot. In that pot the chicken was stewed, lifted out and boned, and the meat returned. Then freshly made noodles, cut square, were added to the broth, always with potatoes tossed in, along with other vegetables at hand. Were they egg noodles? "There was no law on eggs, it was your choice," he said, "but did you notice that in the German tradition, there would be two starches in the same dish?"

Over the years, it's understandable that *bot boi* became corrupted to *pot pie.* And so the inevitable question asked by the server whenever someone requests chicken pot pie. Though we know it as a chicken pie, it could just as easily have been a beef pie. In that case, peas would likely be added.

With the modern efficiencies of the poultry distributors and retailers, it's a challenge to replicate the deep, full flavors of the chicken pot pies once served from our immigrant kitchens. The basis for a full-flavored stock came from day-long simmering of an old, tough bird, the stewing chicken, a rare bird in today's markets. Surely too tough for frying or even roasting, a large stewing chicken would at least yield up its richness and deliver tasty chicken meat after hours of cooking. It's just as tough to imagine anyone doing anything for that long as well as finding a stewing chicken in any of our nearby retail shops. Understandably, we reluctantly resort to the best brand of chicken broth we can find to prepare chicken pies. With the vegetables, we have an easier chance of freshness, as long as we head straight for a local greengrocer

Cooking chicken pot pie at home:

If you can't grab a stewing chicken, you can boost the chicken flavor in a couple of ways. Select the largest and fattest roasting chicken, since there is a lot of flavor in the fat. Then brown the whole chicken or its parts in a heavy pan before simmering the bird. After browning, deglaze the pan with a white wine so as to add all of that flavor to the stewing pot.

Note that the cooking time for the classic German bot boi calls for a full 20 minutes of simmering the noodles in the broth. While it may seem too long in today's preference for al dente cooking, the noodles are rather thick and the longer simmering releases more starch for a thicker sauce. If you like, add peas and carrots, too.

The noodle pie recipe below calls for canned chicken broth as that is how most of us would make it, but by all means prepare your own fresh broth if you can.

German Chicken Bot Boi

Serves six to eight

4-5   pound stewing or roasting chicken
 2   teaspoons salt
1/4   teaspoon pepper
1/2   cup celery, diced
 5   medium all-purpose potatoes,
      peeled and diced
 4   small onions, quartered
1/4   cup chopped parsley
    Bot boi noodles, see below

Simmer chicken in 3 quarts of water with salt, pepper and celery until tender, about 1-1/2 to 2 hours. **Remove** chicken from pot, bone and return chicken. Add potatoes and onions and simmer another 5 minutes. **Drop** in noodles, home prepared or store bought, one by one, and simmer until tender, about 20 minutes.

Add boiling water if more broth is desired. If a thicker broth is desired, add 1/4 cup of flour mixed in 1/2 cup of water.

Continued from previous page:

Bot Boi Noodles:
- 2   cups all-purpose flour
- 1/2 teaspoon salt
- 2   tablespoons lard or shortening
- 1   egg, well beaten with 1/3 cup water

Combine flour and salt. **Cut** lard or shortening in until very fine with one or two knives. Lightly stir in beaten egg with water. **When** it reaches a dough consistency, remove from bowl and cut into quarters. **Roll** out quarter until paper thin, using a sprinkle of flour if needed to keep it from sticking. **Cut** into 2-inch squares and lay on a drying towel until ready for use.

The Barnegat Bay Sneakbox, the "Devil's Coffin," used for duck hunting and sometimes clamming, is popular throughout southern New Jersey. It traces back to the original boat built by Hazelton Seaman in 1836 at West Creek, NJ on Barnegat Bay. Built with well-seasoned Jersey white cedar, it is usually 12 feet long and approximately 4 feet wide, with a three-foot daggerboard and a little more than seven inches of freeboard. The design is such that the boat can be pulled up on a beach and can be sailed in very little water. In fact with the board up it is often possible to "sail" through areas marked as land on coastal maps. This makes it extremely well adapted to the shallow waters of the bays.

English Chicken Pot Pie

Serves four

This English version of chicken pot pie might seem unremarkable at first glance, yet it is surprisingly homey when this recipe is followed. Turkey meat can be substituted as an alternative. This pie makes good use of leftover chicken.

For the filling:

3/4 to 1 pound cooked white chicken meat
4 tablespoons butter
1 small onion, finely diced
2 tablespoons all purpose flour
1-1/2 cups chicken broth
2 carrots, diced
1/4 cup fresh or frozen peas
1 teaspoon sage powder
1/2 teaspoon Worcestershire sauce
1/4 teaspoon salt and freshly ground pepper
1 package ready made crust, top and bottom
1 tablespoon milk to glaze crust, optional

Preheat the oven at 350 degrees F.

In a medium-sized saucepan over medium heat, melt the butter.

Add the onions and cook until clear, about 4 minutes.

Sprinkle the flour over the onions and stir in, cooking two more minutes.

Pour in the chicken broth and add the carrots; cook for 5 minutes.

Add the peas, sage, Worcestershire sauce, salt and pepper; cook for 2 minutes more

Add the chicken meat, stir in to combine, test for seasoning adjustment.

Remove from heat and allow to cool somewhat.

Line the bottom of a 9-inch deep-dish pie pan with one of the piecrusts. **Moisten** the edge.

Pour the filling in the pie pan, topping with the other crust. **Trim** off excess with a sharp knife. **Using** a thumb and the aide of a knife, crimp the edges of the crust into a scallop pattern. **Poke** several times with a fork to allow steam to escape.

If you wish, brush the top crust with 1 tablespoon of milk.

Bake at 350 degrees F. on a middle rack for about 45 minutes, or until the crust is lightly browned.

Ritter Chicken Barbecue

Serves four

This recipe was given out by Ritter's to their customers, and to no surprise, included use of their ketchup and another local-born product, Hires Root Beer. Though called a chicken roast, it is actually a roasted chicken with a barbecue style sauce.

1   (3 to 3-1/2 pound) broiler fryer chicken, cut in pieces
2   cups Ritter Ketchup
2   cups Hires Root Beer or cola

Place chicken skin side up in a 13 by 9 by 2-inch baking pan.
Combine Ritter Ketchup and Hires Root Beer and pour over chicken.
Bake at 375 degrees F. for 45 minutes to 1 hour, basting occasionally.
Note: My trial indicates that 400 degrees would be more appropriate. After baking, the skin can be removed if you wish.

The Ritter Story: It was Louisa Ritter's plum preserves that launched the Ritter family into the food business in 1854. She had delighted her Pennsylvania Dutch neighbors during the winter holidays with jars of plum preserves made from a prized family recipe. These gifts were so highly sought after that her husband Phillip saw an exciting marketing opportunity. Their kitchen was soon bustling with activity as the Ritters delivered their preserves by horse and wagon throughout the Delaware Valley. Eventually, the family kitchen was outgrown and production facilities were established first in Philadelphia and later expanded into Delaware, Kentucky and New Jersey.

Ritter Foods won "Top Awards" from the Philadelphia Centennial of 1876, the Louisville Fair in 1883, the Cincinnati Fair of 1884 and the Columbian Exposition held in Chicago in 1893. In 1917, a cannery was established along the Cohansey River in Bridgeton, NJ, and by the mid-1920's the P.J. Ritter Company's production was consolidated there.

South Jersey was the birthplace of the tomato industry in 1820 and soon became the heart of East Coast tomato production. In late summer, long lines of farmers with tomato laden horse drawn wagons and trucks waited to unload their bounty of red ripe "love apples" to be simmered into Ritter Catsup. Barges from as far away as Maryland delivered their precious cargo of "red gold." The spice added during cooking created a rich aroma that enveloped the entire town and remains a pleasant memory of past travelers to the Jersey shore.

Ritter served as a food arsenal for democracy in two world wars shipping their products across the globe to American troops from France to the South Pacific. As innovators, Phillip J. Ritter was in a partnership in California that was the first to pack asparagus. His brother Christian made preserves affordable for the consumer by discovering that apple jelly could be utilized to make the body of the product. The second generation of Ritter leadership, William H. Ritter, put production on an assembly line basis for the first time and pioneered the use of machine-made glass bottles. The third generation of Ritters, William Jr. and Paul, introduced a planned program of tomato development that enhanced the color and flavor of their catsup. Today, P.J. Ritter III, John Phillip and David A. Ritter continue the family tradition of bringing the Ritter Catsup to a fifth generation of American families.

Chicken or Turkey
in Chestnut Wine Sauce

Serves four to six

It's been estimated that one fourth of our Eastern forests were once comprised of American chestnut trees. Yielding an excellent rot resistant wood for homebuilding fences and shipbuilding, chestnut trees also yielded a tasty chestnut to eat; some would say that they were the tastiest of all those grown around the world. No doubt our Native Americans consumed them as part of their diet as had others for thousands of years.

Sadly, a deadly disease in the early 1900's wiped out virtually all chestnut trees. Today, a few growers are trying to revive them with resistant hybrids. Unfortunately, chestnut cookery has likewise gone with the trees and their nuts, except for the popularity of imported roasted chestnuts during its December peak season of availability. However, dried or precooked chestnuts can be gotten at Asian food markets, which makes it possible to bring them back into our cookery. The chestnut can hardly be called a nut as its quality is so different than other nuts. The fresh nuts are basically a carbohydrate with a high water content containing virtually no oil. Their sweet flavor is due to the conversion of starches to sugars during curing. Due to their high moisture content, they do not store well, which is one reason why they are often dried. In Europe, chestnuts, which were a staple during the lean war years, are still used today in savories and pastries.

Here, Chef Neil Elsohn from Cape May's Water's Edge Restaurant shares his chestnut sauce, the defining element of this recipe.

```
2   pounds grilled chicken or turkey cutlets
Olive oil for coating cutlets
Salt and pepper to taste
4   ounces dried chestnuts, soaked for one hour
2   tablespoons butter
2   ounces white button mushrooms, minced
1/4  cup dry red wine
2   tablespoons brandy
Sprig of parsley, minced
Salt and pepper
```

Lightly coat each cutlet with olive oil, then salt and pepper. **Slowly** grill until cooked throughout, turning as needed. **Set** aside on a serving platter and keep warm. **In** a saucepan with water, boil chestnuts until soft, about 20 to 25 minutes. **Puree** the chestnuts with 1/4 cup of their boiling stock. **Melt** the butter in a saucepan and add mushrooms and simmer for 3 minutes. **Add** the puree, wine, brandy and parsley and simmer for 5 minutes, stirring often. **Add** a few tablespoons of water if necessary. **Serve** over the cooked chicken or turkey cutlets. **Note:** Pan sautéing the chicken is an acceptable alternative to grilling.

Variation: For a smoother sauce, add 2 tablespoons light cream to the sauce.

Ruby Chicken

Serves eight

The Burlington County Times has flushed out recipes from local cranberry growers that will bring more of these bouncing berries high in fiber, rich in vitamin C and low in calories onto your own family table. This recipe is shared by Bill Cutts, a 4th generation cranberry grower, and Ginger Cutts. It is their family favorite.

2	(4-pound) chickens, cut into serving portions
Salt	
1	cup butter, plus 2 tablespoons vegetable oil
1/2	medium onion, diced
1-I/2	cups orange juice
1-1/4	teaspoon Tabasco sauce
1-1/2	teaspoons cinnamon
1-1/2	teaspoons ginger
1/2	cup Craisins (sweetened dried cranberries)
1-1/4	cups sugar
1-1/4	cups molasses
1	tablespoon cornstarch
2	tablespoons cold water

Sprinkle chicken with salt. **In** a large stewing pan, brown the chicken pieces, skin on, in butter and oil a few pieces at a time. Don't crowd the pan.
Add the onion, orange juice, tabasco, cinnamon and ginger. **Cover** and simmer 30 to 35 minutes until chicken is tender. **Remove** chicken to a serving platter; keep warm.
Add cranberries, sugar and molasses to a skillet. Cook uncovered 5 minutes; stirring occasionally. **Blend** cornstarch with cold water. **Add** to the skillet, stirring rapidly. Cook until sauce thickens, about 1 minute. Pour sauce over chicken and serve.

Out of the past, recipe from the Baltimore & Ohio:

PORK CHOPS NORMANDY

If you want to create a stir with something new and catchy in cooking, here's a Baltimore and Ohio favorite that willhave your friends secretly copying you. It's savory, satisfyingand simple.

Pork chops (1 per person) Brown sugar
Apple cider Cinnamon
Cooking apples Butter or margarine

Ask butcher to cut chops about one and three-quarters of an inch thick. Place chops in greased baking dish. Now add apple cider until it is level with top of chops. Put thin slices of apples on the chops, then sprinkle chop tops with brown sugar and cinnamon and dot with butter. Bake in medium oven (350 degrees) about 45 minutes.

Congo Chicken Moambé

Serves six

Glassboro's Joyce Williams has been researching her African-American roots, a quest which has taken her down to Gullah territory in South Carolina. Along with Williams study of the basket making crafts brought over from Sierra Leone, she has taught area children several African recipes, one of which is Congo Chicken Moambé adapted from Bill Odarty's book, "A Sahara of African Cooking." Always in search of ways to avoid simply saying that a dish tastes good, this author asked Williams how good it was. She answered, "When I prepared it at a church supper, I got a marriage proposal, ...and his wife was standing next to him!"

3-4	pounds chicken parts, cut in serving sized pieces
1/2	teaspoon salt and black pepper to taste
1/4	teaspoon cayenne pepper
1	medium onion, minced
	Dash of nutmeg
1	(8-ounce) can tomato sauce
1	tablespoon butter
1	cup creamy peanut butter, unsalted preferred

Place chicken in a 6-quart soup pot with water to cover; add salt and pepper. **Bring** to a boil, lower to simmer and cook for 1 to 1-1/2 hours. **Remove** chicken and reserve 1-1/2 cups of the chicken broth. **In** another pan, sauté onion, nutmeg, tomato sauce, and butter for 3 minutes. **To** the pan, add the cooked chicken, 1-1/2 cups of broth and simmer, covered, for 15 minutes.

Add peanut butter to thicken, place in a 350 degree F. oven for 30 minutes, uncovered. **Serve** warm with cooked rice.

Note: Moambé in central Africa means stew.

SOUTHERN NEW JERSEY BLACK HISTORY

Dr. James Still 1812~1877

self-taught healer and early advocate of school integration

Then, few medical schools existed~it was not unusual for both black and white doctors to be self-taught. Dr. Still treated all ~succeeding often when others had failed...His brother, William Still, is shown aiding a runaway slave's flight in the National Geographic Magazine engraving...Descendants of the Still Family held their 114th annual reunion in Lawnside during the summer of 1983...The settlement of Lawnside served as a waystation for the escaped slave's flight to freedom...The Solomon Wesley Church also served as a hiding post...Friendly whites aided the fugitive slaves — often risking their lives...

This calligraphy copy was prepared for Black History Month in Gloucester County to accompany paintings submitted by the late Blackwood artist Alfred Foster. He had researched such luminaries in black history as Harriet Tubman, known for her efforts in aiding the underground railroad, and John Brown, the abolitionist who, with his Provisional Army, carried out the ill-fated raid on the federal arsenal in Harpers Ferry in 1859.

Alfred Foster's work can be viewed at the Gloucester County Justice Building in Woodbury

Main Family Courses..... 121

German Fricassee Chicken

Serves four to six

When you understand the background of this recipe, you can understand how it fit into the German-style of cooking before the turn of last century. Providing meals for hearty appetites for a hard working farm family meant cooking something ready at hand and plenty of it. Even if there were grocery stores nearby, there was neither the time nor the money to indulge in such luxuries. Fricassee, a method of cooking that overlaps stewing—note the original recipe's use of the word "stewing,"—makes the best use of tough, stringy, but of so much more flavorful hens past their egg-laying time. The moist cooking insures tenderness from an old bird. Notice that ready at hand farm products of eggs and milk, plus flour constitute the ingredients for thickening the rich sauce. It's comfort food at farm's best.

The original recipe, by Adele M. Baden's grandmother, hand-written perhaps in 1889 or 1890, exemplifies the style of the day, presuming you know how to cut up and stew a chicken. We have clarified and updated the original record below:

Cut up a nice tender chicken into pieces; stew till tender. Remove the chicken, let the liquor come to a hard boil; add quickly four tablespoons flour, yolks of two eggs, one cup of milk mixced together; boil a few minutes; sprinkle with a little chopped parsley; pour over chicken and serve.

1	(6-7 pound) stewing or "oven roaster" chicken
3	tablespoons butter, plus 1 tablespoon vegetable oil
1-1/2	cups chicken broth or water
1/4	cup fresh parsley, chopped
	Salt and pepper to taste

Sauce mix:

4	tablespoons flour
	Yolks of two eggs
1	cup milk, whole milk preferred
	Juice of 1/2 lemon, optional

Wash and cut chicken into leg, thigh, wing and breast parts. Use wing tips and scraps for stock for another use. **Sauté** chicken parts in a large, deep skillet using the butter and oil until golden, about 3 to 5 minutes, repeat for other side. **Repeat** for parts that didn't fit in first sautéing. **Return** all pieces to the sauté pan, add 1-1/2 cups of chicken broth or water, and bring to a boil. **Reduce** heat, cover tightly, adjust heat to a bare simmer, and cook for 20 to 30 minutes. **Test** for doneness by poking meat with a fork. **When** juices run clear, the meat is cooked. Breast meat will be cooked first, so remove while dark meat finishes cooking. **Remove** all meat, bring back to a light boil, add sauce, and stir for two minutes. **Return** meat, reduce to simmer, add parsley and cook for another minute, remove from heat, add lemon if using, and serve. Traditionally, this fricassee is served with boiled potatoes.
Note: Onions, carrots, and thyme are often added.

Chicken in Chocolate Mole Sauce

Serves four to six

Our Mexican community is no longer a group of itinerant farm workers working their way north as the picking season advances. They have found a permanent home in Down Jersey, bringing their families with them as they advance in the workforce to responsible positions in the farm and nursery industry.

Their presence also brings about the bodega, Mexican food stores. Bridgeton has several of them. Now that Mexican ingredients are more accessible to us, we can more easily venture into some of their dishes. In this case, I share a recipe given to me by my late friend, Isaias Rocha. By using a prepared mole condiment, making this dish is do-able for us. Anyone who has attempted any one of the wonderful Mole sauces knows that there are no shortcuts to preparing the sauce from scratch.

2   pounds mixed chicken parts, bone-in
2   cups chicken broth or water
1   small onion, chopped
2   cloves garlic, minced
1/2 teaspoon salt, or to taste
3   chile anchos
3   tablespoons prepared mole condiment
2   bananas, sliced
Up to 4 ounces additional semi-sweet or sweet
     chocolate
Cooked rice for serving

In a large sauté pan, place chicken in 2 cups of chicken broth or water with the garlic and onion.

Bring to a boil and simmer, covered for 20 minutes, turning the pieces midway. The chicken will be almost done at this stage.

In the meantime, place the anchos in a pot with water to cover and bring to a boil, reduce to a simmer and cook for 5 minutes.

Drain anchos, and in a blender, blend until smooth, adding water if necessary.

When the chicken has simmered 20 minutes and is almost tender, add anchos, mole sauce, bananas and an amount of chocolate to suite your taste, if any.

Serve warm over rice.

Mole: (MOH-lay) From the Nahuatl *molli*, meaning "concoction," mole is a rich, dark, reddish-brown sauce usually served with poultry. There are many variations for this spicy Mexican specialty, usually depending on what's in the cook's kitchen. Generally, mole is a smooth, cooked blend of onion, garlic, several varieties of chilies, ground seeds (such as sesame seed or pumpkin — known as *pepitas*) and a small amount of Mexican chocolate, its best known ingredient.

From "Food Lover's Companion" by Sharon Tyler Herbst

Ginger Chicken
Japanese Style

Serves four to six

When the Japanese Americans arrived in Seabrook near Bridgeton during WWII, raising of poultry in nearby Rosenhayn was still at a high level and readily available at reasonable cost. We need to be reminded that chicken for the family table was once a rather expensive treat unless you raised your own chickens. The fresh poultry was welcomed by them as it helped to carry on their native style of cooking, such as with this recipe for ginger chicken. While Rosenhayn has virtually stopped production of poultry, the Japanese Americans continue to rely on extensive use of chicken meat.

1   pound chicken breasts, boneless, cut into serving
         size pieces
1   pound chicken thighs, boneless, cut into serving
         sized pieces

For coating:
Flour for dredging
3   eggs, beaten
Mixture of 3/4 cup flour, 2 teaspoons paprika and
      1/2cup Panko-style breadcrumbs, preferred

Ginger sauce:
1   cup soy sauce
2   cups sugar
2   tablespoons grated fresh ginger root, preferred, or
         2 teaspoons powdered ginger

Prepare the ginger sauce by mixing the three ingredients and bringing the liquid to a boil, and either reduce to a light simmer or turn off heat altogether. **Dip** chicken pieces in flour, then the egg wash, then the seasoned flour mixture. **Deep** fry in 350 degree F. vegetable oil until golden; drain and dip immediately in ginger sauce.

In 1994, the Seabrook Educational Cultural Center was opened in the Municipal Building in Upper Deerfield Township. I think it's best to relay their own story of the Japanese-American experience, that in Down Jersey, is so closely interwoven with Seabrook Farms:

Charles Franklin Seabrook's Legacy

What do the Japanese American Citizens League, Chow Mein Dinners, and the Buddhist Church all have in common? They all were brought to this area by a man named Charles Franklin Seabrook. Mr. Seabrook founded and owned Seabrook Brothers and Sons, which was a frozen food industry needing workers to keep his industry going.

The Japanese in Down Jersey

The Japanese attack on Pearl Harbor during the time of World War II in December of 1941 made the Americans fear that the Japanese-American population would also turn against the United States. Because of this, President Franklin Roosevelt signed Executive Order 9006 that allowed 110,000 Japanese Americans to be considered "enemy aliens" and to be moved into internment camps away from their home on the West (Pacific) Coast. These individuals were given one week to pack and be evacuated to ten different, overcrowded internment camps around the country.

While barred in these camps, farms around the country were in need of workers. One of these was Seabrook Farms. Because of this, small groups were allowed to leave the camps and work at these farms. Later the government established a seasonal leave policy.

In 1945, the government closed the ten camps and relocated anyone who didn't have an offer to work anywhere except the West Coast. Many of these decided to work for Charles Seabrook.

Seabrook granted the new coming workers some pay and a place to live. This is where the Hoover village came in. These prefabricated homes were constructed by Seabrook to house these employees. On the other hand, an increase in the Buddhist religion occurred. For this reason, Seabrook also set up a Buddhist Temple for these members.

After years at the Seabrook Company, many have moved on into different areas in the U.S. For the ones who have stayed in Upper Deerfield, the Japanese American Citizens League (JACL) was formed and sponsors community-wide events such as the annual Chow Mein Dinner held at Woodruff School.

In October 1994, a big accomplishment was completed whereby future generations can learn the history of Upper Deerfield. This feat was the dedication of the Seabrook Educational and Cultural Center. This is a museum that explains the story of Charles Seabrook and how he made this township what it is today. It is located at the lower level of the Municipal Building and is open for the public to enjoy. Inside, models of the old Seabrook Factory and water tower are displayed. Also, there is a very detailed exhibit of a three dimensional map of Upper Deerfield.

Roasted Duck

Serves four

Barry Perlow of Bridgeton can trace his family's roots back to the Kiev region of Russia where the forests and fields supported wild game that provided sustenance for the folks. Here in Down Jersey, his family has continued their appreciation of duck in the form of farm-raised Muscovy ducks in lieu of the wild ducks caught back in Russia a long time ago. This recipe is the way he has always made it, and he doesn't think it will ever change. Actually, it's his wife Barbara who cooks it.

This method that poaches the duck before roasting removes much of the fat that lies under the duck's skin. Roasting then finishes the cooking while browning the duck for a crisp skin.

1	Muscovy duck, about 5-6 pounds, thawed, wing tips removed, neck trimmed, fat trimmed, part of tail removed where musk glands are
1/2	cup honey
3	carrots, diced
2	celery stalks, diced
1	medium onion, diced
2	tart apples, peeled, cored and cubed
1/4	cup currants or raisins
4	ounces almonds, slivered
	Salt, pepper and paprika for dry rub

Remove duck from refrigerator, set on counter for 20 minutes at room temperature. **With** a fork or knife, prick holes around the duck, especially the fatty areas. **Fill** a sufficiently large pot to hold the duck with water and bring to a boil. **Add** the honey and carefully and slowly immerse the duck into the boiling water, filling the cavity to help it stay down. It may need to be held down further with a weight. **Bring** back to a boil, reduce the heat and simmer for 25 minutes to render some of the duck's fat into the water. **Meanwhile,** mix the carrots, celery, onion, apples, currants, almonds, salt and pepper for the stuffing. **Preheat** the oven at 325 degrees F. **When** the duck is finished poaching, carefully remove from the stock (the broth becomes a rich stock for use elsewhere), tilting the duck to drain any cavity liquid. Pat the duck with paper towels and allow to further air-dry for a crisper skin when roasted. **When** cool enough to handle, fill the cavity with the stuffing mixture. Rub with salt, pepper and paprika mixture. **Place** the duck in a roasting pan on a rack about 1 inch above the bottom for the fat to drain away. **Roast** at 350 degrees F. until the skin is well browned, about 1-1/2 hours. For medium-rare, insert a thermometer in the thickest part and cook until the temperature reaches 145 degrees F. **Remove**, rest for 20 minutes and carve.

German Style Green Bean and Potato Stew

Serves six

This is an excellent example of the German sense of thrift that has resulted in a dish that is worth resorting to whenever beans from the kitchen garden have matured beyond the tender stage for most recipes. The beans' fibery and deeper flavor come though to enhance the stew that, rather than being mushy, are just right in texture. The green or snap beans referred to here are those that have become a bit stringy and with the beans in the pod prominent, but not to the point where the pod has yellowed or become dry. If you don't have a kitchen garden, look for beans at farmers market where they would not be considered tender fresh, but are at reduced prices. Otherwise, with more tender beans, reduce simmering time accordingly.

3 pieces slab bacon, or 5 pieces regular sliced, diced, optional
1 pound maturing green beans, cut to bite size
3 medium boiling potatoes, peeled and cubed
1 medium onion
2 tablespoons cider or rice vinegar
1 tablespoon sugar
2 tablespoons vegetable oil
Salt and black pepper to taste

In a heavy stewing pot set over medium heat, add the onion and the bacon.

When bacon has browned to your taste and releases some of its fat, add potatoes, barely cover with water, and bring to a boil.

Reduce heat and simmer for 10 minutes.

Add beans, vinegar, sugar; salt and pepper to taste.

Simmer for another 12 minutes, less for more tender beans.

Remove from heat, adjust seasonings and serve.

Notes: As this is a sweet and sour dish, the choice of vinegar is pronounced. Choose a quality vinegar as standard white vinegar can be rather harsh. Doubtless the cider vinegar available at most markets today is a far cry from what our early German immigrants would have used.

Vegetarians and vegans can easily adapt this recipe to their guidelines by using a vegetable fat instead of bacon and adding smoked vegetarian bacon in the same amount as the bacon.

Battaglia Porkette

Makes two dozen sandwiches or more

An enduring tradition at numerous Italian-American festivals throughout Down Jersey has been the serving of porkette sandwiches of which the sauce may be more appreciated than the pork itself. Although the highly seasoned porkette takes on seasoning variations loyally carried from the cook's native region of Italy, it typically contains generous amounts of coarse black pepper, sage and or rosemary, plus wine to deepen the gravy. Our version presented here is an adaptation of my late brother-in-law Fred Battaglia's porkette. We have also elected to relay the braised method, which means browning on top of the stove and cooking in partial liquid, as an inexperienced cook can more easily control the cooking process. Because pork shoulder, the choice cut of pork to use, can vary much in size, and since it is the custom to cook sufficient quantity to feed a large gathering or for putting up, braising becomes a preferred method. We suggest here a "pulled pork" style, which has a natural texture and far less animal fat remaining.

4-5	pound boneless pork shoulder
5-7	cloves garlic, cut in half lengthwise
4	tablespoons coarsely ground black pepper
4	tablespoons olive oil
2	tablespoons powdered rosemary
4	tablespoons powdered sage
1-1/2	teaspoons salt
1/2	cup red or rose wine

Wash and pat dry pork shoulder, removing netting if it has one. **Coat** the pork shoulder with the black pepper, pressing on the surface as best as you can. Any residual black pepper remaining can be added the pot later when simmering. **In a large,** heavy Dutch oven over medium heat, add the olive oil. **Brown the meat** by turning until all sides are lightly browned, adjusting heat to brown slowly, while watching to keep the meat from burning. **When meat** is browned, move meat to one side and add the salt, garlic, rosemary and sage to the oil and stir for a short minute over medium heat. **Add the wine,** stirring in with the seasonings and cook for 5 minutes. **Add sufficient water** to come up to half of the shoulder and bring to a boil, then reduce to a simmer, partially covered, watching to keep at a simmering level. **Remove** surface scum. **From time to time,** turn pork and replace evaporated water. **As** 2 hours of cooking approaches, check internal temperature with a thermometer. Final temperature in the center should reach 170 degrees when done. **Remove** meat from pot; set aside to cool. Check for seasoning adjustment of gravy, adding 1 tablespoon of soy sauce if a richer gravy is desired. Gravy can be cooled for removal of most of the surface fat. **When meat** is cool to handle, pull meat apart with your hands to achieve "pulled pork" texture while at the same time removing as much fat as you feel comfortable with. **Portion** the pulled pork with the gravy and refrigerate or freeze. If desired, add extra-virgin olive oil when reheating to replace the generous amount of fat in the original shoulder.

Sausage and Peppers

Serves six to eight

It's terribly difficult for an Italian cook to say the word "sausage" without say the word "peppers." When I prepare this Italian favorite for church suppers, I lean on my 13-inch cast iron pan so that it can attempt to satisfy the demand. Cast iron itself helps this dish along since nothing beat cast iron for its ability to brown meats. Browning the sausage properly happens to be one of the keys to bringing out the fullest flavor. Because peppers and sausage keep well in the refrigerator as leftovers and freeze well, our recipe is a generous one.

> 2 tablespoons olive oil
> 2 pounds sweet Italian sausage
> 3-4 bell peppers, red and green, cut in large pieces
> 1 large onion, sliced in crescents
> 2 tablespoons tomato paste
> Salt to taste

Cut sausage in 2-inch pieces. If you prefer more browning and have a sufficiently large skillet, cut each piece in half lengthwise.

Select the largest cooking pan you have, preferably cast iron about 12 inches in size.

Over medium heat, add olive oil to the pan and slowly brown the sausage, uncovered, turning the pieces to brown throughout, about 12 minutes.

Add the peppers and onions and stir in. Reduce heat to slowly simmer; check to prevent burning of the peppers. **Add** more oil if needed. **Cook** until peppers soften, about 5 minutes.

Add tomato paste, salt and stir in. **Cook** for another 10 minutes, stirring and checking often.

Notes: In season, select instead (and use more) sweet "frying" peppers, the long, thin peppers are ideal for frying as they tend to be less bitter. Some may prefer to choose hot sausage, or add one or two hot peppers to the sweet ones. A crusty, peasant bread is almost mandatory to sop up the rich sauce that surrounds the peppers and sausage. Upon reheating, consider adding a few tablespoons of Italian style tomato sauce, as the sauce from the original batch will be the first to disappear.

"Cooking" Peppers: Unfortunately, they have been called frying peppers, which implies oily cooking. Generally, they are the thin-walled peppers, such as Hungarian, Cubanelle or Italian Long Sweets. Again, since most long sweet peppers sold at supermarkets are hot peppers, the assumption has been that this group of peppers are all hot and so are unnecessarily avoided.

Their distinguishing feature is that they are far less bitter upon cooking and have a relatively thin outer skin that is far more agreeable than the thicker skin of bell peppers when they are cooked.

Main Family Courses..... 129

Pork Sausage
Lower Alloways Creek Style

As maple syrup is to New England cooking, so is molasses to Down Jersey heritage cooking. This recipe for seasoned sausage is found only in the region of Lower Alloways Creek in Salem County and has been passed down for generations. I first encountered this sausage during a LAC Historical Committee Day at the Cabin on Smick Road in LAC.

This LAC sausage's flavor is quite unique and instantly likable, and unlike traditional breakfast sausage with its defining sage seasoning. For this recipe, I thank Wally Bradway from LAC, which, by the way, is pronounced Lower Alloways Crick by locals. Hence, they are known as "Crickers," a name they are proud of.

Wally Bradway passed along his portions for spices based on use of 25 pounds of pork. When he and his family and friends make sausage, they make more than enough to share. Scale it down to portions that suit your own needs. Bradway cautions against using too much molasses as it will cause the sausage to burn too easily when cooked. Pork shoulder is preferred as it has the right level of fat for a sausage

- 25 pounds pork shoulder, coarsely ground
- 1/2 cup sugar
- 1/4 cup table salt
- 6 tablespoons coarse ground black pepper
- 1/2 cup molasses, mild or full flavored as preferred
- Dash ground ginger
- Cayenne pepper to taste

Mix all of the seasonings and spices together, except a partial amount of the cayenne. **Take** a small, one ounce or so portion of the seasoned mix to fry and taste in order to adjust seasoning as necessary, especially the cayenne. **Complete** the mixing with the remaining batch and either stuff into casing or form into patties.
Note: Patties are best frozen in freezer bags with as much air excluded as possible.

Sausages with Apples and Cider: The Historic Foodways Society of Delaware Valley uncovered this recipe (called receipts in colonial times) from an anonymous source. I tested this recipe and found that it suits anyone with a sweet tooth. Even so, it is recommended to use tart apples, such as Granny Smith or Winesap instead of sweet apples. The browning of the sausages is not mentioned in the original receipt, but is suggested.

    Peel 6 large tart apples, core and cut in sections. **Heat** a pan and add the butter. **Cook** the apples, turning them gently so as not to break them. Prick 1 pound of sausages sauté in a skillet to evenly brown. **Add** 1-1/2 cups cider and simmer for 20 minutes (I suggest use of a cast iron pan).

Stuffed Peppers

Serves four to six

Bell peppers, the choice for stuffing, become locally available at farm markets in July, but in a few more weeks the green peppers mature to red. As the season progresses, more red peppers will be at the market, and depending on the weather, can be available till October. The red peppers are far sweeter, and more importantly for cooking, are far less bitter as well. It's worth waiting for peppers in season as more and more the imported greenhouse peppers seem to lack that full flavor of the field grown. Note that this recipe uses wheat germ in the stuffing for a richer flavor, but feel free to use corn flake or breadcrumbs if you prefer.

8   medium bell peppers, preferably mature red
1   (16-ounce) can tomato sauce

Stuffing mixture:
1   pound ground beef, usually ground round
1   cup wheat germ, or breadcrumbs
1   onion, diced
2   eggs, beaten
1/4   cup ketchup
1/2   cup Cheddar cheese, grated
2   tablespoons Worcestershire sauce
1   teaspoon salt
1   teaspoon freshly ground pepper

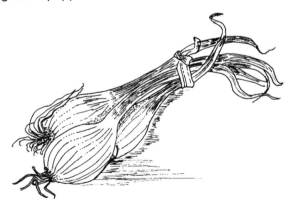

Preheat oven to 350 degrees F.
Wash and cut away top of peppers and set aside for another use; remove the seeds and veins from the inside.
Pour 1/2 of the tomato sauce into the casserole.
Mix the stuffing mixture and proportionately stuff each pepper; Stand each pepper upright in the casserole.
Pour the other half of the sauce over the peppers.
Bake at 350 degrees F. for about 1 hour, uncovered, until the sauce is bubbling and the stuffing is lightly browned.

Fall, a time for railbirding.

Wild Rice

Rice, wild rice? Are you kidding? Would you believe that wild rice is growing in South Jersey? Well, believe it, Uncle Ben! Lining the banks of the Maurice River are stands of wild rice, and there are thousands of little birds that know it.

During this time of year, the wild rice in the salt marsh meadows is ripening, and the sora rail, a small chicken-Iike marsh bird, along with other species come to feast on this Delaware Estuary delicacy as they migrate south. However, along with the railbirds come hunters. The first hunters were the Native.Americans. Next came the local hunters, and later hunters from other areas who learned of this distinctive form of birding came to South Jersey. Included in the list of visiting hunters were President Benjamin Harris, and later, President Teddy Roosevelt.

You might ask: "What is so distinctive about this form of birding?" Among other things, it is the challenge. The small, swift railbirds feast on the wild rice and stay out in the marshes where many boats cannot maneuver. Not to be defeated by nature, our New Jersey Baymen developed the specialized railbird boat! The railbird boat is shallow drafted and propelled by a pole, uniquely constructed with a broad pronged tip that helps keep the pole from sinking in the mud as the long handle adjusts to variable depths through the inlets and flooded plains.

Imagine the peace, tranquility and quietness of our own Bayshore Region as one person in the stem of a boat with no engine pushes through an autumn marsh. Yes, it is a challenging opportunity to hunt railbirds. Their coloring makes them hard to see, their small size makes them difficult to shoot and their location makes retrieval just plain difficult -yet the sora rail add another dimension of beauty along the banks of the Maurice River.

By Bob Walker, Education Director
Bayshore Discovery Project

Chapter 5
Seafood From Bay to Shore

Of all the influences on the food of Down Jersey, the harvest from the fisheries off the coast and bays have a most profound impact. From the earliest times when Native Americans developed trails to the Delaware River region down to the Delaware Bay and over to the Atlantic coast, seafood has had a major influence on our cuisine.

Today, we fall into a yearly pattern of anticipating the fishery season awakened each March with the annual shad spawning run up the Delaware River, on through the fall and winter as the fish move offshore. Clams, one of our biggest catches, however, are available year round, unless the rarel event of a back bay freeze-over occurs.

After the press fascination with the history-steeped shad season fades, excitement heightens with the subsequent blue crab catches. Each year comes with an uncertainty of availability, thanks to fickle weather and nature's unfathomable hand at work. While enjoyment of crabs certainly means a luscious potful of steamed crabs generously tossed with crab boil seasoning, it doesn't stop there. As with other fish and shellfish preparations presented here, our diversity of ethnic groups has brought us other wonderful ways with crabs and other seafood dishes, which we have adopted.

For the seafood afficionado, one of the many seafood festivals occurs at the annual Delaware Bay Day held on the first Saturday and Sunday of June. Certainly much more than a foodie event; it is a family day full of activities for everyone, this maritime event that celebrates the natural resources of the Bay sure pleases the seafood lover's palate. The hosting towns of Bivalve, Shellpile and Port Norris have names that point out the thriving oyster industry that once was and, to a lesser extent, still is.

A garvey is a work boat designed with a shallow draft for use in the shallow waters of the back bays. It is usually made from Jersey white cedar, a wood that is light, durable and rot-resistant. Once poled, rowed or sailed, they are now powered by inboard motors. Today, as was seen generations ago, you can still see this stable utility craft used for tonging and raking clams, as well as for oyster and crab fishing.

Seafood..... 133

Waterman's Seafood Beer Batter

Makes two and one-half cups

At Bay Day in Port Norris on the first Saturday in June, the New Jersey Waterman's Association sure draws a crowd at their softshell crabs, oyster and fish fry stand.

Seafood lovers come back each year to grab their fill of fresh bay seafood coated with crisp and tasty batter. Though some might reckon that any beer batter recipe is trendy, Jean and Bob Munson, in Newport, have leaned on this recipe as it does not have any ingredients that would pose a health risk, such as eggs or milk.

1   (12-ounce) can of flat beer
1-1/4 cup sifted flour
1   tablespoon salt
2   teaspoons baking powder
A few dashes of your favorite spice, Old Bay™, etc.

To allow the beer to go flat, pour the beer into a bowl and have it rest at room temperature for about two hours.

In the beer bowl add the flour, salt and pepper and baking powder. **Mix,** cover and let it rest for 1 ½ to 2 hours to thicken. Whisk just before use as this mix tends to separate. Be sure to dry the fillets before dipping. **Until** you get the hang of it, check the frying oil temperature to insure it hovers around 375 degrees F. At that temperature the fillets will fry to a golden brown color with minimal oil absorption. **Any** remaining batter can be stored in the refrigerator for 3 to 4 days.

Union Hall, on Main Street in Dividing Creek, was not as you would expect, built as a church. Rather, it is one of the oldest public, non-church buildings in existence in southern New Jersey. It was built by the Good Intent Beneficial Society, the Odd Fellows and the Junior Order of United American Mechanics. The first record of a meeting there was on June 24, 1897.

The interior of the two-story structure is rather unique. In the entrance hall, there is a ticket office with a fancy iron door. At the far end of the first floor is a stage with two dressing rooms and a roll-up stage curtain designed and hand painted with a scene by Clement Orr in 1903. From the entrance hall, an open staircase, with a metal grate, leads to the spacious upper floor. At the onset, this area was strictly for lodge activities.

Currently preserved and maintained by the Dividing Creek Historical Society, Union Hall still serves the community today.

Barbecued or Broiled Bluefish

Serves four

As a full-flavored fish, bluefish has its lovers. Due to its high oil levels, bluefish fares best with high acid ingredients, such as abundant lemon juice or lime juice and with spices that enhance but don't overpower the bluefish's flavor.

4   6-ounce bluefish fillets (skin is usually left on)
1   tablespoon lemon pepper
Salt, if not included in lemon pepper seasoning
Juice of 2 lemons or limes

Rinse fillets and pat dry. **Heat** barbecue grill to medium or preheat broiler.
Rub fillets with lemon pepper and salt if needed.
For barbecuing, lightly coat each side with oil and grill, skin-side down, covered, for 8 minutes, or until the fillets begin to flake. Do not turn as it is too flaky.
For broiling, place on lightly greased baking pan, place about 6-8 inches from the broiler and broil, skin-side down, testing at 5 minutes. Fillets are done when they flake easily.
When done either way, splash fillets with lemon or lime juice and serve.

Broiled Mackerel with Honey Mustard

Serves two

Sharing fortunes with bluefish, mackerel is an oily fish (read omega-3 fatty acids), caught off the New Jersey coast that does not keep well, so it must be bought when fresh and cooked straight away. That means those living farther away rarely have the opportunity to enjoy mackerel as the tasty fish it can be. The memory of lingering aromas from canned mackerel does no justice to the treat of fresh caught. Our Atlantic mackerel's main season is in the spring.

4   mackerel fillets
2   tablespoons honey
1   tablespoon mustard, your choice
Dash of nutmeg, optional
Juice of two lemons

Prepare honey mustard sauce, mixing in nutmeg, if using.
Place fillets on a broiler pan and brush fillets with sauce.
Place mackerel skin-side down on a broiler rack.
Broil 4 to 6 inches from broiler element, test for doneness at 5 minutes.
Serve with lemon juice spritzed on each fillet.
Note: Make more honey-mustard sauce to serve along with the fillets.

Dill's Jersey Cioppino

Serves six to eight

With our abundance of fresh and varied seafood, along with our super tomatoes, locals for a long time have been preparing their own form of cioppino, the fish soup (stew, really) of San Francisco fame. The Marino family, owners of Dill's Seafood Store and Restaurant, has offered to share their recipe for Cioppino. It is somewhat similar to daunting bouillabaisse, which, besides its name, scares you with a long list of ingredients, the most troublesome for a home cook being the making of a fish stock from fish carcasses.

While Bouillabaisse's defining ingredients include saffron and fennel, cioppino steers towards basil, and maybe a bit of anisette for a licorice touch. No rule against using saffron, either.

Here, we rely on the relatively recent availability of agreeable commercial marinara sauce as a base, reducing the difficulty drastically over tomatoes and purees, which come from a can anyway. I'll not dissuade anyone from using fresh Jersey tomatoes.

One final comment, while we have listed fish and shellfish indigenous to the Delaware Bay and off the Jersey coast, this is one situation where you might as well rely on your fishmonger to work out a selection for you. The guidelines are to use oil and firm white fish, and either clams or mussels, clams being more a bit more Jersey-ish.

1/2	pound sea bass, croaker or perch or snapper (low oil)	1	green pepper, diced
1/2	pound swordfish or salmon (oil)	2	stalks celery, diced
1	pound large ocean shrimp, 16-20 count, peeled	3	cloves garlic, minced
2	dozen topneck clams	1/2	cup white wine
1	pound sea scallops	16	ounces marinara sauce
1/4	cup extra-virgin olive oil	6-8	fresh basil leaves, minced, or
1	large onion, diced	1	teaspoon dried basil
			Salt and pepper
			Garlic bread for serving

Wash and pat dry the fish fillets, cut into bite-size pieces; set aside in the refrigerator. **Scrub** the clams thoroughly, discarding any that do not close when tapped. **In a large,** heavy pot, add 1/2 cup of water and steam the clams, covered, until they open. **Remove** the clams, set aside. **Carefully** decant the liquid so as to keep the grit at the bottom of the pan. Repeat if necessary. **In a large,** heavy soup pot over medium heat, add the olive oil, onions, peppers, and celery. Sauté until clear, about 5 minutes. Toss in the garlic; sauté briefly. **Add** in the wine, marinara sauce, clam juice, basil, and a light seasoning of salt and pepper; bring to a simmer and cook for 30 minutes. **Add** the seafood, except for the shrimp and clams, stirring gently to avoid breaking the pieces apart. **Cook** for 2 minutes, add the shrimp and clams; cook for 2 minutes more. The residual heat will finish the cooking. **Serve** with garlic bread. **Variations:** Consider adding orange zest or oregano, as you wish.

Rohrman Family Clam Pie

Serves six to eight

This recipe, according to Albert C. Rohrman, Jr., has been used by his German-American family for at least 80 years. In passing along this recipe to me, Rohrman cites use of 1 quart of clams without specifying what size clams to use. When clams came to their kitchen following a day of clam digging along the back bays of the Jersey coast, they were happy to use whatever size was dug. When minced, of course, the size mattered less as the mincing tenderized the larger, tougher clam meats.

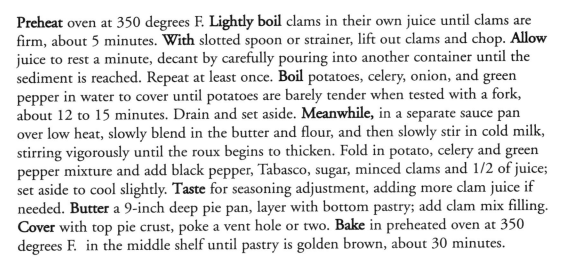

1-1/2	pounds hard clams (yields about 6 ounces clam meat), juice saved
2	cups red-skinned potatoes, 1/2-inch cubed
1/2	cup celery, cubed
1	medium onion, chopped
1/2	cup green pepper, diced
1	teaspoon sugar
1	cup milk
3	tablespoon butter
3	tablespoons flour
	Black pepper and Tabasco sauce to taste
1	(9-inch) deep dish pie crust, top and bottom

Preheat oven at 350 degrees F. **Lightly boil** clams in their own juice until clams are firm, about 5 minutes. **With** slotted spoon or strainer, lift out clams and chop. **Allow** juice to rest a minute, decant by carefully pouring into another container until the sediment is reached. Repeat at least once. **Boil** potatoes, celery, onion, and green pepper in water to cover until potatoes are barely tender when tested with a fork, about 12 to 15 minutes. Drain and set aside. **Meanwhile,** in a separate sauce pan over low heat, slowly blend in the butter and flour, and then slowly stir in cold milk, stirring vigorously until the roux begins to thicken. Fold in potato, celery and green pepper mixture and add black pepper, Tabasco, sugar, minced clams and 1/2 of juice; set aside to cool slightly. **Taste** for seasoning adjustment, adding more clam juice if needed. **Butter** a 9-inch deep pie pan, layer with bottom pastry; add clam mix filling. **Cover** with top pie crust, poke a vent hole or two. **Bake** in preheated oven at 350 degrees F. in the middle shelf until pastry is golden brown, about 30 minutes.

Getting the grit out. The bane of enjoying any clam dish is lingering grit. Clams, after all, spend their lives half-buried in mud or sand on the ocean floor. Several approaches are suggested by cookbook authors: Sifting through multiple layers of cheesecloth, or carefully pouring from one container to another. I find the cheesecloth-straining method tedious and seemingly takes forever, rarely appreciated when the finishing the dish is the goal. Decanting from one bowl to another to remove the grit is relatively fast and easy.

Wilson Family Clam Pie

Serves four

Sharon Wilson passes this thick, homey clam pie recipe she inherited from her husband's grandmother, who retained this dish from her English heritage. Bob Wilson, her husband, who has been clamming off of Brigantine, near Atlantic City, since he was eight years old, passes this along. For one, opt for the larger clams as they have more flavor, and "For goodness' sake, try to use fresh-shucked Jersey clams, not those insipid interlopers from Florida." Sharon would add to that, "Never use canned clams. That's a sacrilege to my husband."

12-15 chowder clams
2   large potatoes, peeled and diced
1   large onion, diced
2   ribs celery, diced
2   tablespoons chopped parsley
Pepper to taste
Pinch of thyme, optional
1   egg, lightly beaten
Roux of 2 tablespoons each of melted butter and
        flour
2   tablespoons light cream, plus additional for
        brushing crust
Homemade or store-bought dough for a 9-inch pie
        plate, rolled out thinly

Preheat oven to 350 degrees F. Scrub clams thoroughly and shuck into a bowl to catch the juices. **Remove** clams from the bowl with a swishing motion in order to allow any clinging grit to fall back into the juice and pulse the clam meat in a food processor until coarsely chopped, or use scissors with the clam meat in a container. Chopping on a cutting board is rather messy. **Carefully** decant the clam juice to free it of its grit by having the container rest for a few minutes and then slowly pour the juice into another container, leaving the last portion of the juice with the grit in the pouring container. Repeat several times. You may prefer to use a fine mesh strainer instead. **Place** the potatoes, onions, and celery in a skillet with the clear clam juice and just enough water to cover the vegetables. Simmer over medium heat, covered, until vegetables are tender, about 10 minutes. **Meanwhile**, make the roux by melting the butter in a saucepan over medium heat. Stir in the flour, stirring for 2 minutes. **Add** cream, stirring a few seconds. **Add** to the skillet the parsley, clam meat, thyme, and pepper to taste, return to a simmer. **Add** beaten egg and cook for 4 minutes. **Stir** in roux, let cool. **Spoon** filling directly into pie shell and cover with dough and brush with milk. **Bake** in a preheated oven at 350 degrees F. for 30 minutes, or until the crust is golden. The clam pie is even better the next day. **Variation:** A twist on this recipe by is to add sliced fennel, as does Philly's Samson Street Oyster House.

Clams Seabrook

Curried Spinach-Stuffed Clams on Half-Shell

Serves six

With New Jersey's long coastline yielding up plentiful, fresh supplies of clams virtually year round, and Jersey's mild winters allowing spinach to over winter four years out of five, this combo of spinach and clams comes about naturally. Once the clams are cleaned and shucked, the rest is easy. This preparation is every bit as rich as Oysters Rockefeller
In a pinch, canned clams can be used.

18 topneck clams
1 (9-oz.) frozen package Seabrook Farms
   Creamed Spinach
1 tablespoon curry seasoning
4 ounces Parmesan cheese, freshly grated

Thaw frozen spinach package.

Clean and shuck clams into a large container, removing and discarding the top shell.

Free the clam meat from its shell by cutting below and around in a circular motion. Swish the clams to free them from grit, carefully lift out and then chop. Some prefer to use a scissors as the clams on a cutting board will ooze considerable liquid. Decant the remaining juice. Save juice for other uses, it freezes well. Carefully clean the half shells; set aside.

Mix clam meat, curry seasoning and 1/2 of the Parmesan cheese with the spinach. Top cleaned, set aside clam shell halves with the mixture, spread remaining Parmesan cheese on top of mix and place stuffed shells on a baking tray. Broil until cheese browns slightly.

Optionally serve with a squeeze of lemon.

Variations: Should you prefer more tender clams, select littleneck clams instead and use two dozen littlenecks instead of 18 topnecks. Also, unflavored breadcrumbs may be added for a more substantial filling mixture. In that case, mix the breadcrumbs, about 1/2 cup, with 1/2 of the parmesan cheese and curry seasoning.

> **Clam Shucking Tip:** Unless you are confident that all of the clams are fresh and have discarded all those that fail to close shut even after a rap or two to entice them to do so, play it safe. Instead of shucking all of your clams into the same container, shuck each one into a separate test container and only toss the shucked clam into the main container after you are sure the clam is fresh. It can save the ruinous result of having one bad clam contaminate the whole batch.

Salem County Deviled Clams

Serves four

This is another recipe recorded by the late Frances Blackwood, a former food writer for the Philadelphia Evening Bulletin and resident of Alloway Township.

24	medium (cherrystone) clams or
	12 chowder hard clams
1/4	cup butter
1/2	medium onion, chopped fine
1-1/2	cups bread crumbs
1	tablespoon flour
1-1/2	cups rich whole milk
1	cup liquid from clams
1	teaspoon Worcestershire sauce
	Sprinkling of cayenne pepper
2	egg yolks

Sometimes you can buy clams already opened. If you have to do this yourself and do not have (or are not familiar with) a "clam knife," don't worry. **Scrub** each clam shell with a small brush. Place them in a large dish pan, not too many at a time. Pour boiling hot water on them. The minute they open their shells, take them up one at a time and run a sharp little paring knife between the two shells to cut the muscles that are on each side. This releases the shells and it is a simple matter to cut the clam completely free of the shell.

Hold clams over a bowl while you cut it free so you can catch all the juice. Put clams with juice and go on to cut the next. **When** all have been opened, set a colander over a bowl and pour the clams into it so they are separated from their juice. Then run them through the meat grinder to chop, or chop them in your blender.

Set half the butter aside to use to dot over tops of clams when deviled. Melt the rest in a large skillet. Simmer the finely chopped onion in it until tender and golden. **Add** the chopped clams, breadcrumbs, 1 cup liquid from clams, seasonings and milk; sprinkle the flour over it all. **Add** egg yolks and stir everything together over moderate heat until it thickens. Have scallop or large clean clam shells well buttered. **Fill** with clam mixture. **Sprinkle** a light coating of crumbs on top of each and add a dot of butter. **Place** in 350° F. oven to bake about 25 to 30 minutes, until golden brown. They can be kept over night when refrigerated.

It is handy to remember that in all shellfish cooking, a small amount of cayenne pepper brings out their delicate flavor. This is especially true with crab and lobster.

Pasta with White Clam Sauce

Serves six

While linguine pasta is a popular pasta cut cited in recipes and at restaurants, I choose the small orecchiette (little ears) pasta as they allow bits of clam and delicious sauce to be captured when scooped with a spoon. With linguine, the clams and sauce fall to the bottom of the plate, which means dredging with a lot of bread instead. Note that as clam sizes vary, it's more accurate to give weights even though they are sold by the dozen.

- 4 pounds topneck or cherrystone clams, shucked and juice reserved, or 3 (10-ounce) cans chopped clams
- 1/3 cup extra-virgin olive oil
- 4 cloves garlic, minced
- 1/2 teaspoon dried oregano
- 1/4 cup dry white wine
- Hot red pepper flakes to taste
- 2 tablespoons chopped parsley
- Fresh ground black pepper to taste
- 1 pound cooked orecchiette or other pasta
- Parmesan cheese for garnish, optional

Relative clam sizes: Topneck (upper left), littleneck (upper right), chowder (lower left), and cherrystone (lower right)

Wash and scrub the clams. Shuck over a bowl to retain the juices; toss clam meat into its own container. Before removing to mince, swish meat around to free them from grit and gently lift out, squeezing the meat somewhat if you intend to use a cutting board. Mince clam on a cutting board or place in a container to use scissors to cut into small pieces. **Decant** clam juice by carefully pouring from one container to another. **In a saucepan**, heat olive oil, add oregano and garlic; sauté until garlic is barely golden, about 1 minute.

Add the white wine, clam juice, parsley and hot pepper flakes.
Simmer for a few minutes and add minced clams and black pepper and simmer for 3 minutes more.

Remove from heat and grind fresh black pepper to taste. The residual heat will finish cooking the clams. Serve with freshly cooked pasta. If you do use Parmesan cheese, use it sparingly.

Note: If you don't have orecchiette, "little ears," at hand, use any spaghetti and break into 1-inch pieces before cooking to make it easier to eat with a spoon.

> **Shopper's Tip:** If you are a regular at your seafood shop, you may want to ask for a spare container or two of the white plastic pails that wholesalers use to pack scallops. They are food-grade plastic and are very handy for shucking and decanting the clam juice, among other uses in the kitchen.
>   Ask for the lids, too.

Fresh Cod, Baccala Style

Serves four to six

The memory of dried salt cod served during Christmas remains strong in the memory of Italian-Americans, and so did its aroma. Reconstituting with water took several days, all too aromatic, but the end result was worth it. As much as we reminisce about this traditional dish, few of us have the time or inclination to continue its preparation. Bearing that, by using fresh cod in place of dried salt cod, virtually all of its merits can be carried forward. Potatoes are common in salt cod recipes, for they offset the saltiness of the cod. Here, we retain the common use of potatoes.

1-1/2	pounds of fresh, boneless cod fillets
3	tablespoons olive oil
3	medium potatoes, diced in 3/8-inch cubes
1	red bell pepper, diced in 3/8-inch squares, more or less
2	medium onions, diced
2	cloves garlic, minced
2	tablespoons raisins, soaked in brandy or water
1/4	cup parsley, chopped
	Salt to taste

Wash cod fillets, pat dry, and cut in 3-inch pieces; it will break apart further during cooking. Set aside.

In a large, non-stick skillet over medium heat, pour in the olive oil, add potatoes, peppers and onions. Sauté until potatoes are lightly browned and vegetables lose their liquid.

Add garlic into the oil with the vegetables, stir, and heat for 30 seconds, stirring to keep garlic from burning.

Add cod and raisins; stir in gently, cooking over medium heat until cooked, about 5 minutes. At the last minute, toss on the parsley, mix in and serve.

Variations: For the tang of tomatoes, add 2 tablespoons tomato paste after the garlic is golden. For more sauce, add 1/2-cup dry white wine after the garlic is sautéed.

Hemispherical Kettle

Historical reproduction handmade by Peter Goebel. The original example was dated 1550 - 1650, however his research has found that this style kettle was in use for over 200 years. Examples can easily be found in Dutch paintings of the period. Dated: 1550 - 1650
Origin: Dutch for domestic

Drawings courtesy of Goosebay Workshops

Conch Seaville

Serves six to eight

Chef and owner of Mama Mia Restaurant in Seaville, Joe Massaglia is quick to prepare conch (pronounced konk) in the Ligurean style from the Italian Riviera when he has fresh conch from local watermen. Though quite common in Italian and Asian cooking, few of us are aware that conch is caught in commercial quantities off the New Jersey coast. Shoppers can find conch in cans at supermarkets, restaurants can source it frozen, but naturally conch is best when obtained fresh. Ask your fish store counter person to get it for you fresh if he can, or at least frozen. This recipe calls for the conch to be sliced thinly, otherwise it can be tough and chewy. Partially freezing the meat allows for easier slicing.

3/4 pound fresh conch, sliced very thin (frozen conch is an acceptable alternative)

Marinate:
1 small red onion, chopped fine
1/2 green bell pepper, chopped
1 stalk celery, chopped
1/4 cup pitted black olives, sliced
Juice of one lemon
1/4 cup extra-virgin olive oil
1 tablespoon brandy
Dash of Anisette
Dash of orange liqueur
Dash of oregano
Romaine lettuce, sufficient to cover plate
Roasted peppers, sufficient to garnish

A wooden conch-trapping pot used in earlier times.
—Drawing courtesy Carlton Pancoast

If conch is fresh, blanch the meat in boiling water for one minute; remove and cool.
Mix all marinating ingredients; combine with conch meat.
Allow to marinate for at least 1/2 hour in the refrigerator, covered. **Taste** for salt, it may not be needed. **Spread** marinated conch over the lettuce and top garnish with roasted peppers. This dish is quite agreeable served at room temperature, *al fresco,* but avoid keeping at room temperatures more than a few minutes.

What is a conch? It is a marine snail, related to clams and squid, caught off the New Jersey coast. Our species, whelk, is related to the queen conch found in the Caribbean. The edible meat of conch shares the same fate as clams and squid in that its meat, when cooked, must either be cooked for no more than 2-3 minutes, or simmered about 45 minutes to an hour, in liquid to tenderize the meat. Some recipes call for pounding the meat vigorously to mechanically tenderize the meat. Beware, the cooking odor can be intimidating.

Rice Sticks with Crab and Broccoli

Serves four

For this recipe, Carlotta Santaniello, a farmers' wife who immigrated from the Philippines, combines familiar Asian seasonings with locally-grown vegetables and available blue crab meat. There is no need to go for the expense of jumbo lump crabmeat here, crab's flavor contribution is what you are after.

2	tablespoons vegetable oil
2	cloves garlic, minced
1	medium onion, diced
1-1/4	pounds broccoli, florets and stems cut into bite sized pieces
1/2	pound crab meat, or surimi
1	tablespoon soy sauce
1	teaspoon sesame oil, optional
8	ounces rice sticks, also called rice noodles, soaked in water for 1 minute

In a large skillet over medium heat, add oil and onions.

When the onions are almost clear, add garlic and stir for 30 seconds.

Add the broccoli and 1/4 cup of water; cover and steam for 3 minutes.

Add crabmeat, soy sauce, sesame oil, and rice sticks. Simmer, stirring occasionally, for 2 minutes and serve.

Blue Crab Meat Grades

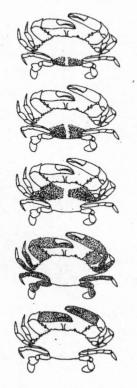

Jumbo Lump and Colossal: This top-line grade consists of the two largest unbroken muscles previously connected to the swimming legs of the crab.

Backfin: Smaller and broken portions of jumbo lump with large flakes included.

Special: The remaining body white meat, with some lump and flake meat.

Claw Meat: The brown meat from the claws and the legs of the crab.

Claw Fingers: Brown meat from the tip end of the crab claw with part of the shell removed.

Red-Sauced Crabs and Linguini

Serves six

This recipe developed by Antionette Battaglia represents a typical approach to using the smaller, cheaper crabs that have too little picking meat to be cooked for their meat alone. The use of the small barely legal size crabs for pasta has earned them the name of "spaghetti crabs" by the watermen. The ritual cleaning of the crabs has been dutifully preformed outdoors by the men willing to kill the feisty crabs and then clean them by copious hosing with water

The standard way of serving these crabs is to present the crab-sauced pasta as a separate dish with the tomato-laden crabs on a separate platter for those undaunted by picking away for the scant, but delectable, crab meat.

Olive oil to coat bottom of crab pot
2 dozen small (number 3's) crabs, cleaned
Salt and black pepper
1/4 cup fresh chopped parsley, or 2 tablespoons dried
1 medium onion, chopped
3-4 cloves garlic, minced
1/2 cup white or red wine
1 28-ounce can of crushed tomatoes, plus 1 cup water
1 6-ounce can tomato paste
Pinch of ground cloves
2 tablespoons dried oregano
2 tablespoons dried or 1/3 cup fresh chopped parsley
2 tablespoons dried or 1/3 cup fresh chopped basil
1 pound linguini or spaghetti, cooked

In a large crab pot **over** medium heat, add sufficient olive oil to film the bottom. **Add** crabs in one layer and sprinkle on the salt, pepper and dried parsley (curiously, it doesn't tend to burn). Adjust heat to singe the crabs but not burn them. Turn the crabs to brown each side. **Repeat** until all crabs are seared.

With all of the crabs removed, add the onions and cook until clear. Add the garlic and cook until garlic is golden. Add more oil if necessary.

Deglaze the pan with the wine, stir to scrape the bottom; simmer for 5 minutes.

Add the crushed tomatoes, paste, and water.

Add the cloves, oregano, parsley, and basil; give a good stir.

Raise heat to bring to a boil, reduce to a simmer and cook, partially covered, for 1 to 1/2 hours, stirring occasionally.

In the meantime, boil water, add salt, and cook the linguini.

Return the crabs to the crab pot and cook at a simmering level for 15 minutes.

Remove crabs to a separate plate, taste sauce for seasoning adjustment and serve sauce over linguini or other pasta.

Sicilian-Style Sautéed Blue Crabs

Serves four

The Italian cooks soon discovered that the blue crabs from the Delaware Bay were buonissimi for inclusion in red gravies (sauces) made from local tomatoes, but they didn't stop there. This recipe was learned and then adapted by Andrew DeNardo, Gibbstown, from a Sicilian-American neighbor.

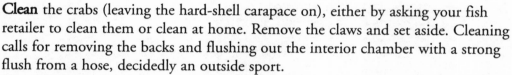

1-1/2   dozen number 1's blue crabs, or 2 dozen number 2's
1/4   cup olive oil, approximately
Salt and black pepper to taste
2   cups fresh parsley, chopped
1/2   cup dry red wine
Roasting pan which fits over two burners, with cover
Sturdy spatula to press down on the crab bodies

Clean the crabs (leaving the hard-shell carapace on), either by asking your fish retailer to clean them or clean at home. Remove the claws and set aside. Cleaning calls for removing the backs and flushing out the interior chamber with a strong flush from a hose, decidedly an outside sport.

Place the oven roaster over two burners, raise burners to medium heat and film the bottom with oil.

Add the crab bodies, back side down. The 1-1/2 dozen should fit snugly in the pan. If not, save them for a second batch.

Add the parsley directly over the crab bodies, sprinkle on the salt and pepper. Drizzle about a teaspoon of olive oil over each crab, using a baster or a spoon, then cover.

Lower heat to medium low, occasionally pressing down each crab body with a sturdy spatula, trying to caramelize as much of the body as practical. Check for possible addition of more oil if needed, add wine and claws; cover and cook for 20 minutes.

Lift cover, turn crabs to belly-side down, check need for additional oil, press down with a spatula, return cover and cook for an additional 15 minutes. When all of the claws no longer show signs of blue, the dish is cooked sufficiently.

Note: It's traditional to serve the crabs on a platter and with a table that has been covered with many layers of newspapers. As they say, count your knives and smashing tools before you start picking crabs as the layers of cracked shells can hide quite a bit. It's also traditional and a great match to serve beer with the salty crabs.

Grilled Soft-Shell Crabs

Serve one as appetizer, two or three for a meal

As we are minutes away from the Bay, in season we have access to the freshest, softest soft-shell crabs that can be had. Once cooked, however, we like them crisp and crunchy and with the sweet taste of butter, and perhaps a touch of garlic or hot sauce. Due to water and air pockets in the soft-shells, it's safer, cleaner and crisper to cook them out on the grill.

> Soft-shell crabs, cleaned, see below
> 1/2 tablespoon melted butter per crab
> Salt to taste
> Lemon wedges

Preheat gas grill to high and cover. **Heat** a charcoal grill (hardwood preferred) until medium hot, covered to thoroughly heat the rack. **Baste** both sides of the crabs with butter and season with salt. **Wire** brush the grate, leave gas burner set to high. **Grill** the crabs, covered on a gas grill, uncovered if charcoal grilled. **Turn** and baste every 2 minutes until spotty brown or orangy, about 6 to 7 minutes for medium sized crabs, and up to 10 minutes for larger crabs. **Serve** with lemon wedges. **Variation:** Add minced garlic and or hot sauce to the melted butter. Garnish with fresh parsley if you like.

Soft-Shell Sauté

Serves two as an entrée

With sautéeing you'll need to cover the crabs for the first few minutes and they'll be slightly less crunchy, but you have a chance to deglaze the pan if you have a mind to.

> 4 soft-shell crabs, cleaned
> Flour for dredging, seasoned with salt and
>   pepper
> 4 tablespoons olive oil or peanut oil
> 1/2 cup dry white wine, optional to deglaze
> Juice of 2 lemons or limes

Heat a sauté pan over medium high heat for 3 to 4 minutes. **When** pan is hot, add the oil. Dredge crabs in flour, shake off excess, raise heat to high; sauté on each side (covered the first 2 minutes) until lightly browned, about 6 to 8 minutes.

Serve with lemons or limes cut into wedges. **Or,** to optionally deglaze, lower heat to medium, add the wine and reduce by 2/3. **Add** the lemon or lime juice, stir in to heat through, and pour over crabs. **Garnish** with fresh parsley if you like.

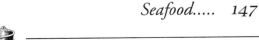

Crabs in White Sauce

Serves six to eight

Dr. Frank De Maio, a Vineland physician, has been working over the years to record and share the cooking traditions of his fellow Italian-Americans. Dr. De Maio introduces this recipe in his book, "Keeping the Tradition," as follows:

> Karen Capano Cifaloglio learned this recipe from her mother-in-law, Sue Cifaloglio. She really liked the flavor and sometimes, on a date before she married, she would cook the crabs for her fiancé and then they would eat them while watching a movie.

As is common with recipes relied upon by new immigrants, this preparation stretches the contribution of crabs by making a white sauce that flavors the pasta eaten beforehand.

- 2 dozen crabs, more or less, cleaned
- 6 cloves garlic, chopped
- 3 (12-ounce) cans beer
- 3 tablespoons vinegar, plus 3 cups water
- 1/4 cup grated Locatelli (Pecorino Romano) cheese
- Olive oil
- 1/4 cup parsley, chopped
- 1 tablespoon dried oregano
- 8-10 basil leaves, or 1 tablespoon dried
- Black pepper, optional
- 1 pound linguine or other pasta, cooked

In a bowl, mix together the beer, 2 tablespoons of olive oil, water and vinegar.
In a separate bowl, mix the flavorings of basil, oregano and black pepper.
Into a large crab pot pour sufficient olive oil to cover the bottom.
Over medium heat, add the garlic and cook until golden. **Place** a layer of crabs on the bottom of the pot. **Pour** a fourth of the beer liquid and fourth of the spice mix over the crab layer. **Repeat** the layering with liquid and spice until pot is full, adding any remaining liquid and spice on top of all the crabs. Cover with a tight-fitting lid.
Steam the crab pot for 15 minutes over medium heat, occasionally shaking vigorously. **Turn** off the heat, remove the crabs and set aside.
Add the Locatelli cheese to the liquid, which is then used to sauce the pasta. Serve with an additional toss of parsley on the serving platter.

When is blue crab season? Delaware Bay blue crabs, the same species that the Chesapeake Bay area is famous for, become active when the Bay water warms sufficiently. Warm, sunny days may have them emerging from the mud perhaps in mid-May after a winter of hibernation. Crabs, of course, are available at the market earlier from sources farther south. With favorable conditions, our watermen catch crabs in their pots into November, and extended further during the dredging season when crabs are inactive.

Port Norris Steamed Blue Crabs

This recipe has found its way around Port Norris for so long that no one claims to be its originator, so let's just call it Port Norris Steamed Blue Crabs.

In a large pot with a 2-inch high steamer rack, pour equal amounts of water and cider vinegar to within half-inch of the rack. **Alternately** layer a dozen blue crabs and several tablespoons of crab boil seasoning such as Baltimore Spice, J.O. or Old Bay. Cover tightly, add a weight if necessary and steam for 18 minutes. Have many layers of newspapers handy for cracking and picking the crabs. Count your cracking hammers before you dig in.

Vietnamese Style Garlic Crabs

At Woodbury Seafood, the former owner, Gang Le, would hand out samples of his style of cooked crabs. It's surprising how much flavor is derived from the added combination of garlic, sugar and salt. An old trick to handling crabs if you are squeamish is to immerse them in ice; that way they will then relax to a resting state for safe and less intimidating handling.

Clean two dozen crabs, break the body in half and break away the claws. In a large pot that can be covered, film the bottom with vegetable oil; sauté 5 chopped garlic cloves until their aroma is released, about 30 seconds. Do not brown or they will become bitter. **Add** crab pieces and 1/4 cup of salt and stir. Cook, covered for 15 minutes, stirring or shaking the whole pot, if that is possible. **Add** 1/4 cup sugar, stir and cook for 10 minutes more. **Add** 1/4-cup chopped scallions, optional, and cook for 2 minutes more. When available at Asian markets, 1/4 cup of rice powder can be added with the sugar for a light finger lickin' coating. I have not tested use of flour as a substitute, but it should be an acceptable alternative.

Crab Tips:
* Store live crabs in a cool, moist area free of excessive drafts. A dampened newspaper is often placed on top of crab baskets.
* Crabs should be lively before steaming. Don't take a chance with dead crabs; they deteriorate quickly.
* Never allow steamed crabs to come in contact with the surface or container of live crabs.
* Refrigerate crab no less than 3 hours after steaming.

Jersey Crab Cakes

Makes six to eight crab cakes

Since 1922, O'Donnell's Restaurant in Gloucester City has been dishing up American style cooking while specializing in seafood. And in that time they have earned an envious reputation for their crab cakes, which as far as we know, have changed little in preparation over the years.

Their current Chef, Dannis Ekimaglou, shares not only their recipe's ingredients, but the techniques that are every much a part of their final grand South Jersey favorite.

1	pound of your choice of backfin, jumbo or jumbo lump crabmeat
4	tablespoons butter, melted
2	tablespoons flour
1	pint milk, warmed, but not hot
	Pinch of salt
1	teaspoon lemon juice
1/2	tablespoon hot sauce
1/2	tablespoon Worcestershire sauce
1/2	tablespoon dry mustard powder
3	slices fresh bread made into bread crumbs
1/4	cup parsley, finely chopped
	Fresh white bread crumbs for coating.

Carefully pick over crabmeat, removing shells and membranes. **Set** aside and keep cool. **A useful** picking trick for the home cook is to use a large baking pan, placing the unpicked meat at one end and moving the picked-over meat at the other end. **Work** in the butter and the flour together with a fork.

In a sauté pan over low heat, add the butter and flour mixture, milk, salt, lemon juice, hot sauce, Worcestershire sauce and mustard powder. **Stir** continuously for 3 minutes and remove from the heat. Stir in the bread crumbs. **When** the sauce has cooled, add the sauce to the top of the crab meat. **Gently** fold together.

Form mixture into crab cake patties and gently roll in bread crumb mixture.

Add sufficient vegetable oil to a fry pan to a depth of 1/4-inch and bring up to medium heat. Test for hotness by dropping in a piece of bread. It should bubble, but the oil should not be smoking.

Gently sauté the patties on each side until lightly golden; don't overcook. Bear in mind that the crabmeat has already been steamed in order to be picked from the shell.

------------------------------------Cleaning Soft-Shell Crabs------------------------------------

1) Just before cooking, cut off the mouth and eyes with scissors.

2) Lift the pointed side of the crab shell, remove the flap on each side and cut away the off-white gills.

3) Turn crab over and cut away the "T" or triangular apron flap. Wash and pat dry.

Baked Flounder alla Vineland
with Onions and Red Peppers

Serves four

Though flounder wins the name game, you can also opt for weakfish, whiting or cod. This baked seafood dish draws on sweet red bell peppers, a specialty of Vineland growers, that are readily available at local markets, especially from August to October.

Red bell peppers are green peppers that have matured to red, and with some varieties, have matured to yellow or orange. The sweetness of baked red peppers, along with onions, compliments seafood wonderfully. But because the peppers and onions take longer to cook than the fillets, they are baked a few minutes before the fillets are added, yet it's still one-pan baking and still done in minutes. Sure suits today's busy cook, doesn't it?

On a budget note, don't bother using the pricier sweet onions since all onions mellow out during cooking. Use the longer storage, less expensive yellow or white types. While I find green peppers too bitter for this dish, use them if that's your taste.

```
1-1/2  pounds flounder, weakfish or cod fillets
 1/2   medium onion, sliced thinly
 1/2   red bell pepper, sliced thinly in 1/4-inch widths
 2     tablespoons olive oil
Salt and pepper to taste
Juice of one fresh lemon
```

Preheat oven to 400 degrees F.

Wash fillets in cold water, check for pin bones in the center of the widest part of the fillet (nearest the head) cut away if found, pat dry and set aside in a cool location.

Preferably on a baking pan attractive for serving directly, season the peppers and onions with salt and black pepper, spread them roughly in the center area where the fillets will rest on top later. **Bake** at 400 degrees F. for 10 minutes to partially cook the peppers and onions.

Meanwhile, Lightly oil the fillets; season with salt and pepper on each side.

Remove baking pan and add the fillets on top of the peppers and onions.

Return pan to the oven and bake until done as tested with a fork. Fillets should barely flake. We have found that in our oven, medium sized fluke (a species of flounder with usually thicker fillets) bakes for us in about 16 minutes. Your own oven may vary.

Remove pan and generously squeeze fillets with lemon juice, and test for seasoning adjustment; serve warm. The modest amount of sauce flavors a side of baked potato or rice rather well.

Variations: You can add a bit of paprika on top of the fillets that have been lightly oiled. Sparingly dusting cayenne pepper on the fillet also adds a zestier bite, if that's your fancy.

Baked Flounder
with Mayonnaise Sauce

Serves two

At Helen's Greentree Restaurant in Thorofare, Helen Beeunas, owner and chef, often serves flounder with this easy-to-whip-up sauce. In today's households it's helpful to have a quick prep handy. No doubt this sauce draws upon Jersey tomatoes to bring that tanginess that so suits seafood. Bear in mind that other fillets such as cod, whiting and weakfish are acceptable substitutes as all are as lean as flounder.

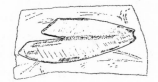

3/4 pound flounder fillets, fluke preferred
   Oil for broiling pan
   Salt and pepper to taste

Sauce:
1/4 cup mayonnaise
1/2 medium onion, diced
 1 round slicing tomato, diced
 1 teaspoon dried dill weed

Preheat oven to 400 degrees F.

Wash flounder with cold water, pat dry and season with salt and pepper on both sides.

Lightly coat baking pan with oil; place fillets on baking pan. **Bake** for 15 to 20 minutes, according to thickness, testing for doneness by flaking with a fork. As soon as the fillets becomes slightly opaque, they are done.

In the meantime, mix all of the sauce ingredients and test for seasoning adjustment. Top the finished fillets with sauce, allowing a minute of cooling after removal from the oven.

Variations: Instead of dill, substitute parsley, cilantro or green onions. A dash of cayenne pepper or hot sauce can be added, too.

> **Fluke versus Flounder?** Fluke (summer flounder) and flounder (winter flounder) belong to the same family of flatfish that are bottom feeders with eyes that move from the both-side juvenile position over to the same side as they mature. With fluke, the eyes move to the left side (viewed with the white belly side down), whereas with the other flounder, they move towards the right side. Note also that with both fluke and flounder, the bottom fillet is typically thinner and pinkish in contrast to the larger and grayer fillet from the top portion.
>
> While thicker fillets fare better in baking because they are easier to keep moist, the thinner flounder, on the other hand, does have its advantages. Thinner flounder will cook more thoroughly when fried, and when a stuffing is desired, such as with crab imperial, the thinner flounder can be stuffed and rolled and baked.

Greek-Style Baked Fluke

Serves four

The abundance of off-shore fluke, also known as summer flounder, has found the waiting Greek chefs eager to bestow their traditional seasonings, and what a match it is. Their style is so easy to prepare and forgiving in ingredient portions that anyone can bake a commendable flounder their way. Because fluke, often sold simply as flounder, is generally larger and thicker than common flounder, it's preferred for baking because its fillets are easier to keep moist. Besides, fluke's larger-flake texture has earned it more fans, as evidenced by its higher prices at fish markets. Though a year-round catch, availability can be spotty at times due to quotas and weather.

        1-1/2 to 2 pounds fluke fillets, pin bones removed
        1/3   cup extra-virgin olive oil, or vegetable oil, as
                preferred, or mixed
        2   teaspoons dill weed, or oregano
        1/4   cup chopped parsley, fresh if possible
        1/2   teaspoon salt
        1/2   teaspoon freshly ground pepper
        1/4   teaspoon cayenne
        Juice of 2 lemons

Preheat oven at 400 degrees F.

Wash the fluke fillets with cold water and pat dry. Do not leave fillets on the counter at room temperature for any length of time. **Pour** the olive oil in a small bowl and add the dill, parsley, salt, pepper and cayenne. Thoroughly mix oil and seasonings with a fork.

Place fluke fillets in a lightly oiled baking pan large enough to hold the fillets in one layer, or use two baking pans. **Give** the oil and seasoning mix one last stir and pour or brush over fillets. **Bake** at 400 degrees F. for 15 to 18 minutes, or until the fluke just begins to flake apart at the thickest portion when tested with a fork.

Remove baaking pan from the oven; squeeze the juice of two lemons over the fillets.

> **Smoked Bluefish:** Even those who find bluefish too strong in flavor relish bluefish when smoked. As you can imagine, it is quite nutritious and a great substitute for those who are looking for an alternative to bacon.
>
> Smoked bluefish is a ready-to-eat fish, yet its goodness can be enhanced when served with rye or pumpernickel bread. Also when served as an appetizer, the citrus tang of sliced oranges compliment bluefish well.
>
> Some may prefer to remove the darker, stronger flavored dark meat along the backbone before serving.

Hog Shrimp

John's Seafood in Paulsboro moves out huge amounts of cooked shrimp, so I asked for their customers' favorite. Wife, Cindy Fergone, who would rather their place be called Cindy's Place, (John's duties often take him away from the shop), said grillers love this one.

Bacon, amount according to number of skewers
Sea scallops, dry preferred (no sodium tripolyphosphate
    added)
Large shrimp, ocean harvested preferred
Crab boil type seasoning. such brands as Baltimore
    Spice, J.O. or Old Bay
Wood skewers

Place one end of a strip of bacon on the skewer. Then run the skewer through one end of a shrimp. On the other side of the attached shrimp, place a scallop next to it on the skewer. Then pierce the other end of the shrimp and the other end of the bacon on the skewer. Repeat this as often as you like, or until you run out of skewers.

Dust the whole skewer lightly with the crab boil seasoning.

Grill on the barbecue until the bacon becomes crisp, turning often.

Note: "Crab boil" seasonings vary not only in their mix of spices, but more importantly, in the amount of salt--the cheapest ingredient--in the mix. If you can, test your selection for flavor and saltiness before you buy.

Edmund G. Booze, a purveyor of spirits from Philadelphia, had his bottles manufactured at the Whitney Glass Works in Glassboro, New Jersey sometime around the 1860's. From that beginning, the Booze name became synonymous with whiskey and then alcohol in general.

The original bottles are quite rare, but the Clevenger Glass Works in Glassboro did make reproductions in the early 1900's that had slight variations such that a collector can distinguish them apart from the original.

Recipes from "Jersey's Best" Brand

At the beginning of the Twentieth Century, the abundance of the oyster harvests from the Delaware Bay was reflected in the number of oyster shucking companies and the brands sold to the public. During that period of intense competition, it's no wonder that on the tins in which oysters were sold there were recipes to help the home cook. We were fortunate to recover a paper tin-covering label from "Jersey's Best" brand from Robbins Brothers in Port Norris listing a number of recipes, as they wrote, "to serve "Jersey's Best Oysters Regularly." Below are three samples of exact recipes as written, ones that still fit in today's kitchens.

Creamed Oysters

Drain and wash "Jersey's Best" oysters. Rub one tablespoon of butter and one tablespoonful of flour until smooth; add one half pint of cream or milk; stir over hot water until smooth and thick-not boiling-add pinch of mace, one half teaspoon of salt, one salt-spoon (1/4 teaspoon) of pepper; stir in the oysters; cool until edges curl. Serve on toast or in patty shells. Note: Patty shells are small shells made of pastry to hold fish, meats and vegetables.

Salvaged brand label

Fortescue Fries

1 pt. small "Jersey's Best" oysters
1/2 cup milk
1/4 tsp. Baking powder
Salt. Pepper. Flour. pinch of soda

Free the oyster from juice, add all ingredients and thicken with flour to consistency of cream. Fry in a very hot fat, having enough to well bottom of pan.

Oyster Fritters

2 cups oysters
2 cups flour
2 eggs, well beaten
1 cup milk
2 teaspoons baking powder

Drain the oysters and chop fine. Combine the flour, baking powder, eggs and milk into a batter that is smooth and free from lumps. Stir in the oysters, mixing thoroughly. Drop from a spoon into deep hot fat and fry for about one minute until golden brown.

Salvaged brand label

Marinated Mussels

Serves four to six

Although harvested mussels along the bays of New Jersey haven't reached commercial levels, they are eagerly picked by licensed gatherers. Mussels are often served steamed, mixed or substituted with other shellfish or added to a seafood salad. On their own they are terribly good served marinated.

A word of caution. Only those harvested from approved sites by the New Jersey Division of Fish, Game and Wildlife should be consumed. Mussels are filter feeders so some locations can be designated off limits to clam and mussel harvesters.

1/2	cup extra-virgin olive oil
3	tablespoons white or red wine vinegar
1	tablespoon capers, minced, optional
1	tablespoon roasted peppers, or pimento, chopped
3	tablespoons parsley, minced
	Freshly ground black pepper
4	pounds mussels
	Lemon wedges for garnish

In a bowl, mix the olive oil, vinegar, capers, peppers, parsley, and black pepper.

Scrub the mussels and remove their "beards." Discard those with cracked shells, or those that do not close when tapped lightly.

In a large pot to accommodate the mussels, add 1/2 cup of water, and the mussels; cover and steam over high heat until they open, about 8 to 10 minutes.

Remove mussels from pot, allow to cool for a moment, then remove the meat from the shells.

Add the mussels to the marinade bowl, toss with first six ingredients, and refrigerate, covered, for a least several hours, preferably for a day before serving. **Serve** garnished with lemon wedges.

Variation: Save 1/2 of the shells, cleaned well, to fill with the marinated mussels.

Brass Pan Spyder

Historic reproduction, handmade by Peter Goebel, of an antique original found at a site in Mississippi. Spyders were essential to cooking for hundreds of years. Most kitchens would have had many of them in various sizes. Goebel has crafted these from examples dating back to 1620. Dated: ca.1729
Origin: French/N. American/English

Drawing courtesy of Goosebay Workshops

Holiday Oysters

Serves six to eight

As oyster consumption in the earlier days of the last century was far higher than today, it's no wonder that we reach back in a family tradition to draw up an old oyster sauce recipe.

We have leaned on Ruth Shiveler, whose mother, Lillian Shiveler, has shared her family recipe. "This is a very rich dish. All of my aunts made it too. We liked it served on turkey or as a gravy over poultry stuffing." The original Shiveler recipe called for 50 oysters, we have reduced that to today's lighter demands.

  2 dozen stewing ("standards" size) oysters
1/2 pint cream
  4 tablespoons butter
  2 hard-boiled eggs, yolk and white separated
Salt and pepper to taste
  1 tablespoon flour mixed with 2 tablespoons milk,
       stirred

Mash egg yolks with butter. Chop egg whites. **Heat** cream in a heavy saucepan until just simmering and add flour/milk thickener. **Add** egg yolk mixture and stir in. **Add** oysters and simmer until the edges begin to curl. Remove from heat immediately. **Add** chopped egg whites and season with salt and pepper to taste; it shouldn't require much salt, if any. **Serve** warm.

Note: Upon reheating, bring up to only warm serving temperature as further cooking will toughen the oyster. Also, for those who are squeamish about eating the oysters themselves, an immersion blender may be used to purees the oysters, resulting in a thicker sauce.

The heyday of oyster plates coincided with the abundance of oysters, mainly from 1860's up to the 1910's. Victorian ladies at that time were anxious to serve the oysters as delicately as possible on appropriate plates. One style was developed to serve oysters on the half-shell on ice, a second type pf plate was designed to serve oysters on the half-shell without ice. The third, depicted here, was made to receive the shucked oyster without its shell.

Drawing courtesy of Patti Levering from a plate loaned by Ruth Shivler

Scalloped Oysters

In keeping with the style of recipe writing from Frances Blackwood, we repeat her recipe for scalloped oysters, and her recipe for oyster batter. which she says you should allow six medium-sized oyster for every serving.

Rinse oysters quickly in cold water, drain, and place on paper toweling. Butter a casserole or other baking dish. Cover bottom of pan with coarse breadcrumbs and dot with butter. Arrange a layer of oysters over the crumbs; sprinkle lightly with salt, pepper and another layer of crumbs. Dot this generously with butter and sprinkle lightly with salt and pepper. Repeat these layers, making the last one crumbs, butter and seasoning. Place in preheated moderate 350 degree F. oven, and bake about 45 minutes.

Note: Whether using oysters to scallop or fry, always drain off excess liquid. Save it if needed and strain before using.

Batter for Frying Oysters

Rinse, drain, and place oysters on cloth or paper toweling. Have ready 2 eggs beaten with 1/2 teaspoon baking powder and stir in 1 cup milk. Dip oysters in very fine crumbs, then in egg mixture and again in crumbs to coat well. Let stand on a rack at least 20 minutes to dry. Heat enough oil, vegetable shortening, or half shortening and half bacon fat to deep fry. Lower 3 or 4 oysters at a time into it. Brown quickly on one side, turn, and brown the other side. Strain out onto brown paper and keep in warm oven with door open until all are fried and ready to serve.

As oysters are sufficiently salty in themselves, if you add salt, do so with care.

Oysters were (once) so plentiful they were advertised in Philadelphia and Baltimore: "All you can eat for 6 cents," and one Colonial recipe writer suggested that "3 quarts of oysters are the right amount to stew for a small family dinner," and "If company comes when you are planning a plain gumbo for supper, 100 oysters thrown in would enrich it pleasantly."

"*Once Upon a Time,*" Frances Blackwood

It's of historical interest to note that the now-named Red Bank Avenue in West Deptford that begins at the Delaware River and leads to Woodbury, was formerly named Oyster Shell Road. Many other roads were so named. That speaks of an earlier time when, as Blackwood alludes to, oysters were far more part of our food economy than today.

Poached Salmon
with Dijon and Horseradish Sauce

Serves four

From Dill's Seafood where they bring in North Atlantic farm-raised salmon, they pass along this easy to do salmon recipe. It's often shouted across the counter when a customer asks for a cooking suggestion. Though classical poaching in the French style calls for a court bouillon broth using onions, celery and carrots, this recipe with full-flavored salmon only asks for a bit of white wine vinegar in the poaching water. We are providing two choices of sauce styles here, an easy mix of Dijon mustard and horseradish or a saucier reduction sauce made from the poaching broth.

> 1-1/2 pounds salmon fillets, cut into 2-3-inch widths
> 1/4   cup white wine vinegar or cider vinegar
> 1/2   teaspoon salt
> Lemon slices for garnishing
>
> **Easy Sauce:**
> 1/4   cup Dijon or other spicy mustard
> 1/4   cup horseradish sauce
>
> **Reduction sauce**: Same ingredients, plus poaching
>   liquid

If you choose to make the easy sauce, mix at this time.

Wash the salmon fillets gently in cold water. Cut the salmon into 2-3-inch widths.

In a large pan, add water to a depth of 1-1/2 to 2 inches; add the vinegar and salt.

Bring to a boil, reduce to a simmer and add salmon pieces, but not so much as to crowd the pan. Poach another batch if necessary.

Poach the salmon, being sure to control the heat to maintain a bare simmer. Poach the salmon to your satisfaction by testing with a fork, it should take about four to five minutes.

Carefully remove with a slotted fork, allow excess poaching liquid to drip off and plate with the lemons as a garnish. Serve with easy Dijon-horseradish sauce.

If you are choosing to make the reduction sauce, keep the salmon in a warming oven.

Pour off about half of the poaching liquid. Raise heat to boil liquid until about 1/2 cup remains. Reduce heat to low and add the Dijon and horseradish sauce, stir a moment and pour into a sauceboat.

Plate by pouring the sauce on the plate with salmon placed above the sauce, or with a dollop on each fillet portion.

Variations: Chopped parsley, dill or capers can be added to either sauce for a more assertive herbal flavor

Sautéed Caramelized Scallops

Serves two

This is another example of a seafood dish that is quick and easy to prepare. Because some retailers continue to sell scallops treated with sodium tripolyphosphate (wet) scallops, we suggest you steer toward your nearest seafood store to purchase untreated (dry) scallops. The wet scallops, a 25% water-added product, ooze so much liquid in the pan that they don't develop the caramelization that brings out their best flavor.

Dredging for scallops is a major fishery off the New Jersey coast. Conservation quota restrictions limit the allowable catch by scallopers and that keeps the prices on the high side. Being so, a preparation for scallops ought to celebrate their full delicate flavor without interference by other stronger ingredients. My friend Clay Cary has suggested a classic recipe for enjoying Jersey scallops to their fullest.

When using a large sauté pan, the limit of scallops that can be sautéed without the steaming effect from crowding is about 3/4 pound. For that reason, we suggest that if you want to increase or double the recipe, clean the pan and prepare it with another separate batch.

3/4	pound untreated (dry) scallops
1	tablespoon olive oil
1	tablespoon butter
Salt and black pepper to taste	
1/2	cup frozen peas, optional
1/2	cup dry white wine
2	shallots or 1/2 small onion, minced
2	tablespoons butter
Juice of 1/2 lemon.	

Carefully wash the scallops in water, rinse and pat dry with a paper towel.

In a large skillet over medium-high heat, add the olive oil and butter. When the butter eases up on foaming, add the scallops. Lightly salt and pepper. Spread apart so they do not steam, and try not to disturb so as to get the fullest browning.

When scallops are browned on one side, flip over and brown the other side.

Lightly salt and pepper again. Remove scallops to a plate and keep warm.

Add the peas, if desired, white wine, and shallots or onions. Reduce heat somewhat to medium and cook until wine is reduced to about half.

Remove the skillet from heat, allow to cool slightly and swirl in the pats of butter.

Add the lemon juice and serve over rice or cous cous.

Variations: If not using the peas, garnish the dish with chopped fresh parsley. For more color, sprinkle a teaspoon of paprika over the scallops. Because the black pepper may appear as "dirty" scallops to some, choose to use white pepper instead.

Salem Oak Diner Shad Roe

Serves two

When shad roe is in season late winter, the Salem Oak Diner, owned by Robert and Barbara McAllister, will serve upwards of four dozen orders a night. Son William, now chef at Salem Oak, maintains that his customers overwhelmingly favor use of bacon fat, though others would sternly insist butter is the choice fat.

This delicacy, for those that treasure it, takes a special approach when cooking. The roe must be handled very gently lest the egg sacks burst. It must be sautéed gently, and not overcooked or the roe becomes dry and tough.

When selecting shad roe at the market, size and color will vary greatly as shad is a wild species. What is important is that the roe be fresh, that is, without any fishy odor. Fish cutters (filleters) will present the roe properly trimmed and ready to cook. Supplies are chancy at the seafood store, so call ahead to have the fishmonger set roe aside for you.

2   pairs shad roe, about 6 ounces each
3   slices bacon, diced
Salt and pepper to taste
Parsley, chopped, for garnishing
Lemon wedges for serving

Very gently wash the shad roe pairs in cold water; pat dry with paper towel.

In a medium sized heavy pan over medium heat, cook the bacon until it loses most of its fat. **Salt** and pepper the shad roe on each side and add to the pan. **Reduce** heat to medium low, cover with a tight lid to allow the roe to steam, and cook until it is firm to the touch, no more. That should take about 12 to 15 minutes. Be careful, as the roe tends to pop, spewing hot fat over the cook.

Serve with parsley as a garnish and lemon wedges on the plate.

Variation: Instead of bacon fat, use 6 to 8 tablespoons of butter, and cook in a similar fashion, covered. **Then** remove the roe, pour off half of the butter, continue to heat the remaining butter until slightly brown.

Add 1 tablespoon of finely chopped capers, stirred in and saute 30 seconds more. **Serve** the butter sauce over the shad roe with the lemon wedges.

Charles E. Hires supposedly was born in Elsinboro, Salem County (his obituary said Roadstown), worked in a confectionary store in Milleville, and then as a pharmacist in Philadelphia. Somewhere along his career, he developed Hires Root Beer, so named after a suggestion that Pennsylvania's hard-drinking miners interested in the temperance movement would find the name more acceptable with "beer" in its name. Whatever its real history, this non-alcoholic, creamy, licorice-wintergreen and vanilla blended soda is still being sold today.

Seafood..... 161

Tales on Filleting Shad, or Trying To

Stories are legion about fishermen trying vainly to rid a shad fillet of its multitude of tiny bones. Of course, it's possible for the rank amateur to try, but doubtless there won't be enough fillet meat remaining to bother serving.

One notable example of the frustrations of the would-be filleter comes from one of my main sources of shad lore, the eminent shad fisherman, Sid Riley, a retired school principal from Elsinboro, near Salem, NJ. He is fortunate to be able to fish literally from the back porch of his house. Nonetheless, with all of his years of netting and catching tons of shad from his back door, here is his tale of woe on attempting to rid the shad fillet of its bones:

"I figured for once and for all, I would master the art of filleting. A friend video taped the whole process and told me to have the right sharp knives to do the job. It takes two different knives, you see. So we ran the tape, and I tried and tried. Even had my wife Joan run it backwards and forwarded a number of times. All I ended up with were heaps of useless waste. After two weeks of trying, I gave up."

To that, I'll add my own fish story. On a day when I happened to be in the presence of an expert shad filleter, he paid me no mind. Cutters, that's what the filleters call themselves, by nature don't let anyone outside their inner circle watch them at their task for they don't want to give away the secrets to their livelihood. Understood. But, he let me watch. That was the ultimate insult to my manhood for he felt that in no way would I ever be able to duplicate his skills. Naturally, he sped up his cutting so fast and with disguised moves it would have been difficult without a slow motion replay to figure out just what he was doing.

So....if you come across a cookbook that instructs you on the skillful art of shad filleting, cut up the book instead.

Baked Shad

This recipe, submitted by Mary Jane Henderson, has been excerpted from "A BOOK OF FAVORITE RECIPES" compiled by the Lower Alloways Creek Mother's Circle and Friends. The book's cover shows a wood burning stove with the date 1929 on the oven door, the date of the Circle's founding and whose stoves have been in use until but a few years ago by locals. This reprinted recipe, however, is still appreciated by today's diners.

Remove back bone. Place in pan skin side down. Pour 1 tablespoon vinegar over fish. Add salt and pepper. Put about 1/4 inch of water in the pan. Cover tightly with aluminum foil, making sure no steam escapes. Pace in 225 degree F. oven for 4 hours. You will be able to eat every bone.

Crisp Broiled Shad

Serves four

By broiling shad skin side up until the skin is crisp, much of the oil drains away and you needn't turn over the soft, flappy fillets. It's easy to do and amazingly crisp and juicy.

2   boned shad fillets, about 3/4 to 1 pound each
Salt and pepper to taste
Juice of one lemon or lime

The late **Bill "Bucky" Buckalew** ranked as one of the best shad fisherman in Salem County.

Carefully wash the fillets and pat dry. **Lightly** salt and pepper both sides of fillets. **Lay** skin-side up on an lightly oiled oven-proof baking pan. **Broil** 6 to 8 inches under the heating element until skin is crisp, about 8 minutes. The fillets should be cooked through without the need to turn over the fragil shad. **Remove** from broiler; plate by lifting with a long spatula, and squeeze lemon juice generously over the fillet. Cut into serving sizes for easier transfer to diner's plate. **Variation:** The epicurean cook may prefer to cut the peel from a fresh lemon and finely mince a scant teaspoon to add at the last minute before the fillet is finished broiling.

A fisherman's wife once said that her husband often returns home with his pickup truck reeking from the smell of less than fresh fish from earlier catches. "But when that pickup smells that bad, that means he is catching fish. So when he is catching fish, he is making money....and I love the sweet smell of fresh money!"

Seafood..... 163

Broiled Shad
with Orange Liqueur or Zest

Serves four

Combining the rich flavor of Delaware Bay shad and the almost-everyone likes fruitiness of an orange liqueur or zest brings about a sure pleaser with ease. If you are using the liqueur, you can choose from the exalted Grand Marnier to the humble Triple Sec liqueurs; they equally enhance the shad. When I prepared this dish for the first time, a fellow from Quinton who ate shad all of his many years, said it was the best shad he ever had. Enough said.

> 2   boned shad fillets, about 3/4 pound each
> Salt and pepper to taste
> Flour for dredging
> 1   tablespoon oil
> 2   tablespoons orange liqueur, or 1 teaspoon orange
>   zest
> 1/4 cup dry white wine
> Orange slices for garnish

Carefully rinse and pat dry shad fillets. Sprinkle with salt and pepper on both sides.
Over medium-high heat, film an ovenproof sauté pan sufficiently large to hold both fillets. **Dredge** fillets in flour, shake off excess, and lay skin-side down.
Sauté over medium heat for about 8 minutes, or until the under side barely begins to brown. Do not turn over as the shad fillets are too delicate.
Add the orange liqueur or orange zest, sauté for another minute and place under broiler about 4 to 6 inches under the heating element until fillet surfaces brown slightly, about 3 to 4 minutes.
Garnish with orange slices around the serving plate.

This restored **Shad Cabin** at the Lower Alloways Creek Museum is typical of cabins the watermen used as retreats when working long hours during shad runs up the Delaware Bay. This cabin could be skidded easily on ice during the freezing months prior to the shad catch and could be floated as well. The Swedish and Finns were known to follow the shad up along the east coast as the water warmed progressively northwards. According to historian Clem Sutton, many cabins had names, such as one that he remembers, "Mudville."

Stuffed Shad Marino

Serve four to six

In Down Jersey, no one fillets as many shad as the cutters at Dill's Seafood in Bridgeton. With their extensive shad cooking know how, I asked the owners, the Marino family, to pass along their favorite version of stuffed shad. It's from Janice Marino, wife of Earl Marino. In a bow to convenience, Janice opts to use Stove Top Stuffing, but certainly you can use another favorite, or one made from scratch, if you prefer.

    1   6-ounce package Stove Top Stuffing Mix for
          Chicken
    2   boneless shad fillets, about 3/4-1 pound each
    Salt and pepper to taste
  1/4   cup fresh parsley, chopped
    1   cup seasoned bread crumbs
    3   tablespoons grated Parmesan cheese
  1/4   medium onion, thinly sliced crosswise
    2   tablespoons paprika
  1/2   cup dry white wine
    3   tablespoons butter

Preheat oven to 400 degrees F.

Prepare stuffing mix according to package directions.

Place shad fillets in lightly oiled baking pan skin side down. **When** stuffing is cool enough to handle, pack the stuffing into the folds of the shad fillets. **In a separate bowl,** mix the salt and pepper, parsley, bread crumbs, and cheese. Spread across top of fillets, allowing stuffing to spill over the sides. **Place** onion rings on top of bread crumbs, and in turn, sprinkle the paprika over it all. **Pour** the wine over the fillets, top with 3 tablespoons of butter and cover with aluminum foil. **Bake** at 400 degrees F. for 25 to 30 minutes or until barely flaky. Uncover and bake for 5 minutes more to brown surface.

Variation: Opt to use lemon or orange slices instead of onion rings.

This **advertisement** appeared in a Bridgeton Newspaper in 1933.
Courtesy of South Jersey Magazine

Slow-Cooker Shad

Serves 3-4 as entree, 6-8 as appetizer

My friend Steve "The Professor" Crane, a waterman from Canton near the Delaware Bay, passed along this recipe for shad that's easy to prepare. It takes care of the bone problem by long and slow simmering in a crockery pot...the bones simply melt away. "If done right, you won't be able to find the bones," Crane told me. By his method you can tell he knows something about shad cooking. This technique works for those of us who find someone knocking at the back door with a whole shad, and doubtless neither they nor you know how to remove the bones from the fillets. Buck shad are often offered whole from the fishmonger as the male shad are smaller and, of course, don't contain roe.

This can be served as an appetizer or as a main entree. See below.

> 1 buck (male) shad, about 3 pounds
> Salt and pepper to taste
> 1 green pepper, diced
> 1 medium onion, diced
> Spicy mustard for topping

Either cut the fillets yourself or have your fish store person do it for you. Have him remove the skin, but don't expect him to always have the knack of removing the multi-layer fine bones.

Cut the fillets to fit in one layer on the bottom of the crock pot. Salt and pepper to taste.

Place shad fillets along with the onions and peppers in the crock pot. **Simmer** over a low setting about 6 to 8 hours. If your lid doesn't have a vent opening, place slightly ajar to allow some moisture to escape. Add water as necessary.

For appetizer: Remove onions and peppers and serve with a spicy mustard topping.

For entree: Serve with onions and peppers.

Planked Shad

The practice of cooking shad on planks (usually thick oak) was passed along from the Lenni-Lenape to the early settlers. Notice that the shad is pinned to the planks with drip pans below to catch the dripping oil.

Baked Striped Bass
with Egg Sauce

Serves four

Stripped bass, also known as rockfish, is entirely a sport fish as it's illegal to sell in the commercial trade in New Jersey . As a feisty fighter it's popular with sport fishermen. Arguably one of the finest tasting fish caught in nearby waters, stripped bass rates as a special dish for company. According to Frances Blackwood, it was commonly served with an egg sauce after the whole fish was poached. Here, in the interest of easier cooking, we suggest the use of her egg sauce recipe over baked fillets. The delicate egg sauce compliments and doesn't overpower the fine, delicate flavor of the stripped bass. You can ask your fishman to remove the skin from the fillets if you wish.

4 (8-ounce) stripped bass fillets
Salt and pepper
Lemon juice

Egg Sauce:
2   tablespoons flour
2-1/2 tablespoons butter
1   cup fish stock or water
Salt and pepper to taste
1   cup light cream
3   egg yolks
Thin wedges of lemon
Sliced hard-boiled egg

Preheat oven to 400 degrees F.

Wash and pat dry the stripper fillets. Lightly salt and pepper and place on lightly oiled baking pan.

Bake in a 400 degree F. oven and check at 10 minutes. They are done when tested with a fork and they are flaky. Do not over cook.

Remove carefully with a long spatula to a serving platter and squeeze fresh lemon juice over the fillets. Keep warm in the oven briefly while the sauce is made.

Preparing the Egg Sauce:

Melt butter over low heat, add flour, stir until it bubbles and turns a faint golden brown. **Slowly** stir in fish stock or water; continue to stir over moderate heat until mixture thickens. Season with salt and pepper to taste. **Add** cream into which the egg yolks have been beaten, stirring it in gradually; continue to cook until smoothly thickened. **Pour** over warm fish on the hot platter; arrange lemon wedges and sliced boiled eggs around edge of platter. For a finishing touch of garnish, arrange a wreath of watercress all around the fish.

Teriyaki Seafood Medley

Serves four to six

My friend Tom Alexandridis, who owned a seafood restaurant for a number of years and has worked with the suppliers at Philadelphia's Wholesale Fish Market, brought this recipe together. He used the freshest of fish with a homemade teriyaki sauce he learned from the Asian workers at the market. By drawing on fresh ingredients instead of the bottled sauce, this teriyaki sauce comes alive to compliment the fish. Any firm fish can be used as long as it is truly fresh, and that should guide you as to choice of fish. This recipe always draws raves from those who say they don't like fish, but they like it this way. It was chosen for serving at my daughter Ann's wedding

Teriyaki Sauce:

1/2	teaspoon grated ginger
2	tablespoons soy sauce
3	garlic cloves, minced
	Juice of one lemon
1	tablespoon vegetable oil
	Zest of 1/2 half lemon, or 1 teaspoon lemon pepper
1/4	teaspoon salt
1/4	teaspoon honey
	Cayenne to taste

1-1/2	pounds firm fish fillets, see note, cut into 1/2-inch cubes
2	tablespoons vegetable oil
	Cooked rice

Prepare teriyaki by mixing all ingredients in a non-reactive bowl.

Wash fish fillets in cold water, pat dry, and cut into 1/2-inch cubes.

Toss fish cubes in teriyaki sauce. Place in refrigerator for about 20 minutes, covered.

Heat oil in a large pan or wok over medium high heat. When oil is hot, remove one-half of the fish from the bowl with a slotted spoon and sauté or stir fry for about three minutes, stirring occasionally. With a knife or fork, check the interior of the cubes for doneness. Repeat for the other half of the cubes without discarding the small amount of teriyaki marinating sauce remaining in the bowl.

Serve the medley over the cooked rice.

Variation: Add the remaining marinating sauce to the pan along with 2 tablespoons orange liqueur simmered for two minutes. Add 1/4 cup of chicken stock or water and simmer for two minutes more. Omit the orange liqueur and use the chicken stock or water to make a sauce to pour on the serving platter.

Note: A wide variety of fresh fillets can be used, and mixing them is even better. The main concern is to choose those that are firm enough to stand up to tossing, such as sword, tuna, shark, mahi mahi, salmon, monk and tilefish.

Sicilian Tuna and Rigatoni

Serves six

This is a recipe that starts best at the fish store, which for us in Down Jersey can't be more than a few minutes away. Fresh tuna, the defining seafood in this dish, forms a basis for many Sicilian recipes. By starting with a doctored commercial sauce that we called "Today's Spaghetti Gravy," this preparation is easy to do. About the only task required is having someone with the dexterity to cut the tuna into bite-sized pieces.

1/2-3/4 pound fresh tuna	
1	quart of Today's Spaghetti Gravy, see page 235
1	pound cooked rigatoni, penne or cavatelli
Dash of hot pepper flakes, optional	

While the pasta is cooking, warm the marinara sauce in a heavy-bottom saucepan. **With** a knife, cut the tuna into bite-sized pieces. If the marinara sauce is not sufficiently warmed to a simmer, place tuna in the refrigerator until sauce is ready. **Bring** sauce to a simmer and add the tuna, stirring; simmer for 3 minutes at which time the tuna should be sufficiently cooked.

Serve as a seafood sauce over the pasta with pepper flakes as a garnish. Cheese, such as a Romano, is not usually served with seafood dishes. Refrigerate the remaining sauce as soon as the diners have finished their meal. This is a habit the author learned when working with the seafood industry.

Variation: Out of a desire to keep this recipe as simple as possible, slices of fennel bulbs were not mentioned as an ingredient, yet back in Sicily use of it is very typical. It's just that, until recently, fennel bulbs were not commonly found at our markets. If you choose to use a fennel bulb, add thinly cut slices to the sauce and simmer for 5 minutes before adding the tuna.

Keeping Seafood Fresh: A good habit when handling any seafood product is to avoid allowing it to reach room temperature for more than a brief moment. While we have good intentions, seafood is too perishable and would suffer from warm temperatures, even for a brief time. I recall that about one hour at room temps equals about one day in the refrigerator. Therefore, after seasoning a filet for cooking, unless the fillet is to immediately go into the skillet or baking pan, return the fillet to the refrigerator until it is cooked. Likewise, after serving an appetizer such as shrimp, don't allow the shrimp bowl to remain on the table for any length of time after your diners are finished enjoying them.

Crane's Weakfish Fingers
with Barbecue sauce

Serves 8-10 as appetizer, 4-6 as main course
When weakfish (known as seatrout by our neighbors across the Bay in Delaware) are running during the summer season, catches are abundant, so serving them with party-style barbecue sauce fits right in. The size limits of weakfish regulations takes them out of pan frying, and so most are filleted. While weakfish fillets are sweet and mild, they are rather flaky. Steve Crane, the contributor of this recipe, handles that by salt-brining the fillets for a few hours before cooking. Though Crane fashions his own barbecue sauce, any good quality bottled sauce will do fine. Weakfish is usually sold with the skin attached.

> 2   pounds weakfish fillets
> 1   quart water mixed with 1/4 cup salt
> Beer batter sufficient for dredging, see below
> Vegetable oil for deep frying
> Homemade or bottled barbecue sauce

Place the fillets in a non-reactive baking pan and cover with the water/salt brine solution. **Refrigerate** for 1 hour or more. **Remove** fillets from brine solution, rinse free of the salty brine and pat dry. **Cut** the fillets, which will now be firm, into finger-sized pieces about 1-1/2 to 2 inches wide. **Dredge** the fillets in beer batter and either deep fry in an electric fryer, or add sufficient vegetable oil in a cast iron pan to a depth of 1/4-inch or more. Try to maintain an oil temperature of about 360 degrees. By frying in small batches, it is easier to maintain temps.
Fry the fillet pieces in small batches until slightly golden and allow to drain on an open rack or paper towels. Serve the weakfish warm on a large platter with your barbecue dipping sauce bowl placed in the center.

Beer batter:
Makes 2-1/2 cups
1 (12 oz.) can of flat
    beer
1-1/4 cup sifted flour
1 Tablespoon salt
2 teaspoons baking
    powder
Black pepper to taste

Mix all ingredients and allow to rest for 30
    minutes.

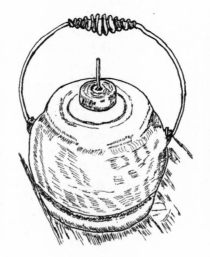

Kerosene bottles such as this one were common in the upstairs or downstairs kitchens in the early part of the 20th Century. They supplied fuel for kerosene stoves before electric and gas ranges became more popular. This bottle bore the inscription: Patented July 1, 1913.

Sweet and Sour Whiting

Serves four to six

Whiting has been an extremely popular fish in Down Jersey as harvests are virtually year round. They are particularly popular with those who have deep roots near the shore and Bay.

For as long back as they can remember, the Marino family, who now own and operate Dill's Seafood and Restaurant in Bridgeton, has prepared whiting straight forward fried and baked. As you will notice, the whiting can be served with the bone as many prefer for its fuller flavor, or boned out by the fishmonger, if that is your preference. Hake (which is often sold as whiting, and usually offered skinless) or other white fish can be substituted with excellent results. Whiting has a short shelf life, so buy immediately ahead of intended preparation.

- 2 pounds whiting, cut in either bone-in 2-inch steaks, or boned and cut in 2-inch cubes
- 1/2 cup flour, seasoned with salt and pepper
- Oil for frying
- 1 medium onion, sliced
- 6-8 fresh mint leaves or 1 teaspoon dill weed
- 3/4 cup sugar mixed with 3/4 cup cider vinegar

Preheat oven to 300 degrees F.

Pour frying oil in pan to a depth of 1/4 inch and bring to frying temperature by testing with a small cube of bread.

Meanwhile, pat dry the whiting steaks; dredge the whiting fillets in seasoned flour. When the temperature reaches the appropriate level, fry on each side until lightly browned. Drain on paper towels. As they are finished, place in a casserole large enough to hold them on a single layer.

When all whiting are fried, pour off all but two tablespoons of oil add onions; sauté over medium heat until onions are soft and clear. Add mint or dill and sauté 1 minute more. **Stir** in mix of sugar and vinegar, turn off heat

Pour deglazing sauce from pan over the whiting fillets in the casserole.

Place in preheated oven for 10 minutes or more, at which time the casserole should reach a light simmer.

Another use for whiting: Because whiting flakes easily when cooked in a sauce, it can turn an ordinary marinara sauce into a delightful seafood sauce. Heat the sauce to a light simmer and add roughly cut pieces of whiting, stir until broken. Simmer for about three minutes. The residual heat of the sauce will finish the cooking. This is great over pasta such as rigatoni or shells.

The wharf at **Bayside** was a busy place during the shad and sturgeon
season at the turn of the 20 Century.
—Drawing from photo, courtesy of Don Wentzel

The port hamlet of Bay Side, also known as Caviar, a few miles west of
Greenwich in Cumberland and on the Delaware Bay, once thrived in the
industry of caviar and shad. Today, only a few visible pilings at water's edge
remain as a reminder of a village that once was. Here is an account published
in "Industrial Directories of New Jersey, 1882 and 1901:

> "The railroad name of Caviar is Bay Side; it is situated on the Red Bank-
> Bay Side Branch of the Central Railroad of New Jersey and on the
> Delaware Bay. The permanent population of Caviar is small, but large
> numbers come there to engage in the sturgeon and shad fishing, which
> begins early in March and usually lasts until the end of June. The roes of
> these large fish, when prepared and salted, become the relish known as
> 'Caviar,' which gives its name to the village. Large quantities of it are sold
> every season, many of the buyers coming from Germany and Russia. There
> are six firms regularly engaged in preparing the fish roe and marketing them
> who employ between them about 140 men."

In the fall, for a five-year period in the 1880's,
the Baltimore & Ohio Railroad and it's affiliated
Jersey Central Railroad carried oysters (and
probably shad roe) daily from the port of Bay
Side (Caviar) up to New York City. The trains
initiated in Baltimore, were floated across the
Delaware Bay, loaded in Bayside and at the
docks at Bacon's Neck and Greenwich Pier
before continuing the evening run northwards.
At Jersey City, rail cars loaded with oysters were
floated across the Upper New York Bay to 23rd.
Street at the Fulton Fish Market.

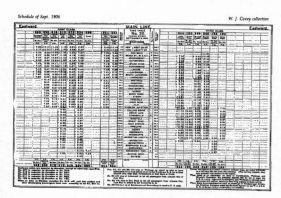

This Jersey Central train schedule of September,
1906 shows an 8:40 p.m stop at Bay Side.

Chapter 6
Vegetarian and Vegan for All

It's time to treat the subject of vegetarian and vegan dishes on their own, even though a number of previous courses printed in this book are already vegetarian or can easily be adapted. In this modest chapter, I have passed along vegetarian dishes that do not include meat or fish to be considered vegetarian, and for some, vegan. As with all the foods covered so far, they have to taste good; simply qualifying as vegetarian or vegan isn't enough.

The definition of vegetarian varies, but here we take it to mean dishes without meat or fish, yet some mistakingly consider themselves vegetarian if they don't eat red meat. Whatever your inclination to include or exclude, I have learned that fresh vegetables can be prepared in exciting ways for full enjoyment that take no backseat to any other choices. My goal here is to pass that along.

The belief of the vegans is that no animal products at all should be consumed, so they exclude milk, eggs, cheese and honey. It may seem daunting at first that any food could be prepared at all without one of the forbidden items, but there are alternatives. That said, it does help if a health food store is nearby and you take a liking to a variety of soy products.

The growing preference for vegan meals is advanced and supported by efforts of a Down Jersey-located Society, the American Vegan Society headquartered in Malaga, Franklin Township. It is fitting that a vegan focus should spring from an area that holds fresh produce in high esteem. From their activities starting in 1960, veganism has spread across the U.S., gathering thousands of members that respect the views of their humanitarian approach to healthful eating.

Despite all the confusion on which path leads to the healthiest diet, the evidence is strongly in favor of lessening our consumption of fatty meats filled with hormones and from animals fed "scientific" diets laced with antibiotics. The way becomes much clearer when we have tasty alternatives, rather than a regiment driven by admonitions of what's healthy.

Here, we will take you to locally inspired foods that may help you to eat more vegetables, just like Doctor Mom always said you should. I thank Freya Dinshah, an Officer in the American Vegan Society, for her guidance and sharing of recipes.

Asparagus Soup

Serves four

This is a fitting example of a soup that meets the vegan standard of being meatless and dairyless.

1	medium potato, diced
1	medium onion
1	carrot, diced
1-1/2	pounds asparagus (weight after trimming bottom ends), cut into tips and stems, separated
1	tablespoon soy or corn oil, optional
1/4	cup fresh parsley, chopped
3-4	leaves fresh spearmint, optional

Prepare the potato, onion and carrot; place in a soup pot with 4 cups of water. **Stir** in the asparagus stems and herbs. **Bring** to a boil, reduce to a simmer and cook for 15 minutes or until vegetables are barely tender. **Remove** from heat and allow to cool somewhat. **In** blender of food processor, pulse vegetables and stock, a portion at a time, until all is smooth. **Pour** back into the soup pot, reheat, and add asparagus tips set aside earlier. Simmer for 3 minutes; stir well and serve.

Variation: Add cooked green peas to the pureed soup. For more body, add cooked brown or white rice when the asparagus tips are being cooked.

Vegetable Time Table

	BOILED	BAKED
Asparagus	15 to 35 min.	
Beans-String	35 min. to 1 hr.	
Lima or other green beans	30 to 45 min.	
Dried	3 to 4 hrs.	
Beets-Young	30 to 45 min.	About 1 hr.
Old	2 to 4 hrs.	2 to 4-1/2 hrs.
Cabbage	15 to 30 min.	
Carrots—Young	15 to 25 min.	
Old	30 to 60 min.	
Cauliflower	20 to 30 min.	
Celery (stewed)	20 to 35 min.	
Corn, green	5 to 15 min.	12 to 25 min.
Egg-plant (stewed)	15 to 20 min.	15 min.
Lentils, dried	3 to 4 hrs.	4 hrs.
Okra	20 to 40 min.	
Onion	30 to 60 min.	2 hrs.
Parsnip	30 to 50 min.	
Peas-Green	15 to 40 min.	
Dried	3 to 4 hrs.	
Potato	30 to 40 min.	45 to 60 min.
Sweet Potato	25 to 30 min.	30 to 45 min.
Pumpkin, cut	30 to 40 min.	
whole		1-1/2 hrs.
Spinach	15 to 25 min.	
Summer Squash	15 to 20 min.	
Tomato (stewed)	15 to 25 min.	30 min.
Turnip	30 to 60 min.	

The Rumford Chemical Works of Rhode Island, manufacturer of Rumford Baking Powder since 1859, now owned by Hulman and Company of Terre Haute, Indiana, published many recipe books to promote their products. One of them, *The Rumford Common Sense Cookbook* (1926, '27, '28) was authored by Lily Haxworth Wallace. In her book, she lists the recommended vegetable cooking times of the day. Notice the extraordinary times compared to the shorter periods we find acceptable today. Reprint editions of *The Rumford Complete Cookbok* are still available today.

Pancakes

Makes 36 small pancakes

Ursula Dinshaw, from Malaga, brought this old recipe with her from Germany where she was born. It has endured as a family favorite over many generations and it happens to fit the vegan guidelines.

2	teaspoons active dry yeast
2	tablespoons water
1/4	teaspoon salt
4	teaspoons unsulphured molasses
2-2/3	cups water
4	teaspoons arrowroot powder
4	teaspoons soy powder
2	cups whole wheat flour, plus extra flour
2/3	cup raisins

Dissolve yeast in the 2 tablespoons of water.

Stir in other ingredients in the order mentioned, mixing well as each item is added.

Let the batter stand in a warm place for about an hour.

In a pan lightly filmed with vegetable oil or soy lecithin over medium heat, drop two tablespoons of batter in the pan for each pancake. Cook on both sides until golden.

Serve with soy butter, apple sauce (below), maple syrup, or blueberry jam.

Applesauce

9	Yellow Delicious apples, about
	2-1/2pounds
1/4	cup apple juice

Peel, core and dice the apples.

Cook the apples in the apple juice for about 10 minutes.

Stir occasionally until desired consistency is achieved.

Hearth Griddle

Escarole Soup

Makes five cups

This recipe is reprinted from Freya Dinshah's cookbook, "The Vegan Kitchen," which demonstrates that a great tasting soup can be made without any animal products. Freya also is editor of the "American Vegan" magazine.

4 stalks celery, diced
6 green beans, cut in 1-inch lengths
1 small onion, diced
1 medium potato, optional, diced
1/8 small cabbage, chopped
1/2 head escarole
1 cup water
1 teaspoon vegetable oil, optional
1 sprig fresh parsley, chopped

After preparing all of the vegetables, place all except the parsley in a 4-quart soup pot in the order mentioned. **Add** the water and cook about 20 minutes, till tender.

Use a blender or a food processor to blend the cooked ingredients with the oil and parsley.

Add extra water to make the soup to desired consistency.

Variations: Add cooked peas, or pole or baby lima beans, or finely sliced vegetables to top off the soup.

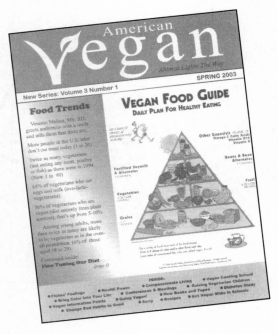

The **American Vegan** is published by the American Vegan Society (pronounced VEE-guns) in Malaga, Franklin Township. They profess to live on products of the plant kingdom, so exclude flesh, fish, fowl, dairy products, eggs, honey, and animal gelatin.

Tomato Bean Soup

Serves six

This soup is an adapted version from Freya Dinshah, my friend from Malaga. Notice that when fresh tomatoes are not in season, opt for use of tomato puree. As Jersey round tomatoes may be a bit tart for a soup, notice that we suggest adding two carrots or a teaspoon of sugar.

```
1-1/2 cups dried black eyed peas(beans), about 10 ounces
1    large onion, diced
2    carrots, diced, or 1 teaspoon sugar
Salt to taste
5    cups water
4    medium tomatoes,
Additional water for blender and for desired consistency
2    tablespoons olive or vegetable oil
```

Sort and wash the black eyed peas in several changes of water. **In** a 4-quart soup pot, add 5 cups of fresh water to a level about 1-1/2 inches above the beans; add the diced onions, carrots, and salt. **Bring** to a boil, reduce to a simmer, and cook for 1-1/2 hours, or until the beans are tender. **Drain** water from the beans into blender, add half of the beans and onions. **Blenderize** and return to pot, or use an immersion blender. **Rinse** blender with 2 cups water and return to pot. **Stir** in the tomato pulp and water to desired consistency; add oil. **Heat** to desired level for serving.
Variation: Chopped celery will add more flavor, along with chunks of butternut squash. **Add** the celery with the onions and carrots; add the squash at the last 15 minutes.

Tomato and Eggplant Soup

Serves six

This is another soup offered by Freya Dinshah. Here, she suggests the use of tahini to bring a creaminess to the soup. If tahini isn't readily available, try peanut butter or almond butter instead.

```
1    large eggplant, about 1-1/2 pounds
2/3  cup water
3    pounds tomatoes
1    tablespoon tahini, or peanut butter or almond butter
Salt to taste
```

Peel and dice the eggplant. **Cook** the eggplant in the water for about 15 minutes, or until tender. **In a blender** or food processor, blend the cooked eggplant and water in which it cooked, with the uncooked tomatoes, tahini and salt. If using a 1-quart blender, do it in small batches. **Return** to the soup pot. **Heat** till hot; do not boil.

Vegetarian & Vegan   177

Panned Broccoli

Serves six to eight

This easy preparation can be taken many ways, all of them delightful. The basic vegan recipe has a small amount of soy sauce to flavor a sauce that makes it wonderful as a topping over rice or pasta. To that, you can add cooked beans or other ingredients. The other vegetarian version takes you to the Mediterranean with a final touch of Parmesan cheese, and it's just as versatile. If it's a side dish you want, reduce the amount of stock.

1-1/2 pounds broccoli, about one bunch
2   tablespoons vegetable oil
1   medium onion, sliced lengthwise
2   cloves garlic, minced
1   (13-ounce) can vegetable stock
2   tablespoons soy sauce
2   tablespoons cornstarch
3   tablespoons water

Peel outer stems and slice stems into 1/4-inch slices. Cut florets into 1-inch pieces. **In** a large skillet over medium heat, heat onions in oil for 2 minutes.
Add garlic and stir for 30 seconds.
Add vegetable stock, soy sauce and broccoli stems. After 1 minute, add florets and simmer for 2 minutes.
Mix the cornstarch and water, give it a stir, and add to pan. Stir for another 1/2 minute and serve.
Variation: Two teaspoons of vegetarian oyster sauce can be added and/or a dash of cayenne. Adding cooked beans over rice or pasta brings enough body to make this a complete meal. Reduce amount of vegetable stock if this is to be a side dish.

Italian (vegetarian, but not vegan) version:
Replace the soy sauce with Parmesan cheese, which is added at the end of simmering. **Add** salt and pepper to taste. **In the** Chinese version, the soy and oyster sauce will contribute sufficient salt.
For those who approach meat as a condiment, use chicken broth instead of vegetable broth, and or add a small amount of cooked julienned beef or other meat to the dish.

Chickpea Stew
with Spinach or other Greens

Serves four

The prevalence of Hispanics and Italians in Down Jersey has brought a plentiful supply of chickpeas (garbanzos) onto grocery shelves. Pairing them with seasonal spinach or a host of other sturdy greens brings about a hearty stew that can be prepared almost any time of the year.

2	tablespoons extra virgin olive oil
1	small onion, diced
3	garlic cloves, sliced thinly crosswise
1/2	teaspoon red pepper flakes to taste
1/4	cup peeled, diced plum or round tomatoes, fresh or canned, or 2 tablespoons tomato paste plus 3 tablespoons water
3	cups cooked chickpeas, or 2 (15-ounce) cans, drained
	Salt and black pepper
1	pound spinach or other greens, well rinsed and coarsely chopped (see comment below regarding stems)

In a large sauté pan, heat the oil over medium-high heat. Sauté the onions and pepper flakes until the onions are clear, about 3 minutes.

Toss in the garlic, stir, and cook for 30 seconds more.

Toss in the tomatoes or paste, chickpeas, partial salt and pepper; reduce heat to a simmer and cook, covered, for 15 minutes. Add water as necessary, a tablespoon at a time.

Add the chopped spinach with its wash water still clinging, cover and cook over low heat for about a minute or a little longer until the leaves have wilted. Remove cover, stir, and cook for another 2 minutes.

Taste and adjust for salt and pepper.

Serve with a light drizzle of extra-virgin olive oil.

Should you cut off spinach stems? Some might automatically remove the stems of spinach believing that they are tough and fibery, but it's not necessarily so. Grown under favorable conditions without stress, spinach, as well as its stems, might be tender and sweet throughout. If your recipe accommodates them, cutting and discarding stems might be a waste of time and a loss of an agreeable bite contrasting with the softer leaves. I suggest that you take a sample bite of a stem to decide for yourself. Of course, with the very large, long stems it would be best to trim them close to the leaves.

Eggplant Parmesan

Serves six

Our climate and soil so favor both eggplants and tomatoes, that the Italian immigrants found happiness with eggplant Parmesan, and so did everyone else. We'll pass (Mom forgive me), the salting routine as today's eggplants at the market are more tender and less bitter. They don't benefit as much from the slating process to lessen moisture and bitterness as they once did. Incidentally, most Italian cooks had more access to Romano cheese, called by a popular brand, Locatelli, than Parmesan, which was less available in earlier times.

> 2 medium or larger eggplants
> Olive oil for sautéing
> Flour for dredging, with a pinch of salt
> Salt and fresh ground pepper, to taste
> 2 cups marinara sauce
> 1/2 pound grated Mozzarella cheese
> 1 cup Parmesan or Pecorino Romano cheese
> Basil leaves or dried basil, if not in sauce

Preheat oven to 350 degrees F. **Peel** and cut eggplants into 3/8-inch slices; dredge in flour. **In** a sauté pan filmed with oil over medium heat, add dredged eggplant slices to fill, but not crowd, the pan. **Salt** and pepper; sauté until lightly golden. Repeat for other side. **Remove** and drain on paper towels. **Continue** sautéing until all slices are done, adding more oil as needed. **Ladle** a portion of the marinara sauce in the bottom of a baking dish. Place a single layer of eggplants, a portion of the Parmesan and Romano cheese, and several leaves of fresh basil or a sprinkle of dried basil. **Repeat** with each layer, topping with a final ladling of sauce and the cheese mix again. **Bake** in a 350-degree F. oven for 20 minutes, or until it bubbles.

Quick Prep Eggplant Parmesan

As much as we praise fresh eggplants, sometimes use of quality frozen pre-coated and sautéed slices are our only sensible choice. No salt should be needed in this version.

> 4 cups marinara sauce
> 1 pound frozen eggplant cutlets, breaded
> 1/2 pound mozzarella cheese, grated
> 1/4 pound Parmesan or Romano cheese, grated

In a large, deep baking pan, ladle a layer of marinara sauce on the bottom. **Place** a layer of eggplants, top with a portion of the mozzarella cheese. **Repeat** until all the cutlets are used. **Top** final layer with sauce and all of the Parmesan cheese. **Bake** in a 375-degree F. oven, covered, for 25 minutes, uncovered for another 10 mintes.

Seasoned Sautéed Eggplants
Easy Farm Market Style

Serves four to six

The Italian farmers of southern New Jersey, along with home gardeners, quickly learned that eggplants thrive in our hot and humid summers. The classic eggplant dish, eggplant Parmesan, however, calls for salting. That step, though not difficult, limits its use to occasiona times. Perhaps that is why eggplant Parmesan is so popular at restaurants.

In this easier to do recipe, flouring the eggplant seasoned with Romano cheese blankets the eggplant rounds set atop sturdy bread slices, without the salting procedure. It celebrates the full flavor of eggplants. The seasoned flour avoids the mess of the three-step process of dredging. Though the flour-only coating permits the eggplants to absorb more oil, it happens to be olive oil and is balanced by the use of bread. Also, instructions call for pre-heating the sauté pan for faster sautéing to lessen oil absorption.

Special Note: While the subtle flavor differences of various eggplant varieties now available at markets are all useable, the long, narrow Asian types, about 8"-10" long x 2" wide, or the newer "baby" eggplants are the most suitable size for slicing.

2	eggplants, sliced 1/4-inch thick
1/2	cup flour
2	tablespoons Romano cheese, grated
1/3	teaspoon salt
2	tablespoon olive oil
1	Italian or French style bread, sliced 1/2-inch thick

Optional additional pan sauce:

1	tablespoon olive oil
5	fresh basil leaves, chopped
2	tablespoons Romano cheese
1	cup, or more, marinara sauce

Prepare eggplants by peeling, removing tip end and peeling away the calyx at the stem end. **Slice** into 1/4-inch slices, sliced thin so that they sauté a bit more quickly. **Combine** and mix flour, cheese and salt in a wide soup bowl or a small baking pan. **Meanwhile**, preheat a non-stick sauté pan and add the olive oil. **Dredge** each slice in seasoned flour mix, shake off excess, and add to sauté pan when the oil is near smoking. **Add** the dredged slices. **Moderate** heat somewhat and sauté on first side until lightly browned. **Turn** over slices and repeat. If you need to sauté more than 2 panfuls, clean pan with a damp towel after second batch before continuing to avoid burning the flour that remains in the pan. **Add** more oil as needed. **Remove** the sautéed slices from the pan and place atop slices of bread. **Serve** as is, or follow saucing option. **While** pan is still warm and over low heat, add another tablespoon of olive oil, 2 tablespoons of cheese and chopped basil. **Stir** for 30 seconds and add spaghetti sauce; simmer for 2 minutes,
Spoon pan sauces over slices of bread topped with eggplants.

Greens and Beans

Serves six

This dish doesn't sound inviting, nor does it look all that appealing to the uninitiated. Yet, it's one great combo that's easy and quick to do, and you don't have to be a nutritionist to figure out it's good for you. Whenever I prepare it at demonstrations, it always gets second requests. Proportions given are estimates as they can vary. This is a family favorite.

2	tablespoons vegetable oil
1	large onion, sliced
1	pound fresh greens, such as spinach, kale, collards or bok choy washed and roughly chopped
1	quart baked beans, any meatless style

Heat oil in a large skillet or soup pot; cook onions until clear.
Add fresh greens with their washing liquid, cover and simmer for 5 minutes.
Add beans and when they are heated through, remove from heat and serve.
Applesauce makes an ideal accompaniment.
Variations: Any number of other greens can be used in addition to those mentioned such as Swiss chard, rape and a sturdy lettuce such as Romaine. However, should you use lettuce as your greens, add them after you remove the pot from the heat. When added, there should be enough heat to barely wilt the lettuce as you don't want to cook it to the point of losing all texture.

Curried Spinach

Serves four to six

To those who like curry, this dish is a fine example of how good a simple to prepare dish can be. Try to use a high quality curry that hasn't been on the shelf too long.

2	tablespoons vegetable oil
1	medium onion, sliced in crescents
1	teaspoon curry powder
1	pound spinach, washed, stems trimmed if necessary, and chopped coarsely and patted dry

In a wide skillet, deep enough to hold the spinachlater, over medium heat, add the oil and the onions; sauté until barely clear as you want to retain a bit of a crunch.
With a spatula, move a few onions aside in the middle of the pan and add the curry.
Stir into the oil for about 30 seconds until you can smell its fragrance. **Stir** and combine the infused curry oil with the onions. **Squeeze** spinach of excess water, add to the pan, cover, and steam for one minute or a little more until it has wilted.
Uncover, stir in with the seasoned onions and cook one minute more.

Grilled Portabella Sandwich
with Grilled Vegetables

Makes two sandwiches

Though vegetarians or vegans—if the option of cheese is sidestepped—will find this way of preparing portabellas rather agreeable, this powerfully tasty sandwich will appeal to almost anyone. In this sandwich prep, portabellas add their juicy, meaty textures while the seasonings and vegetables round it out. Free feel to substitute your own vegetable choices of whatever is found fresh at your local market.

2　medium portabella mushrooms, stems
　　　removed and used elsewhere
Salt and pepper to taste
2　tablespoons extra-virgin olive oil
2　cloves garlic, minced
For grilling:
　　Zucchini, sliced lengthwise
　　Eggplant, peeled if skin is tough, and sliced
　　Red bell pepper, halved and flattened
　　Onion slices, root end kept attached

Wipe the mushrooms clean with a damp paper towel.

Brush mushrooms with olive oil, season with salt, pepper and garlic; rest for about 20 minutes.

When grill is medium hot, coat grill with oil and grill mushrooms until slightly browned, turning to grill each side.

While mushrooms are grilling, lightly sprinkle vegetables with oil and then the salt and pepper; place on an oiled grill. Try not to disturb them so as to create grill marks.

This Colonial-ers **blender** reproduction shows us that, although operated by hand, few kitchen appliance ideas are new.
Drawing courtesy Goosebay Workshop

Assemble sandwich, using optional shredded cheese, perhaps one made with hot peppers.

Variation: Consider using a sprig of rosemary tossed in with the seasonings. McCormick's Montreal Spice™ is another alternative spice seasoning for mushrooms.

Broiled Cabbage
with Apple Breadcrumb Topping

Serves four

This is a sister recipe to Cheesy German Cabbage in the Vegetable Chapter. Its difference is that it's a vegan version and in no way is any less for it. With the apple breadcrumb topping, you might favor it even more so.

    1/2 small to medium green cabbage
    1/2 medium onion, sliced
         Salt and generous black pepper to taste
    1/2 cup unseasoned breadcrumbs
     2   tablespoons vegetable oil
     1   apple, sweet preferred, washed, and cut in small
            dice
         Whole wheat bread as a side

Select a large skillet that is attractive to directly serve from because the dish keeps its presentation best when presented straight from the cooking pan. Also, since it will be in the broiler, select a pan with a heatproof handle. Cast iron pansall have that, and seem right when placed directly on the table, on a trivet or pad, of course.

Wash the cabbage, removing any damaged or wilted outer leaves. Carefully with a large knife, cut the head in half, put aside one half for another use and cut the other in half again. Take the quarters and slice away the core section to use for pepper hash or discard.

Thinly slice the two quarters into shreds with a sharp knife or mandolin.

Before cooking cabbage, prepare topping by mixing together the breadcrumbs, oil and apples. Season lightly with salt.

In your pan over medium-low heat, film with vegetable oil, sauté the onions for one minute, or until just before they become clear.

Add the cabbage shreds, stir in to mix. Add salt, pepper, and continue cooking, covered, stirring occasionally for 4 to 5 minutes until the cabbage is tender.

Meanwhile, preheat the broiler.

When the cabbage is cooked, spread the breadcrumb topping evenly on the surface and place the pan under the broiler, about 6 to 8 inches away from the heat source.

Broil until the breadcrumbs are lightly browned, about 3 to 4 minutes.

Serve directly from the pan with a dense whole wheat bread as a side.

Vegan Pepper "Steak"
with Wheat Gluten

Serves four to six

For a short period in the 1980's, Peter Uprichard, the chef at the Frog Pond Cafe in Rosenhayn, prepared this dish for his vegan customers. His recipe lives on with the American Vegan Society in their various publications. Wheat gluten (also called Seitan), the protein derived from wheat flour, can be purchased at health food stores and at Asian markets.

Wheat gluten often is sold prepared with other high protein flours and soy sauce seasoning as it is rather bland itself. On the other hand, wheat gluten has a satisfying chewy, meaty texture. For this recipe, we are considering the Seitan form that has been shaped into meat-like pieces.

This dish is typically served over white or brown rice; a modest amount of sauce is made from the pan's juices.

10	ounces white button mushrooms
1	tablespoon vegetable oil
2	large green bell peppers, sliced
2	medium onions, sliced
2	cloves garlic, sliced thinly
2	tablespoons soy sauce
8	ounces wheat gluten, sliced
1	cup of water mixed with 2 tablespoons cornstarch
	Cooked brown or white rice

Wipe mushrooms with a damp cloth and slice.

In a large skillet, add the vegetable oil and mushrooms and cook over medium-low heat for 5-6 minutes until the mushrooms have lost most of their water.

Add the peppers and cook for 3 minutes.

Add the garlic, stir in, and cook for 30 seconds.

Add the onions and wheat gluten and continue to cook over medium-low heat for another 4-5 minutes. This cooking portion allows the onions to become clear and the wheat gluten, which is already cooked, to absorb the pan's flavors.

Give the water and cornstarch mixture one last stir, add to pan and stir in. Cook for about one minute to thicken the sauce and get the raw taste out of the cornstarch.

Serve over rice.

Variations: Some vegans will use tofu instead of wheat gluten. For this dish, they place the tofu in the freezer before use. Upon thawing, the tofu takes on a more textured consistency that compliments this dish. Tofu can be purchased in Asian and other markets already seasoned with anise, soy sauce and other flavorings.

Comforting Potato Soup

Serves four

Though I favor leeks from my garden, I didn't identify this as a leek soup, as onions could just as well be substituted. Since leek and potato soup is a classic that shouldn't be messed with, I go on to another way to enjoy this combo of the onion family with the comfort of potatoes. From my experience of making this soothing soup for friends when they are ill or have lost a loved one, this soup has evolved to its current form.

At first, I automatically added diced bacon or ham at the start to give a foundation of a rich, salty smokiness. When someone is sick though, while they need sustenance, they would rather not have any hint of meat. And since I would prepare a gallon of the potato soup for a big family, more than likely there would be a vegetarian in the bunch.

But by taking out the bacon or ham, something was missing. After scratching about, I reckoned that by roasting the potatoes first, the caramelization, or browning, would more than make up for the lost of the smoky meat flavor. It does add to the cooking time, however. Instead of the mess of puréeing, I prefer the simpler and more rustic method of hand-mashing the potatoes at the end of the cooking. Mashing can be as little or as much as you please. I like it chunky.

This soup lends itself to being built upon. Adding carrots comes to mind first, then there are diced red peppers, and so on. This soup recipe can easily be multiplied to make more. I also like a mix of russet and boiling potatoes (I like our local "Superior" variety), as the russet potatoes tend to break down upon boiling, thereby thickening the broth.

3　medium potatoes, peeled and quartered
1　tablespoon butter or extra-virgin olive oil,
　　　plus extra for brushing
2　large leeks, washed and chopped,
　　　or 2 medium onions, chopped
4 cups chicken stock, plus 2 cups water
Salt and pepper to taste

Preheat oven to 450 degrees F.

Place the quartered potatoes on a lightly greased baking pan and brush with butter or olive oil. **Roast**, uncovered, until browned, about 1 hour or more.

Thoroughly wash the leeks by quartering them lengthwise and rinsing vigorously in a deep pot of water; then chop. **As** the potatoes are becoming lightly browned, prepare soup by placing a heavy soup pot over medium heat and adding the butter. **Lightly** sauté the leeks until very lightly browned. **Remove** from heat until potatoes are ready. **Continue** by adding the chicken stock and water and potatoes.

Partially add salt and pepper, the chicken stock may be salty. **Simmer** until the potatoes are tender, about 15 minutes, bearing mind that the roasting has partially cooked them. **Remove** from heat, adjust for seasoning and hand mash.

Add a dollop of heavy cream if you wish, vegans can garnish with green onions.

Chapter 7

Fresh Salads, and Tomatoes, of Course

Our relatively long growing season gives us lots of salad makings from the first of the dandelions harvested in March to the last of the greens in October. And it doesn't stop in early fall because with our moderately cold winters, we can extend the season with hardy crops such as carrots, beets, radishes, kohlrabi, and the like.

Every year, more and more farmers are operating farm stands that tempt us to indulge in the season's freshest. Recently, we have seen the opening of city farmers' markets where serving urban ethnic diversity makes them even more exciting for shoppers.

I will repeat hints for the popular salad items that might help you prepare a salad:

Tomatoes: When we think of a salad tomato, a round, slicing tomato usually comes to mind. Our summer, field-grown tomatoes are peerless, although it's fine to consider local greenhouse tomatoes as an interim choice. Since its flavor is so powerfully assertive, consider a salad where the tomato itself fills the bowl, to be complimented with just a dressing and perhaps one other ingredient. It could be tomatoes and basil, mozzarella or diced onions.

For a tossed salad, and one that is prepared ahead of time, think of using plum tomatoes. They are sturdier and will stand up to rougher handling.

Cucumbers: I'll never understand why so many put up with the tough-skinned, waxed cucumbers in the supermarkets and at some farmstands. Usually, the smaller cucumbers we call pickles are not waxed. It is so easy to wash and slice pickle cucumbers into a salad with their skins on. Be sure to cut the growing end, as it is usually quite bitter.

Lettuce: Romaine lettuce is *the* lettuce of Down Jersey. Crisphead lettuce (Iceberg) has a tough time maturing in our summer heat. Besides, the Italian farmers have done a good job of seeing to it that we learn to like Romaine, an all-purpose lettuce, with crunch *and* flavor. Other looseleaf lettuce varieties have been coming on to the market. The flavor interest and color blends of the mixed lettuce types carries salads to more exciting levels.

Asian greens: South Jersey growers have been diversifying into Asian crops, many of them quite good for our salads. Chinese cabbage, for example, is much milder than European green cabbage, so it's easier to fit into a salad. Try one or more of them on your own to see what you think of them.

Carrots, kohlrabi, beets and radishes: These winter-hardy vegetables ought to be considered all year, especially when our tender summer crops have passed their season. These are often appreciated when shredded in a salad.

Wheaton Village Mixed Salad
(Bulgarian Shopska Salad)

Serves four

At Wheaton Village's Folklife Center in Millville, one of their many cultural events included a Bulgarian Wedding Feast followed by a sampling of Bulgarian foods. At that feast, this salad was served; it made fine use of our summer season vegetables along with an exquisite cheese, Bulgarian feta. The heady, robust flavors of this salad takes on a whole new-to-us flavor with Bulgarian feta cheese. This cheese is now available in Vineland-area shops.

3-4	medium, round Jersey tomatoes, diced
2	pickles (small cucumbers), sliced, see note below
1	medium onion, sliced in rings
2	tablespoons parsley
1/4	pound Bulgarian feta cheese, crumbled
1	tablespoon red wine or other vinegar
3	tablespoons extra-virgin olive oil

Salt and pepper to taste

In a salad bowl, mix all ingredients, add the salt, vinegar and oil, and toss; add the crumbled Bulgarian feta cheese on top.

Note: In our area, small pickling-sized cucumbers are called pickles by locals, sometimes kirbys in other markets. They are especially liked since they are rarely waxed and therefore, need not be peeled.

Peasant Tomato and Bread Salad

Serves eight as appetizer

Called panzanella in the south of Italy, this salad served newly arrived families who had little else to place on the table. It's remarkably good; the cheese is today's extravaganza.

> 1-1/2 stale Italian or French bread, sliced 1/2-inch thick
> 6   tablespoons extra-virgin olive oil
> 2   tablespoons wine vinegar
> Salt and freshly ground black pepper to taste
> 6   large round tomatoes, diced
> 1   medium onion, chopped
> 1/2 pound mozzarella cheese, plus a toss of Romano
>   or Parmesan cheese
> 6-8 fresh basil leaves, or 1 tablespoon dried
> Additional seasoning herbs: oregano, mint or parsley

Soak the bread in water and allow to soften; squeeze out excess and crumble.
Toss with remaining ingredients and rest for 15 minutes before serving.

Romaine Rollups

Romaine, it's a wrap! Down Jersey has for a long time been big on Romaine lettuce, thanks to the farmers of Vineland and its favorable soil. Romaine delivers far more flavor to a salad, or in this case, a wrap, and is available for a much longer season than Iceberg lettuce, locally, that is.

> Romaine leaves
> Deli beef or turkey, sliced thin
> Shredded carrots
> Thin slices of fresh red peppers or pimentos, optional
> Cheese to please

Suggested dressings: Mayo and horseradish, or chopped tomatoes, dill, paprika, finely chopped sweet Spanish onions.
Prepare the romaine leaves by slicing the white rib with a v-cut, and folding over half of the leaf. **Spread** the sauce on the lettuce, and then add the other ingredients as you please. **Gently** roll the leaf to enclose the ingredients. Slice this roll in half and place on a serving platter.

Cucumber Raita

Serves six

Though this cool and refreshing dip or sauce doesn't have roots in southern New Jersey, our love of anything with cucumbers should adopt this one quickly. Use the smallest cukes you can find, for they have the smallest seeds that are almost indistinguishable.

3   cups yogurt
2   cups grated cucumbers, preferably unwaxed
Salt and pepper to taste
1   teaspoon ground cumin, preferably roasted
Cilantro or mint for garnish

If the yogurt is watery, allow it to drain for 10 minutes in a strainer. **Whisk** the yogurt in a serving bowl until smooth, and salt and pepper. **Add** the grated cucumbers, which have been peeled if they are waxed. **Stir** in the cumin, and if desired, a pinch of cayenne. **Allow** to rest in the refrigerator for about a half hour and serve cool.

Country Fennel Salad

Serves four

My friend, Carmen Zampaglione, passes this delightful salad that celebrates the full flavor of fennel. When fennel isn't handy, he uses the stalk end of Romaine lettuce to similar effect, except he doesn't cut it quite as thin as fennel. The thin lemon slices might seem a bit too powerful for some, but Carmen says his family always serves fennel salad this way and loves the tangy bite of the slices, skin and all. This salad is usually served after the pasta course and it accompanies some sort of meat and crusty bread.

1   fennel bulb, ferns cut away and set aside
2   teaspoons balsamic vinegar
2   tablespoons extra-virgin olive oil
Salt and pepper to taste
Juice of one lemon
1/2 lemon, well washed, sliced very thin, seeds
        removed, optional

Slice fennel bulb in half. **Remove** the tough core and stems, and discard. Using either a sharp knife or a mandolin slicer, cut each half into very thin slices. **In** a large salad bowl, add and mix vigorously the balsamic vinegar, olive oil, salt, pepper, and lemon juice. **Add** the fennel slices to the dressing, tossing to coat evenly. **If** using, add the lemon slices and toss to coat with the dressing. **Serve** at room temperature with a garnish of chopped fennel ferns. A few minutes of rest improves the flavor.

Dandelion Salad Dressings

Dressings for two pounds of greens

One of the most colorful cheerleaders for southern New Jersey vegetables was the late and colorful former Mayor of Vineland, Patrick Fiorilli. We have excerpted one of his "Pat's Pantry" columns from "The Press of Atlantic City" in which he offers three salad dressings for dandelions. But first, here is his introduction:

Around the end of February or the beginning of March, a visitor comes to our home. It's not always popular, and you may spend scads of money to get rid of the visitor. Maybe it would be cheaper and healthier to make friends.

The unwanted visitor is the dandelion, the same dandelion you have been doing battle with for years, and you haven't won the battle yet. If you can't beat them, why not join them?

Cleaning the dandelions: Cut the root off to separate the leaves. Soak them in tepid water, moving them around while they soak. You should always use three times as much water as dandelions. After swishing them around in the warm water, put them in a strainer and drain. The warm water will loosen up any sand clinging to the leaves. Soaking the dandelions: Soak in cold water at the same 3 to 1 volume. Swish, drain and repeat 3 times. After recent rains, you may need to repeat once more.

Oil and Vinegar Dressing

1/4 cup olive oil
1 tablespoon red wine vinegar
1 clove garlic, peeled
1 large onion, peeled and chopped
6 hard-boiled eggs
1 teaspoon oregano
1/4 teaspoon salt
1/4 teaspoon pepper

Creamy Dandelion Dressing

1/4 cup olive oil
1 tablespoon cider vinegar
1 teaspoon oregano
4 hard-boiled eggs
2 basil leaves
5 rosemary leaves
1 clove garlic
2 tablespoons mayonnaise
Salt and pepper to taste

Blend olive oil, vinegar, garlic, and onion in a blender.
Remove yolks from eggs; blend in.
Slice the remaining egg whites to decorate the salad.
Pour dressing over dandelion greens and decorate with the egg slices.
Variation: Add diced anchovies and/or roasted red peppers to the dressing.

Slice one of the hard boiled eggs for garnish.
Put remaining 3 hard-boiled eggs in a blender with other ingredients and blend well.
Pour dressing over the dandelions and garnish with egg slices.

Dandelion Salad

Serves six to eight

My friend, Carlton Pancoast, passes along this dandelion salad recipe that he remembers well as his German-American family prepared it often during dandelion season. With due credit to the Italian-Americans for proclaiming their loyalty to this early spring, pleasantly bitter salad green—as evidenced by the Vineland's former Mayor Patrick Fiorilli and his inauguration of the Annual Dandelion Festival—the earlier German settlers found this bitter green just as refreshing as a spring tonic. In the German style, the preference is for salads with a touch of bacon for a sweet and salty contribution.

Though not a native plant, dandelions soon naturalized themselves in American soil much to the chagrin of lawn purists. If there is an admonition with dandelion greens, it's to harvest them as young as possible, and certainly before they begin to flower. Upon flowering they are terribly bitter.

3	quarts young dandelion greens, washed, drained and chopped
4	strips bacon, fried and crumbled
1/2	cup sugar
2	tablespoons flour
1	egg, beaten
1	cup vinegar
1	cup water
1/3	cup chopped walnuts, optional

In a heavy pan over medium heat, render the bacon fat from the strips, about 10 minutes. **Remove** bacon with a slotted spoon and set aside. **Mix** the sugar, flour, egg, vinegar and water; pour into the bacon drippings. **Simmer** and stir with a wooden spoon until it is thick enough to coat the back of the spoon. **Pour** the warm dressing over the dandelion greens; toss and serve while still warm. **Crumble** the bacon, add it and the walnuts, if using, to the salad. Test for salt, being mindful that the bacon may have contributed enough saltiness.

Variations: Instead of common strip bacon, use slab bacon, cut into 1/2-inch cubes. Also, add 1 teaspoon of Dijon mustard, if you prefer.

In earlier times when cooking oil was virtually unavailable at stores, most folks rendered their own pork lard for cooking fat. It meant chopping the fat into small cubes or putting it through a grinder. The pieces were then placed in a cast iron pan or pot and partially filled with water. Then the pan was set over low heat on the stove or in the oven at around 225 degrees F. On the top of the stove it took about 45 minutes, in the oven about 1-1/2 hours. After partially cooling, the fat was then strained of its cracklings before cooling and storage.

German Escarole Salad

Serves four to six

Ursala Dinshah, a well-known herbalist and a committed vegetarian from the Malaga section of Franklin Township, remembers this recipe from her grandparents. Now she makes it herself using imitation bacon, an essential flavor ingredient. Understandably, here we will use real bacon. The Italian farmers have always grown acres of endive and its cousin, escarole, as they brought their European taste for this delightfully bitter vegetable with them. But since this recipe uses only endive, the soaking called for reduces the bitterness somewhat.

    1 full head of escarole or endive
    6 strips of bacon, or vegetarian bacon
    2 tablespoons butter, optional
    Salt and pepper to taste

In a large container of warm water that allows the whole head to be immersed, soak the escarole for about an hour. Swish in a manner to have any clinging grit fall to the bottom of the water and remove.

Chop coarsely and set aside.

In a large sauté pan over low heat, add the bacon and allow it to render its fat and become crisp, about 10 minutes.

If using, add the butter at this time.

With the heat still on low, add the endive, salt and pepper to taste, and toss only a moment to wilt the endive. Serve warm.

Romaine Hearts

Carmen Zampaglione, of Carmen's Deli in Paulsboro, passed this recipe along that his mother prepares. It's a clever use of an otherwise discard, as she would be inclined not to waste any part of the lettuce that wasn't suitable for their salads.

    Saved cores of several romaine hearts
    Balsamic vinegar

Wash and cut romaine cores into bite sized pieces. **Drizzle** balsamic over the cores to taste. **Serve** at room temperature.

Greek Tomato Salad

Serves four

Anyone who has ever enjoyed a salad in Greece would understand that our Greek immigrants found the full tangy taste of a Jersey tomato worthy of continuing their fondness for a summertime salad. As classical Greek salads don't lean on lettuce, this marriage of fresh tomatoes and feta cheese celebrates the union that has stayed together so long.

Salad:
15-20 Kalamata olives
1/2   medium onion, red preferred, thinly sliced
 4   medium tomatoes, cored and diced
1/2   pound feta cheese, crumbled

Oregano Dressing:
 1   tablespoon red wine vinegar
Juice of one small lemon
 1   clove garlic, minced
1/2 teaspoon dried oregano
Salt and freshly ground pepper to taste
 1/4 cup olive oil

Combine all salad ingredients except feta cheese, and toss with oregano dressing.
Allow to stand 15 to 30 minutes at room temperature.
Sprinkle with feta cheese and serve.

In Salem County on New Bridge Road (Rt. 523), residents continue to refer to this bridge as" The **New Bridge**," even though it was constructed in 1903.

Sillsallad

(Herring Salad)

Serves eight to ten

The Swedish share with other Northern European countries a fondness for herring in many ways, especially when the tang of vinegar is added or, as they would say, "soured." The oiliness of herring lends itself to pickling, yet it is not unduly fat. This recipe has been taken from "Historic Old Swedes' Trinity Episcopal Church Recipes."

    1   salt herring or 2 fillets (at least one cup)
1-1/2 cup chopped cold boiled potatoes
1-1/2 cup chopped cold beets, freshly cooked or canned
 1/2 cup chopped apple
 1/4 cup chopped onion
   1   teaspoon dill weed
   2   tablespoons white wine vinegar
Salt and pepper to taste

Fillet fish and soak overnight, covered, in cold water in a refrigerator.
Remove small bones and skin from the herring. Rinse and drain;dice.
Mix herring, potatoes, beets, apple, and onion.
Mix dill weed with the vinegar and pour over the salad ingredients.
Add salt and pepper to taste; toss gently with a wooden spoon.

   Dressing:
   3   chilled, hard-cooked eggs
   1   tablespoon prepared mustard
   2   tablespoons white wine vinegar
 1/4 cup vegetable oil
   3   tablespoons heavy cream (whipping cream)
   Dill weed

Remove yolks from the eggs. Mince whites and reserve. **Force** the yolks through a sieve into a small bowl and then mash into a paste.
Add the mustard and mix. Gradually beat in the vinegar and oil, then add the cream a tablespoon at a time. **Pour** over the salad and mix lightly, but thoroughly.
Cover and chill for at least two hours. Transfer the salad to a serving bowl or platter.
Sprinkle with dill weed.

Sauce: Mix and pass around a blend of 1 cup sour cream, 3 tablespoons beet juice and 1/2 teaspoon lemon juice.

Seabrook Style Cucumber Salad

Serves six

The Japanese love for cucumbers and Down Jersey's abundance of them throughout the growing season have found a match. From mid-June to September, cucumbers and their smaller pickling-sized versions, called pickles by locals, are available fresh at local farmstands when not grown in kitchen gardens. The advantage is that they won't be waxed as are those bound for distant markets where shelf life needs to be extended. Notice the wide number of variations that bring in other ingredients, consisting of both seasonal vegetables and specialty Japanese items.

This recipe was shared by Fusaye Kazaoka from Seabrook.

> 1/2 cup sugar
> 1/2 cup vinegar
> 1 teaspoon salt
> 1 teaspoon Accent (MSG), optional
> 3 medium-sized regular cukes, or 6 pickle cukes

Mix all dressing ingredients until all sugar and Accent is dissolved. **Clean** cucumbers and pare skin, leaving a few strips of green for color. **Cut** cucumber in half lengthwise, and if seedy, scoop out the seeds with a spoon. **Cut** into thin half-rounds. **Marinate** at least 10 minutes in dressing before serving.

Variations: Add one or more of the following:
Thinly sliced celery, drained crabmeat, drained canned whole baby clams, thinly-sliced carrots, lettuce pieces, bean sprouts, boiled and drained cellophane noodles, and 1/2-inch cut strips of Chinese cabbage.

Restored **Historical Cabin** on Smick Road by the Lower Alloways Creek Historical Society. Behind the cabin is a reconstructed canning factory similiar to those once common in Down Jersey towns.

Cucumbers in Taziki Sauce

Makes one cup plus

Taziki, a tangy, yogurt-based sauce, is virtually unknown by some, but some of our immigrant groups know it well. Our immigrant Greeks have found it perfect for enhancing the abundance of our warm-season vegetables. You can choose full, low or non-fat yogurt as you like. This sauce keeps in the refrigerator for up to one week.

Taziki Sauce:
1 cup plain yogurt
1 tablespoon extra-virgin olive oil
Juice of 1/2 lemon
1 garlic clove, minced
Salt to taste
3 sprigs fresh dill, minced, or 1/2 teaspoon dried dill
     leaves, crushed
Cucumbers for the salad

In a non-reactive bowl, mix all of the ingredients, adjusting seasonings as desired. **Rest** in the refrigerator for a half hour before serving to blend and mellow flavors. **Prepare** your cucumber salad as you prefer; use generous amount of taziki sauce. **Variations:** You may prefer cumin along with or instead of dill.

Beet and Fennel Salad

Serves four to six

Granted, unless you opt for canned beets as a substitute, this salad will take a short time in order to boil and peel the beets. For all their freshness, it's well worth it when you have the chance. Fennel and beets are a terrific match.

1 pound beets, about 4 medium
1/2 fennel bulb
Juice of 1/2 lemon
2 tablespoons olive oil
Salt and pepper

Boil beets in salted water, covered, until tender when tested with a knife tip, about 30 minutes. **Drain** water, allow to cool, remove rootlet, stem, and slip off skin. **After** removing the core at the base, slice the fennel bulb thinly from top to bottom. **In** a jar or cruet, combine and shake together the lemon, olive oil, and salt and pepper. **Pour** dressing over beets and fennel, toss and set aside to marinade a few minutes before serving. **Note:** 1 tablespoon Anisette can substitue for the fennel.

Tomato Salads

Thinking of salads, it's understandable to imagine the world of green, leafy lettuce and its companions. When tomatoes are in season in southern New Jersey, they come to mind first over all other ingredients for salads. In this change-up of recipe style, we want to impress upon you that tomato salads are easy to prepare and don't need that rigidity of amounts, it's whatever pleases you. Perhaps, too, loosen up on your practice of serving a salad before or after, and go with having your salad nearby during the entire meal.

In keeping with the wealth of ethnic diversity and current interest in a variety of cuisines, we bring you recipes that respect the full, bright flavor of our summer tomatoes. Whereas gardeners have held onto those exquisite heirloom tomatoes over the years, farm markets have been re-introducing them. Bear in mind that they are much softer and therefore have less shelf life, so be more forgiving when you pick up the tomato to test its firmness. As I have said elsewhere, shoppers talk of taste, but buy firm tomatoes. A pity.

Sliced Tomato Salad

As with cookery that uses the fewest ingredients, when serving a tomato salad without any other addition, it's of prime importance to use the best salad dressing you can manage to buy. A straight-forward serving platter of sliced tomatoes, arranged individually or in a fanned-out manner, also benefits from use of the simplest tossing of a superior grade of olive oil and wine or balsamic vinegar.

Tomato Salad with Onions

It's amazing how a few sliced or diced sweet salad onions can do wonders to a tomato salad. Don't overdo it; the tomatoes are the star.

Tomato Salad with Cucumbers

Arriving at farm markets at nearly the same time as tomatoes and departing somewhat earlier, the tender, heat-loving cucumbers surely compliment tomatoes with their crisp, cool crunch. Choose the smallest, most immature cukes you can find, preferably those that have not been waxed. By tradition, the small pickling cucumbers, known as pickles in area markets, are not waxed by local farmers, so farm markets are safe to source from.

Tomato and Mozzarella Salad

The mild, salty and smooth body of the mozzarella contrasts with the rich soft texture of tomatoes. Simply drizzle the best olive oil you have at hand over ripe tomatoes tossed with knobs of mozzarella sprinkled with diced fresh basil leaves. This salad has it all: looks, color and aroma. Dried basil is OK in a pinch.

Juicy Tomato and Green Bean Salad

Serves four to six

When exceptionally tender green beans become available, such as from a local farm market or from a home garden, this salad comes to mind as ordinary beans won't do. Green beans become more fibery as they mature, shipping varieties from other areas simply won't work for this salad. You need the farm market or kitchen garden. Fortunately, when fresh beans are available, so is the essential flavoring ingredient, Jersey tomatoes.

1/2	pound fresh and tender green beans, washed and trimmed to 1-1/2-inch lengths
1/4	teaspoon salt
1/4	sweet onion, sliced thinly
2	medium fully-ripe Jersey round tomatoes, diced
	Juice of one lemon, or 2 tablespoons red wine vinegar
3	tablespoons extra-virgin olive oil
	Fresh ground black pepper to taste

Bring 3 quarts of water to a boil in a medium pot, add 1/2 teaspoon of salt. Add green beans, reduce to a simmer and cook for 12 minutes, uncovered.

In the meantime, add diced tomatoes and onions to a salad bowl; toss with lemon juice and olive oil.

Check beans for tenderness at the end of 12 minutes; cook for a few more minutes if necessary. **Remove** from heat, splash with cold water from the faucet and add to the salad bowl.

Toss all ingredients together, allow to rest for 15 minutes if you can, and serve at room temperature.

Variations: Although not as fresh, a 5.5-ounce can of Campbell's V8 can be used if fresh tomatoes are out of season. The richness of the eight ingredients in V8 makes for an agreeable alternative.

Sautéed Onion Salad

Instead of an exact recipe to relay, farmer John Santaniello's wife, Carlotta, simply sautés a pan of sliced onions in salad oil until clear, removes from the heat, adds them to her salad greens and tosses. She prefers Romaine and radicchio, but will use whatever is at hand as long as it is fresh. She adds no vinegar and relies only on the oil she has sautéed the onions with to coat the lettuce leaves. Parmesan cheese is grated over the top of the salad.

Waldorf Salad

Serves four to six

Though Chef Oscar Tschirky of the Waldorf Astoria Hotel in New York City created this salad in the late 1890's, it has found a welcome home in Down Jersey for several reasons. First, the apples grown in our region are seldom waxed and only undergo short periods of storage, making them far more suitable for versions of this salad where it is desired to leave the skin on. Secondly, our vast acres of cranberry production have given us a taste for the tart berries and in their recent incarnation, the dried version called Craisins. Together, the red-skinned apple cubes and the bits of cranberry-red Craisins make for an exciting, appealing Waldorf salad.

> 1 cup diced celery
> 1 cup diced, red-skinned apples, such as Gala, Molly or Rome
> 1/2 cup coarsely chopped walnuts, optional
> 1/2 cup Craisins, or substitute raisins
> 1/2 to 3/4 cup mayonnaise

Wash apples and cut a slice off both ends, leaving the skin on.

Quarter the apples and remove the seedy, corky interior. Cut into 1/2-inch dices, more or less.

Mix all ingredients together, starting with 1/2 cup of the mayonnaise, adding more if desired. Set aside for about 20 minutes and serve either chilled or at room temperature.

Variations: Chopped dates, about 1/2 cup, are delicious additions, as are other dried fruits. For another, try one of the new-to-the-market red pears, mixed with, or instead of, apples.

Apple growers in New Jersey deliver a major portion of their fruit to the local markets fresh and juicy from the tree. Picked closer to prime eating quality and without waxing or long-term storage, they are exceptional in quality when available. Growers have also found customers that have come to like special varieties that offer a change up from the common types such as the ever popular Red Delicious and Golden Delicious. Sketched here are Gala apples, well liked for their tasty out-of-hand eating and use in cooking.

Chapter 8

Desserts and Pastries with Love

It's understandable that one wouldn't consider Down Jersey as a region notable for its desserts and pastries. Yet, in doing research for this book, I changed my presumption; I learned that our peaches, apples, blueberries and cranberries are farm-fresh. What better dessert ingredients can you get? Add in our diverse ethnic contributions, and once again we have a tradition that is Down Jersey.

In the doughnut category, we have the Dutch crullers, which have so immersed themselves into our dessert palette that we regard them as American. Lesser known and not in the mainstream of American fare, but deserving of more recognition are the Polish Pacziki (doughnuts).

Pizzeles and biscotti, no stranger to anyone, are still made by Italian cooks holding on to family favorites. But unlike doughnuts, these pastries are more often made for special get togethers as opposed to desserts following weekday meals.

Continuing the assortment, we have Irish Potatoes, Japanese Mandarin Cake, plus a number of popular blueberry and cranberry desserts. We continue on to a sweet potato pie that heralds our southern immigrants who welcomed using the familiar sweet potatoes we grow in abundance. Near the end of the dessert chapter we bring a Moravian sugar cake in remembrance of the once-strong presence of the Moravians in Down Jersey.

To encourage conviviality, we have included in the last page of this chapter drinks that call for ingredients indigenous to southern New Jersey. However, I reached a few miles into central New Jersey to Laird's AppleJack, as it is the oldest operating distillery in the country. Don't forget that Welch's Grape Juice had its start in Vineland, so we have a another memorable drink with roots in New Jersey to celebrate.

Apple Fritters

Makes one dozen

From Mood's Farm Market, Mullica Hill, this recipe for apple fritters has been passed along to their customers "over the counter" and in their cookbook, "Recipes From Friends of Mood's Farm Market."

2 cups flour
1 tablespoon baking powder
1/4 teaspoon salt
1 teaspoon sugar
2 egg yolks, well beaten
1 cup milk
2 cups tart apples, peeled or unpeeled, and diced
2 egg whites, optional
Oil for frying

Sift flour; add baking powder, salt and sugar; combine.

Add egg yolks and milk; stir to combine.

Add apples and mix in with the batter.

Gently fold in stiffly beaten egg whites, if using.

Drop carefully from a tablespoon and deep fry at 360 degrees F. for 3 minutes. Place on paper towels to drain. Dust with powdered sugar and serve.

Variation: Add 1 teaspoon of cinnamon with the flour, or stir in 2 tablespoons of rum or applejack with the milk and eggs.

The Celebrated Jersey Apple Grinder is Everywhere

THE FAVORITE

The Butterworth Patent Apple Grinder.
Advertisement from a catalogue published around 1865.

Biscotti

Makes about four dozen

Thanks to the generosity of Anita DeVitis of Deptford, this biscotti adaptation has risen to the top choice of biscotti fanciers. It's an example of a traditional Italian cookie that has been updated to today's kitchen. The name here is a misnomer as biscotti means twice cooked; this one isn't. The practice of twice baking, which is what biscotti means, came about in earlier times as a practical way of drying a cookie for storage when no freezer was at hand.

This version, instead of being twice baked, is poured into baking pans for baking once as a batter instead of a rolled dough. This results in a lighter, moister cookie that doesn't hang around long enough to make storage a concern. That said, it freezes well.

Anita found that of all the possible flavorings, her friends found Sambuca to be their favorite. Still, see the list of suggested alternatives.

> 3   cups sifted flour
> 2   teaspoons baking powder
> 1/2 teaspoon salt
> 5   eggs
> 1/2 pound sweet butter
> 2   tablespoons Sambuca
> 2   cups sugar

Preheat oven to 350 degrees F.

Combine the flour, baking powder and salt.

In a separate mixing bowl, cream sugar and butter together about 2 minutes.

Add eggs, one at a time, beating in well.

Add the Sambuca, stir in well.

Add flour, baking powder, and salt mixture to the butter and egg mixture.

Pour the batter into 2 greased and floured 9 x 13-inch baking pans.

Bake at 350 degrees F. for 25 minutes or until an inserted toothpick comes out clean.

Allow to cool somewhat; cut into 1/2-inch thick bars and sprinkle with powdered sugar.

Variations: Anise has been a long-time favorite flavoring, with other possibilities being Triple Sec, Amaretto, lemon or orange zest, among other choices. Use them at the same strength as Sambuca.

Three-Season Fruit Muffins

Makes twelve muffins

This multi-season recipe reflects Betsy Pliner's awareness of baking with respect to the seasonal fruit at hand. Not only that, Pliner lists the dates and adjustments for each fruit.

Betsey Pliner is a member of the Pinelands Commission planning staff and lives in Tabernacle, deep in the heart of the Pinelands. She loves to go farm marketing and enjoys pick-your-own farms, too.

  2   cups flour
  1   tablespoon baking powder
  1/2 teaspoon salt
  1/2 cup sugar
  1/2 cup milk
  1   egg, slightly beaten
  1/4 cup melted butter

Select from the following Pinelands grown fresh fruits according to the season:
April: 1 cup of chopped Rhubarb mixed with 1/4 cup sugar
May/June: 1 cup of coarsely chopped Strawberries
July to Mid-August: 1 cup Blueberries
August: 1 cup of Blackberries mixed with an additional 1 cup of sugar
or
1 cup of Peaches coarsely chopped and sprinkled with 1/4 teaspoon of almond extract
September: 1 cup Raspberries
October: 1 cup finely chopped tart Apples, such as Winesaps

Preheat oven to 350-degrees F.
Mix the flour, baking powder and salt together with a fork.
Gently fold in the remaining ingredients including one cup of the selected fruit, which is folded in last to minimize smashing and loss of color.
Stir to combine, but don't over mix.
Spoon the batter into muffin pans lined with paper baking cups.
Sprinkle additional sugar or sugar/cinnamon mix on top, if desired.
Bake in a 350 degree F. oven for about 20 minutes.

Chef's Tip: the bulk of the blueberries bred for the mixed market are large, tasty cultivars useful from eating out of hand to baking and fruit compotes, and more. Yet, savvy bakers know that the varieties close to their wild ancestry, such as Rubel, have more intense blueberry flavor. Where do you find them? The best way is to call ahead to a U-Pick farm and ask if they have the wild types, and if they are in season.

Blueberry and Ricotta Dessert

Serves six to eight

At the turn of the last century, for field labor, blueberry growers relied on the latest wave of Italian immigrants, who were bussed in each workday from nearby Philadelphia.

Farmers came to rely on the accepted practice of the padrone, who was the leader, interpreter and problem solver all in one. Most of the Italian immigrants at that time lacked formal education and not only did they not speak English, but they had distinct regional dialects.

From Jersey's blueberry farms came the custom of paring a popular Italian cheese, ricotta, with blueberries served together. It reflects the Italian notion of great foods based on simple, but fresh, ingredients. Quality varies considerably with ricotta cheese, so select carefully by quality, not by price. No doubt you will recognize that this recipe as a healthy, light dessert.

> 1   pint fresh blueberries, washed
> 1   quart ricotta, full fat preferred
> Honey for drizzling, optional
> Fresh black pepper, optional

Place the blueberries and the ricotta each in their own attractive serving bowls. Give each diner a small dessert dish and allow them to place a heap of ricotta on their plate. Then serve the blueberries as a topping, suggesting they crush a few berries with a fork if they care to.

Pass the honey for drizzling and pass to each the pepper grinder for a fresh grind. This method is preferred as the use of one large dish to serve from would result in a rather unattractive affair.

Variations: Almost any other ripe fruit can be used, and if none is available, try using one of the marmalades, such as orange marmalade for a topping.

Blueberries Top the List: Of 40 vegetables and fruits tested at the Human Nutrition on Aging Research Center at Tufts University in Boston, Massachusetts, blueberries ranked the highest in levels of antioxidants. Ron Prior, USDA, said that antioxidants fight those free radicals that are found in things such as tobacco smoke. With up to four times the antioxidant activity as vitamin C and E, when ingesting high levels of blueberries, the dietary implications mean longer life expectancy, lower cancer risk and lower arteriosclerosis.

Blueberry Sauce

Makes approximately 1-1/2 cups

The reasons for considering this sauce are many, not the least because it is so easy to make. Once you follow the recipe, you will discover that experience will guide you as to ingredient proportions rather than a precise recipe. This sauce finds a home when used as a topping for mixed fruit desserts, cakes or pancakes, among others. It freezes well; a suggestion is to freeze the sauce in small containers.

1	cup blueberries
1/2	cup water
1/3	cup sugar
1	teaspoon cornstarch
1/8	teaspoon salt
1	teaspoon butter
2	tablespoons lemon juice

Combine 1/2 cup of blueberries and water in a small saucepan. Bring to a boil, reduce to simmer; cook for 3 minutes, stirring occasionally.

Combine sugar, cornstarch, and salt; stir into the blueberries. Cook over moderate heat, stirring constantly, until mixture boils and thickens, about 1 minute.

Add remaining blueberries and cook 3 minutes longer.

Stir in lemon juice, butter and serve.

New Jersey Has the Blues for You

In and around the region known as the Pine Barrens, New Jersey farmers grow a considerable amount of blueberries, ranking second in national production after Michigan. Given a publicity boost from a recent study finding that blueberries have high levels of antioxidants, they are welcome in more and more preparations. We say preparations purposely as they lend themselves to uncomplicated cookery that often is quick and easy to do.

In southern New Jersey, blueberries are fresh in season from late June to the latter part of August, with the weather having the final say, of course. While the popularity contest is won by the large cultivated varieties, savvy chefs will seek out the wild varieties, such as *Rubel*, for their intense fruitiness so refreshing in baking. To web search the nearest blueberry farm, use the keywords "Pick your own farms, New Jersey."

Blueberry Tea Cake

Serves eight

Nancy Fehlauer, who with her husband Werner, operates a small blueberry farm in Gibbstown, said that this recipe is her and her customers' favorite. It was printed in the then Woodbury Times *newspaper in 1968.*

3/4	cup sugar
1	egg
1/4	cup butter
1/2	cup milk
2	cups flour
2	teaspoons baking powder
1/2	teaspoon salt
2	cups blueberries

Cream the sugar and the butter and add the egg; then beat. Alternately add milk, with the flour, baking powder and the salt sifted together. **Fold** in blueberries. Pour into batter into an 8 by 9-inch baking pan, lightly greased.

Topping:

1/2	cup sugar
1/4	cup flour
1	teaspoon cinnamon
1/4	cup butter

Mix all the topping ingredients together with fingers and sprinkle over cake batter. **Bake** in a 375-degree F. oven for 40 to 45 minutes.

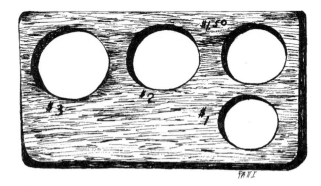

Elizabeth White, a pioneer in the search for improving the cultivars of blueberries, used this gauge as an incentive for scouts to find large, wild blueberries. Notice that they were rewarded with ever-larger amounts, in dollars, for those berries that wouldn't pass through the larger-gauged holes.

Sketch courtesy of Patti Brown.

South Jersey Corn Bread

Serves two or three

This southern way of cooking corn bread brought to Down Jersey uses a cast iron pan as is common in the South.

Elizabeth Barrick, whose family arrived from the South, shares this recipe since it is so easy to make. She said that corn bread is seldom eaten alone; it is enjoyed with greens or beans. Either way, the use of modest amounts of bacon fat adds immeasurably to the flavor of corn bread. Southerners disdain the use of sugar in their corn bread. Here in Down Jersey, we add a mere teaspoon of sugar, but feel free to increase the amount or delete it. Also, as corn bread does not have good keeping qualities, we suggest making this modest amount. Once you become familiar with making it, it doesn't take much effort to add its goodness to your meal.

As with any baking mixture containing baking soda, mix the ingredients immediately prior to baking.

> 1 cup yellow stone ground cornmeal
> 1/2 cup all-purpose flour
> 1/2 teaspoon salt
> 1-1/2 teaspoons baking powder
> 1/2 teaspoon baking soda
> 1 tablespoon sugar
> 1 egg, beaten
> 1 cup buttermilk
> 1-1/2 tablespoons bacon drippings or lard

Preheat oven at 425 degrees F.

In a large bowl, combine the dry ingredients of cornmeal, flour, salt, baking powder and baking soda. **In** another bowl, mix together the sugar, egg and buttermilk; combine with the dry ingredients .

Fold in 1 tablespoon of the bacon drippings and mix until smooth. Add more buttermilk, if necessary, to get a thick batter that can be scooped out with a spatula. **Pour** in a hot skillet, preferably cast iron, which has been greased with 1/2 tablespoon of bacon drippings. **Bake** at 425 degrees F. for 20 to 25 minutes, or until an inserted knife comes out clean. **Variation:** Mix in the batter finely diced jalapeno jack cheese.

In case you are concerned about the use of lard, Paula Wolfert, in her book, *The Cooking of South-West France*, says, *"An interesting fact I discovered in a U. S. Department of Agriculture Publication—Handbook 8-4 (revised 1979)—is that rendered poultry fat (goose, duck, and chicken) contains 9 percent cholesterol, and lard contains 10 percent, compared with butter's 22 percent. Since one needs less poultry fat, oil, or lard than butter to sauté vegetables, one will ingest far less saturated fat if these cooking media are used instead of butter. One needs less of these because butter breaks down and burns at high temperatures, whereas others do not.*

Cranberry Pudding

Serves six

This sweet and tart dessert recipe comes to us from Nancy Pedrick, Bridgeport, who has prepared this pudding since her college days and continues to do so. She tells me it freezes well.

1	cup sugar
2	cups all-purpose flour
2	teaspoons baking powder
1	cup whole milk
2	cups whole uncooked cranberries fresh or frozen

Preheat oven to 350 degrees F.

Mix and sift sugar, flour and baking powder.

Add and mix in milk and cranberries, thawed, if using frozen.

Pour into greased 8 by 8-inch baking pan.

Bake for 25 minutes or until done by testing with a toothpick; it should emerge free of any batter sticking to it.

In the meantime, prepare butter sauce with the recipe given below.

Serve warm with the butter sauce:

Butter Sauce

1	cup sugar
1/2	cup butter
1/2	cup cream

Add all three ingredients in a double broiler, stirring for 15 minutes.

Serve warm over cranberry pudding.

Pickled Pears

Once again, we post a recipe from Adele M. Baden's German grandmother who wrote this recipe in ink sometime around 1889:

To eight pounds of fruit, add three and one-half pounds of sugar, one pint of vinegar and one pint of water. Dissolve the sugar in the vinegar and water; let it boil, and skim till clear; then put in the pears, and cook slowly, till done; take them out and boil the liquid till quite thick, and pour over them. The pears should be pared, and a few cloves stuck in them.

Soft Ginger Cookies

Makes three to four dozen cookies

The Haines family, owners of Haines Pork Store, Mickleton, who trace their roots back to England, have compiled a book of family recipes. One of them, this soft ginger cookie, shows the long popularity of molasses and lard in baked items in Down Jersey. In case you might shudder at today's use of lard, bear in mind that butcher's lard (not the hydrogenated store lard) is all-natural and has one-third the cholesterol of butter.

> 1 teaspoon baking soda, plus one cup boiling water
> 1 egg
> 1 cup molasses
> 1 teaspoon ginger powder
> 1/4 teaspoon cinnamon powder
> 1/4 teaspoon salt
> 1 cup sugar
> 1 cup lard, melted
> 4-1/2 cups all-purpose flour

Preheat oven to 375 degrees F. **Dissolve** soda in one cup of boiling water.
Beat egg in a large, separate bowl. **Mix** in remaining ingredients together and blend well.
Drop by rounded spoonfuls on lightly greased baking pans. **Bake** at 375 degrees F. for 12 minutes or until done, but do not allow to brown further at which time they will then overcook, despite being somewhat soft. **Variations:** Today's baker might prefer to add a teaspoon of ground allspice, a pinch of cloves and a dash of black pepper.

Thumb-Print Cookies

Makes 1-1/2 to 2 dozen

> 1/2 cup (1 stick) butter
> 1/4 cup firmly packed brown sugar
> 1 medium size egg, separated
> 1 cup sifted all-purpose flour
> 1 cup finely chopped nuts
> Welch's Grape Jam

In an electric mixer bowl, cream butter and sugar until light and fluffy. **Mix** in egg yolk. **Add** flour and shape into small balls. **If dough** is hard to handle, chill. **Place** on fork and dip into slightly beaten egg white, then into nuts. **Place** cookies on an ungreased baking sheet. **With** your thumb, press a hole in center of each. **Bake** in a preheated 350-degree F. oven for 8 minutes. **Remove** from oven and press in center of each cookie again. **Continue** baking 15 minutes longer. **Cool** slightly. **Fill** centers with grape jam.

Welch's Grape Juice Story

Welch's Grape Juice had its foundings in Vineland in the 1870's as an alternative to alcoholic wine then served at many churches. At the time in Vineland there was a law prohibiting the sale of liquor.

Born in 1825 in Glastonbury, England, Thomas Bramwell Welch sailed to the United States in 1831, eventually settling in Vineland. At first he studied to become a minister, but having trouble with his voice, became a doctor instead. He then chose to become a dentist and served as a communion steward in his church.

Using the theory of Louis Pasteur for sterilization in the processing of grapes, Dr. Welch was able to create and bottle on a small scale an alcohol-free "Unfermented Sacramental Wine" for his church, thus creating the first produced grape juice.

In 1870, Dr. Welch promoted his unfermented grape juice to area local churches, an initial failure at first. His son, Dr. Charles E. Welch took over his father's interest in the business in 1883 and changed the name to Dr. Welch's Grape Juice.

In 1893 at the Chicago World's Fair, they dropped the "Dr." in the name. They made Welch's Grape Juice a nationwide favorite after handing out samples of their product.

The grape juice was eventually to become so successful that he gave up his practice of dentistry. Eventually he moved his factory from Vineland to New York State where there was a greater production of concord grapes than in New Jersey.

Welch's continued to grow in the following years through impressive advertising and promotion, sponsoring such programs as the 1930's top rated program, The Irene Rich Show, Howdy Doody, Walt Disney's Mickey Mouse Club and the Flintstones.

And Welch's Grape Juice started flowing in Vineland.

Japanese Mandarin Orange Refrigerator Cake

Mandarin oranges, which we know from their cousins, the clementine and tangerine, are seedless, so are suitable for this cake. Their intense citrus taste lifts it to a pleasant oriental delight. The recipe is shared by my friend Fusaye Kazaoka of Seabrook, near Bridgeton.

- 2 (11-ounce) cans Mandarin oranges, drained and juice saved
- 1 (6-ounce) package lemon Jell-O
- 1 cup cold water
- 2 packages lady fingers, (18-20 count), or other soft cookie
- 2 cups heavy cream, whipped

Pour reserved orange liquid in cup and add sufficient water to make 2 cups and bring to a boil in a saucepan. **Dissolve** Jell-O in the hot liquid; add 1 cup of cold water and cool in the refrigerator until it is syrupy, about an hour. **Line** bottom and sides of a 9-inch springform or a 9" by 11" pan with lady finger halves. **Fold** syrupy Jell-O into the whipped cream and add orange slices and fold in. **Pour** into the cake pan lined with lady fingers; chill for several hours, remove springform pan and serve. **Garnish** with mandarin orange slices. **Variations:** Use sliced fresh strawberries when in season and add 3 cups of water instead of 1 cup since there is no strawberry juice.

Irish Potatoes

Makes sixty candy balls

Irish Potatoes are a local specialty that magically appear in Philadelphia and our Down Jersey region before and during St. Patrick's holiday in March. Perhaps locally popular cream cheese is the foundation that inspired these favorites that our children remember. Deptford's Rosemary Salmon, who spent her childhood in Philadelphia, passes this recipe along to us.

- 1/4 cup softened butter
- 4 ounces softened cream cheese
- 1 teaspoon real vanilla extract
- 4 cups confectioner's sugar, sifted
- 2-1/2 cups flaked sweetened coconut
- 4 teaspoons cinnamon
- 1 teaspoon cocoa

Beat the butter and cream cheese together until smooth. **Add** the vanilla and confectioner's sugar. **Beat** until smooth. **Mix** in the coconut. **Refrigerate** the mix for about 30 minutes to make it easier to handle. **Meanwhile**, mix together the cinnamon and cocoa. **Roll** the dough into balls or potato shapes and roll in the cinnamon and cocoa mixture. **Place** on a cookie sheet and chill to set.

Molasses Cake

Makes about two dozen large cookies

In a quiet sticky way, molasses has retained its hold as a popular ingredient in Down Jersey from the early colonial days when it was a key item of trade in what has been referred to as the sailing triangle. Wind-driven ships from Europe would sail westward riding on the prevailing westward tropical breezes, stop at the Caribbean Islands, pick up molasses and sail northward to the east coast ports. In all likelihood, ships manifests arriving at Greenwich, on the Delaware Bay below Bridgeton, would have recorded significant tonnage of molasses. Molasses, which was cheaper than sugar, remained the main sweetener until after WWI when sugar became less expensive.

The adapted recipe below has been shared by Lorraina Shidner-Sharp from Canton in Salem County. It traces its lineage back to her great grandmother, JoHanna Hancock, along with Shidner-Sharp and her siblings, who lived in the historic town of Hancock's Bridge. Lorraina Shidner-Sharp says that she is obliged to send her cakes to her son in Arizona; he is so dependent on them. They're that good. Note that tradition has it called a cake, whereas most of us today would refer to it as a cookie recipe.

5	cups all purpose flour
1	teaspoon salt
2	teaspoons cinnamon
1	cup white sugar, or 1/2 white and 1/2 cup brown sugar
1	cup butter, softened
1	cup Grandma's Molasses
1	cup milk, soured with 1 teaspoon white vinegar
2	teaspoons baking soda
2	eggs

Adjust oven rack to middle position. **Preheat** oven to 350 degrees F.

Mix together the flour, salt and cinnamon and set aside.

Mix together the sugar and butter in a separate bowl; beat until fluffy.

Mix the milk, baking soda and vinegar together in a separate cup.

Alternately mix together the flour, sugar and milk mixtures in a large bowl. Add the eggs and blend well.

Using two teaspoons, drop cookies by the teaspoonful on a greased baking sheet.

Bake for 8 to 10 minutes, one sheet at a time. Bake until edges are set but centers are still soft; do not over bake.

Variations: Some may prefer to use baking trays lined with parchment sheets instead of the practice of greasing the trays. For those interested in spicing up this recipe, add 1/4 teaspoon of black pepper and 1/2 teaspoon freshly ground allspice with the flour when mixing.

Yummy Blueberry Muffins

Makes one dozen

This is an always welcome recipe shared by Pat DellaRova from West Deptford that brings out the best of New Jersey blueberries.

1	egg
1/2	cup milk
1/4	cup salad oil
1	teaspoon vanilla
1	teaspoon lemon or orange zest
1-1/2	cup flour
1/2	cup sugar
2	teaspoons baking powder
1/2	teaspoon salt
1	cup blueberries and 3 teaspoons sugar, mixed
1	dozen cupcake liners

Preheat oven to 400 degrees F.

Beat egg; stir in milk, oil, and vanilla. **Add** in and mix other ingredients, leaving a desirable lumpy batter; add blueberries and fold in.

Fill cupcake liners 3/4 full and bake at 400 degrees F. for 20 to 25 minutes, or until tops are lightly browned.

Spaghetti Cake *(Migliaccio)*

Serves eight

It is quite common in Italian cooking to use pasta from leftovers in baked dishes. In this recipe from Vineland's Frank De Maio, M.D., that he shared from Jennie De Maio, his memory was that there was seldom leftover pasta; the only time he ate it was during Easter.

1	pound spaghetti, dried
5	eggs
12	ounces sugar
1-1/2	ounces butter
	Grated peel from one lemon

Preheat oven at 350 degrees F. **Cook** the spaghetti in the usual fashion in rolling boiling water with salt added. **Drain** the spaghetti and place in a bowl. **Mix** the eggs, sugar, butter and lemon thoroughly with the pasta. **Coat** an 8 by 11-inch baking pan with oil. **Transfer** the pasta mixture into the baking pan. **Bake** at 350 degrees F. for until top is golden, about 30 minutes. **Remove** from oven, sprinkle with powdered sugar and serve.

Pizzelles

Makes about 48 pizzelles

I have sharp memories of my mother making pizzelles countless times down in her second basement kitchen. She used a hand-iron pizzelle maker that she held over the stove's open flame, deftly removing each hot pizzelle by hand as she opened the hot iron. Perhaps since they were probably favored for their ability to dry quickly and store well back in Italy where refrigeration was virtually non-existent, pizzelles are practical for today's cook who wants to multiply the recipe and store those not consumed straight away.

While anisette flavoring with its telltale seeds most often comes to mind as the defining spice, it is not the only choice. We have listed several alternatives.

As pizzelles are somewhat flexible while hot off the iron, you might choose to shape them into cones or over a custard cup for later filling, perhaps with that ricotta/sugar mix so common with cannoli. I assume you will be using an electric pizzelle maker.

6	large eggs
1-1/4	cups sugar
3/4	pound butter, melted and cooled
1	teaspoon anise seed
1	teaspoon anise extract or anise liqueur
1	teaspoon vanilla extract
3	cups flour
2	teaspoons baking powder
Pinch of salt	

A pizzele iron was held over an open flame and took deft hands to remove each pizzele without burning fingers. This model is a bit unusual in that it makes square rather than round pizzelles.
—Drawing courtesy of Raymond Colanero

In a mixing bowl or by hand, beat the eggs and sugar together until incorporated. **Add** in melted butter and flavorings of anise, anise extract and vanilla. **In a separate bowl**, sift flour, add baking powder and salt; mix together. **Add** flour mix to egg mix and beat. Batter should be of a consistency for dropping by spoon. **Preheat** pizzelles baker according to manufacturer's instructions. **Prepare** work area by placing a newspaper under the pizzelle baker and place the batter bowl next to the baker. Also, have a large, flat surface area to place the pizzelles as they cool, unless they are to be specially shaped. Have handy two similar-sized tablespoons.

Do a trial of the first one or two by taking up a partial spoonful with one spoon and releasing its batter with the other spoon. Practice will teach you to take up a bit more batter than you need and using the other spoon to control amount released onto the griddle. Once the batter is dropped, it's difficult to add more.

Alternative flavorings: For each 1/2 dozen eggs, use 2 tablespoons of liqueurs such as Triple-Sec (orange flavored), Sambuca, Cuarenta y Tres, Amaretto, rum or others. Orange and lemon zest can be used to add bright, citrusy flavors.

Krullen

Makes one dozen

The Dutch presence in Colonial America has been neglected by historians, yet the 17th century bore the non-English presence of the Dutch. Until the English reigned supreme in 1674, the territory of New Netherlands ranged from New England to Virginia. One of the lingering marks left by the early Dutch settlers has been their baked goods. This recipe, for krullers that still are popular here today, is reprinted from "The Sensible Cook," translated and edited by Peter G. Rose, published by Syracuse University Press.

Rose introduces the recipe by the following: ..."The recipe is adapted from a nineteenth century Dutch cookbook that survived only as a fragment without a title page. This version resembles more closely Washington Irving's description in his "Legend of Sleepy Hollow." The author describes a Dutch tea table set for guests, which included "Such heaped up platters of cakes of various and almost indescribable kinds, known only to experienced Dutch housewives. There was the doughy dough nut, the tenderer oly koek, and the crisp and crumbling cruller..." (Irving, 287) This recipe creates a crisp and crumbling cruller, or cork-screw krul (curl).

9	tablespoons butter (no substitutes)
1	egg
1-2/3	cups flour (tapped down)
2	tablespoons heavy cream, if needed

Cream the butter until light and fluffy. Add the egg and incorporate. **Add** the flour a little at a time. If the dough is too stiff, add some cream. **Roll** to a thickness of 1/6-inch and cut into strips of approximately 3/4-inch wide (it does not matter how long they are). **Twist** around the handle of a wooden spoon to make a corkscrew curl. **Gently** slide off the handle into a hot oil at about 350 degrees F. (This take a bit of a knack, but don't dispair; it takes practice. J.C.) **Fry** until golden brown and slightly puffed. **Drain** on paper towels. **Sift** confectioner's sugar over each curl before serving.

This special skillet with indentions is made specifically for **poffertjies**, tiny puffed pancakes made by the Dutch.

Polish Doughnuts (Paczki)

Makes about one and one-half dozen

At Polish celebrations, the celebrants are likely to indulge in the delight of paczki (pronounced in local dialect, punch-key). They were a Polish cook's thrifty way to use up their supply of eggs and butter. Whereas the Dutch Olicooks were to become the now common doughnuts, Polish paczki have yet to be known to the general public.

This batch size can be doubled if you wish as the doughnuts freeze well.

1	package active dry yeast, plus 1 tablespoon sugar
1/4	cup warm water
1/3	cup (6 tablespoons) butter at room temperature
2/3	cup sugar
3	egg yolks
1	teaspoon vanilla extract
	Choice of 1 teaspoon grated orange or lemon peel
1/4	teaspoon nutmeg
3/4	teaspoon salt
3-1/2	cups all-purpose flour
	Oil for frying
	Granulated sugar for dusting
	Milk for adjusting dough consistency

Dissolve the yeast and sugar in warm water. Set in a warm place to proof for 5 minutes. **Cream** butter and sugar until fluffy. **Beat** in egg yolks, one at a time. **Add** vanilla extract, orange peel, dissolved yeast, and salt. Beat until well mixed. **Stir** in flour, stopping when the mix makes a stiff dough. Cautiously add milk a teaspoon at a time if needed to get to a workable dough.

Flour a working surface, work dough until smooth and elastic, about ten minutes. Cover and set in a warm location until doubled in size.

Return dough to floured surface. Roll into 1/4-inch thickness, adding flour if necessary to keep from being too sticky.

Cut out with a glass or biscuit cutter, about 2-1/2 to 3 inches in diameter. Place on a lightly buttered baking pan. Lightly cover and allow to rise until nearly doubled in bulk.

Fry small batches in hot 360 degree F. fat in a deep fryer, electric skillet or heavy pan for about 1-1/2 to 2 minutes, turning frequently, until lightly browned. If not an electric fryer, use of a deep fat or candy thermometer helps to gauge the temperature.

Place on paper towels and dust with regular granulated sugar. Optionally, add a dash of nutmeg or cinnamon to the dusting sugar. These are delicious dunking in tea or coffee.

Note: Wrap and freeze those doughnuts you do not serve straight away. Reheat on a baking pan at about 350 degrees F. for about 7 minutes.

Tea Scones with Craisins

Makes 12 to 16 wedges

The popularity of cranberries from our local bogs makes it natural that we would adapt scones using a relatively new cranberry product, Craisins, which are dried and sweetened cranberries. Nudging this movement along has been the recent openings of tearooms in Down Jersey. Although nowhere near the popularity of West Coast coffee shops, tea shops are becoming a part of our local scene. This recipe is a traditional English version adapted to include craisins.

2	cups all-purpose flour
2	tablespoons sugar
2	teaspoons baking powder
1/2	teaspoon salt
1/3	cup Craisins
6	tablespoons cold butter, cut into pea-size pieces
1	beaten egg
1/2	cup milk
1	slightly beaten egg, for brushing scones

Preheat oven to 425 degrees F.

In a medium size bowl, mix together the flour, sugar, baking powder, and salt; stir in the Craisins.

Cut in the butter, either mixing with your fingers or with two knives until coarse crumbs are formed.

Beat the egg and milk; stir until the dough clings together.

Knead the dough on a lightly floured surface just enough to moisten the dry ingredients, about 12 to 15 strokes. Divide dough into two balls. Pat each to a 6-inch round about 1/2-inch thick. Cut into 6 or 8 wedges with a sharp knife.

Place on an ungreased baking sheet with wedges slightly apart. Brush scones with the slightly beaten egg. **Bake** at 425 degrees F. until nicely browned, about 12 to 15 minutes.

Craisins, a dried and sweetened version of fresh cranberries, bring a snappy and colorful new healthy ingredient for us to use in snacks and a variety of baked goods and salads. Who knows, our Native American Lenni-Lenape people probably thought of using them before we did.

Swedish Christmas Bread
(Julkaka)

Every country whose people celebrate Christmas with the baking of Christmas breads, does it in their own distinctive way, both in the recipe ingredients, and especially, in the manner of preparation and presentation. The Swedish tradition has in common with other countries the practice of fashioning the loaf into a circle, often braided, to symbolize the full circle of life.

2 cups lukewarm milk
1 cup sugar
1 teaspoon salt
1 teaspoon ground cardamom
7 to 7-1/2 cups flour
2 cakes of packages of yeast
2 eggs
1/2 citron, chopped
1/2 cup raisins

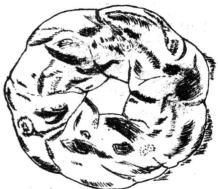

Mix milk, sugar, salt, and cardamom.
Add crumbled yeast, beaten eggs and melted shortening; set aside for 5 minutes.
Add flour and fruit and mix to form a dough. **Turn** onto a floured work surface and knead until silky and elastic, about 10 minutes.
Put the kneaded dough in a bowl, cover with a dish towel, and let rise in a warm area until double in size, about 1-1/2 hours.
Punch down and allow to double in size.
Preheat the oven to 350 degrees F.
If choosing to make into a simple round ring, roll into a 16-inch long rope, and shape into a round loaf.
If fashioning into a twisted ring, divide the dough into two equal pieces, which are rolled into two 16-inch ropes and then twisted together into a ring shape.
Bake in preheated oven for 30 to 40 minutes, until golden and hollow sounding when tapped underneath. Cool on a wire rack.

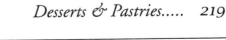

Swedish Pancakes

From Hilda Nileson (VASA)

Historic *"Old Swedes" Trinity Episcopal Church Recipes, Second Edition, 1989*

Serves   six to eight

As in the northern countries of Europe, pancakes were frequently served in the cold climes where, more than likely, there would have been a wood-burning kitchen stove ready at hand. Try to use the freshest milk you can muster, just as the Swedes would have had. Particularly common was the practice of serving pancakes with a berry sauce, especially blueberry sauce in Down Jersey. Some preferred to roll the pancakes spooning the sauce within.

```
   3    eggs
2-1/4 cups flour
   2    cups milk
  1/2   teaspoon salt
   2    teaspoons sugar
Powdered sugar for dusting
```

Beat eggs; add dry ingredients and milk. Beat well.
Add melted butter (or you can put all of it in an electric blender). **Pour** a small amount of batter into a griddle or plett pan, which has been greased once. **Spread** over bottom of pan and fry at medium heat, turning when light brown. **Dust** with powdered sugar and serve with butter, syrup, lingonberries or jelly..

A plett pan is a cast iron pan with circular indentions to make 7 small pancakes at a time.
Lingonberries are a super hardy dwarf perennial evergreen shrub reaching 4 to 16 inches high. As such they were available and rather popular in Swedish cooking, especially for fruit jams and jellies. Difficult to find in area supermarkets, they have been offered at Ikea outlets.

    The Swedes were among the earliest settlers, establishing some of the earliest agricultural and industrial communities. About three hundred years ago Swedish pioneers came into southern New Jersey from Christiana, a town now known as Wilmington, and built their farms and homes in Raccoon, now Swedesboro.

    The settlers were devout church-goers, but having no church, had to sail across the Delaware to worship in Christiana. Eventually this became a hardship, and even dangerous during bad weather. They solved the problem by building their own church on the banks of Raccoon Creek.

    The log cabin church was completed in 1703 and was the first Swedish Lutheran Church in New Jersey. That original church, damaged during the Revolutionary War, was replaced by another in 1784, and a bell tower and steeple were added in 1839. It is this church, Trinity Episcopal "Old Swedes" Church that was the fulcrum of a rapidly growing farming community and that today is the focus of an ever-growing cultural awareness in picturesque Swedesboro and its surrounding area.

Sweet Potato Pie

Makes two nine-inch pies

Some may know this recipe's contributor, Ida Rowe, from her performances with the group, Seven Quilts for Seven Sisters, which, as they say, "Through folklore, skits, music and song, let us share with you the joys of sisterhood and the sorrows of slavery and its influence in the art of quilt making."

I also know Ida Rowe from her reputation as an accomplished baker. Here, she shares her recipe for sweet potato pie, a pie that is quite common in southern New Jersey. Our sandy soils and long, warm growing season are favorable for growing sweet potatoes. Rowe said that she adapted this recipe from a cookbook she bought at Woodstown's Cowtown Market, "Big Mama's Black Pot Recipes," that she says goes well beyond recipes with stories of cooking in the tough times of the South by slaves.

Ida Walker favors the use of yams. "Yam" is the market name in Down Jersey for those true sweet potatoes that are considered moist. Confusing the matter further, southern shippers are grouping yams in with sweets, calling all of them sweet potatoes. I recommend that you consult with your farm marketer for obtaining the variety you prefer for the way you will cook them.

5	cups sweet potatoes
1/2	cup melted butter
2	cups sugar
4	eggs
1	teaspoon cinnamon
1/2	teaspoon salt
1-2/3	cups evaporated milk
1	teaspoon vanilla extract
1	teaspoon lemon extract
2	9-inch prepared pie shells

In a large pot filled with salted water, bring to a boil, add the sweet potatoes and slowly boil, unskinned, for 30 to 40 minutes until tender when tested with a fork. **Remove,** drain and cool sweet potatoes until comfortable to peel. **In the meantime,** preheat the oven to 400 degrees F. **Mash** the peeled sweet potatoes well. **Blend** all ingredients. **Pour** into prepared pie shells. There should be sufficient filling for two pies. **Bake** for one hour, or until firm. Ida Rowe prefers her pies baked firm, but still with some moistness. Different varieties of sweet potatoes will yield various tastes and moisture levels.

> **Joe Tierno,** whose grandparents once farmed in Vineland, tells me how they managed to get a head start for sweet potatoes, which have a long growing season. To get them to mature in time, in late spring they would encourage the "seed" sweet potatoes to sprout by digging a pit deep enough for a man to stand in. They would than built a wooden rack across the middle, lay soil and then the sweet potatoes on top and build a fire below.

Heavenly Sweet Potato Biscuits

Makes two dozen

This recipe has come to us by way of Phyllis Walker, from Mullica Hill, whom I met at the Church of Christ in Pitman. There they hold potluck dinners on Wednesdays to allow their members to attend prayer services following a workday. Phyllis Walker has a reputation for presenting these biscuits often at the prayer services, as well as for her own family.

1   egg, slightly beaten
1   cup cooked and mashed sweet potatoes
1/4 cup sugar
4   tablespoons butter, softened
2   cups flour
1   teaspoon baking powder

Mix all ingredients, stirring in enough flour to make a soft dough. **Lightly** flour a working surface; knead the dough briefly. **Roll** to 1/4-inch thickness; cut with 2-inch biscuit cutter or glass rim. **Place** on an ungreased baking sheet and bake at 350 degrees F. about 15 minutes or until lightly browned. **Serve** with honey or butter.

Sweet Potato Rolls

Makes two dozen or more

Here is another "Talk about good" recipe shared by Phyllis Walker.

1   cup boiled and mashed yams
4 1/2 cups all-purpose flour
1   teaspoon salt
1/3 cup vegetable oil
1/4 cup sugar
1   teaspoon cinnamon, optional
2   eggs, beaten, brought to room
     temperature
1   package yeast dissolved in 1/2 cup
     of warm water

Sift together the flour and salt. **Combine** with sugar and cinnamon. **Add** in the eggs and yeast and water. It should develop a soft dough, which is kneaded for a few minutes. **Allow** the dough to rise, covered, for 2 hours in a warm location. **Punch** down and allow to rise for another 2 hours, pinch apart to a size of a plum. **Place** on a greased cake pan. **Bake** in a preheated oven at 400 degree F. for 10 to 12 minutes. Phyllis Walker likes to place her rolls in a wicker basket wrapped in a homey towel so as to keep them warm for serving.

Ricotta Pie

Makes two 9-inch pies

Ricotta pie is one of the most popular desserts that traveled across the Atlantic from the Province of Abruzzo in Italy to Down Jersey. One of the most loyal keepers of this tradition is the Manzoni family who settled in the town of Paulsboro. I can thank Rosa Manzoni-Friars for sharing her version, which is in the style of the Abruzzo region. "I had to take the recipe from my mother, Aida, who did it from "a little of this and that" to a written recipe that all of us in the family could do.

3   pounds ricotta cheese
2   cups sugar
6   eggs
1   cup whole milk
1   teaspoon vanilla extract
Zest and juice of 1 lemon
2   tablespoons butter, melted
Cinnamon for sprinkling
2   prepared, deep-dish piecrusts

Preheat the oven at 425 degrees F. Adjust two racks in the 2 middle positions.
Most containers of ricotta cheese will have some liquid whey separating from the curds. **Remove** the whey by placing the cheese in a strainer to drain for a few minutes.
Combine the sugar and eggs; whip until well blended.
Add and stir in the remaining ingredients. Pour the batter into the piecrusts and spread evenly with a spatula. Do not cover with a crust top. During baking, the butter will rise to the surface for a pleasing buttery topping.
Sprinkle each pie with a dusting of cinnamon.
Place the pies in the middle 2 racks in the oven.
Bake for 15 minutes at 425 degrees F., then reduce to 350 degrees F. and bake for 45 to 50 minutes more, until the pie batter is just beyond jiggling.

Wheat Cakes

You'll get light fluffy cakes instead of rough, leathery ones if you beat the batter thoroughly. And don't overheat the griddle. It should be hot enough to make the cakes rise, but no hotter. Turning the cakes more than once makes them tough. Wheat cakes, by the way, need even heat. That's why the old-fashioned iron skillet is the best griddle.

This recipe instruction is excerpted from *Dinner in the Diner: Great Railroad Recipes of all time," by* Will C. Hollister.
Wheat cakes were served to diners on the Baltimore & Ohio Railroad during the early part of the 20th century.

Moravian Sugar Cake

Even this author doubted a substantial presence of Moravians in southern New Jersey until I learned of a former Moravian Church in Swedesboro, still standing on Moravian Church Road in Oldman's Creek, south of Swedesboro. The church was formally deeded to the Episcopal Church in 1836. It is now owned by the Gloucester County Historical Society and is on the National Register.

Until a few years ago, occasional gatherings were held at the Oldman's Creek Moravian Church, but they have been discontinued. Most of us would remember the Moravian custom of "Love Feasts," during which many of their traditional foods would be served. Of their foods, the cakes, cookies and pies are best remembered. As the Moravian community has gravitated to the Pennsylvania side of the Delaware River, namely Bethlehem, that area is where their foodways is best preserved.

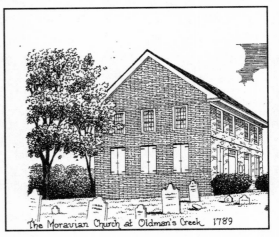

The Moravian Church at Oldman's Creek 1789

The plaque on the wall on this church on Moravian Church Road reads as follows:
On this site the Moravians erected a log Church in 1747 and Dedicated August 31, 1749 by Bishop A. G. Spangenberg.
In June of 1786 this Church was erected and Dedicated July 5, 1789 by Bishop J. Ettwein.
—*Drawing courtesy of the Gloucester County Historical Society*

This following recipe reprinted from "Cooking with the Pennsylvania Dutch" captures one of their recipes the Moravians might have used here during one of their Love Feast services:

At 5 o'clock p.m., set a sponge or batter, consisting of 1 cup of mashed potatoes, 2 cups of sugar, 1 cup of sweet milk, scalded and cooled, 1/2 cake of yeast, dissolved in 1 cup of lukewarm water, 2 eggs, 3/4 cup of a mixture of lard and butter, add 3 cups of flour, beat well, stand in a warm place to raise; at 9 o'clock add about 6 cups of flour. Stand until morning in a warm place, near the range. The following morning turn out on a floured bake-board, roll out cakes one-inch thick, place in pie tins. When ready for the oven; punch half a dozen small holes in the top of cakes, in which place small bits of butter. Sprinkle sugar over liberally and cinnamon, if liked. Bake in a moderate oven.

Party Drinks and Refreshments

Jersey Devil Punch

1 gallon cranberry juice
2 quarts apple cider or apple juice
1 quart applejack
1 apple, sliced

Pour all ingredients into a punch bowl in which a block of ice is floating, and stir.

Laird's Jersey Devil Cocktail

1 ounce Laird's AppleJack
1/3 ounce lime juice
1/3 ounce Cointreau or Triple sec
1/3 ounce cranberry juice
1/2 teaspoon sugar

Shake ingredients with ice. **Strain** into a cocktail glass.

Sparkling Holiday Punch

2 bottles Welch's Sparkling White Grape Juice Cocktail, chilled
1 (11.5 oz.) can Welch's Frozen Concentrated Cranberry Juice Cocktail
3 cups cold water
3 cans (12 oz. each) ginger ale, chilled

Combine sparking white grape Juice, frozenconcentrated cranberry cuice cocktail and water. **Gently** stir in ginger ale. Float fruited ice ring made with sparkling juice and garnished with mint leaves. **Serve** immediately. Makes about 30 1/2-cup servings.

Jersey Bounce

Official cocktail of the "Jersey Derby" once held at Garden State Park in Cherry Hill.

1-1/2 ounces Laird's AppleJack
Dash of Triple Sec
Dash of lime juice
1-1/2 ounces cranberry juice
1-1/2 ounces sour mix
Dash of egg white
Lime wedge

Pour AppleJack over ice. Add triple sec, juices, sour mix, and egg white. Shake well and garnish with a wedge of lime.

Ale Shoe used in taverns to warm ale. The toe was placed in hot coals of the hearth to warm the drink. Copied from a 1700's original.
Drawing courtesy of Goosebay Workshops

Ruby Mulled Cider

1 (11.5 oz. or 12 oz.) can Welch's Frozen Concentrated Cranberry Juice Cocktail, thawed and undiluted
8 cups apple cider
4 cinnamon sticks
20 whole cloves
Butter

Tie spices in a cheesecloth pouch. In a saucepan, **heat** cranberry juice cocktail concentrate, cider, and spices. **Simmer** for 5 minutes. In each mug, put about 1 tsp. butter. **Pour** in hot cranberry and cider mixture. Makes 8 servings.

Swedish Glögg

Makes one and one-half quarts

Glögg emerged in Europe many centuries ago, and among the countries continuing this tradition of a mulled beverage, Sweden cherishes it the most. No wonder as this warmed punch reaches its highest appreciation when served in the chilling months, so not surprisingly this drink is most closely identified with Christmas. It is common to serve this drink with raisins and almonds or hazelnuts.

Our recipe, given to us by Elizabeth Singer, traces its roots back to Sweden from a friend only remembered as Sophia. This drink continues to be served at Swedesboro's Trinity Episcopal Church's covered-dish suppers. It is also a featured drink during Christmas parties at the historic home of Susan and Joe Frank, known as the Seven Stars Tavern, in Sharptown, . Admittedly, there are numerous versions of a "true" glögg recipe, but we think you will find this one worthy of its long-honored tradition. Since it's a high-octane alcoholic drink, reduce the level of vodka should you wish.

1	quart ordinary dry red wine
4-5	pieces cinnamon sticks
20	cloves
	1-inch piece of ginger
1	heaping teaspoon crushed cardamom seeds
1/3	cup vodka
1-1/4	cup sugar
1/2	teaspoon vanilla extract
1	tablespoon orange peels, minced
	Blanched almonds or hazelnuts and raisins

Place the wine, cinnamon, cloves, ginger, and cardamom in a glass jar and pour the vodka over them. **Allow** the mixture to rest overnight, or at least 3 to 4 hours. **Strain** the mixture through a coffee filter. **Pour** spiced vodka and wine in a pot, add the sugar and vanilla and bring to a light simmer, stirring occasionally to dissolve the sugar. Do not boil. **Remove** from heat and serve in small cups, along with a spoon, and a toss of nuts and raisins. Fresh orange peels are often served as a garnish.

Mulling Cone & Bandreth

This drawing of a historic reproduction by Peter Goebel shows a mulling cone and bandreth (trivet) that was used to warm drinks. The mulling cone is nestled in a brandreth, which was used to hold the cone in an upright position and allowed hot coals from the hearth fire to be raked under the cone.
Dated: 1600-1750
Origin: English

—Drawings courtesy of Goosebay Workshops

Chapter 9

Sauces We Have Come to Know

The aspiring cook soon learns that sauces serve to compliment and finish the food prepared, often taking top honors itself. In advancing culinary skills, learning classic sauces is of great benefit. But here, we have brought to you sauces found to have a connection with Down Jersey. In searching out those with ties to our region, we haven't sought to provide a basic text on sauces, but rather to share those with which we have familiarity.

Surely, tomato sauces brought from elsewhere, namely Italy, reached heights that would challenge sauces from anywhere else. Once again, our Jersey tomato counts.

From the days when the scent of canning house operations filled the air of towns in the heart of farm communities, first I present a chilaly sauce derived from a ketchup base. Before store-bought ketchup became affordable, ketchup was made in the home kitchen. For that, we bring you Adele Baden's grandma's recipe for homemade ketchup.

From the Quaker tradition, strong in Salem County, we have lemon butter, a recipe that is still served today at Friends Meeting gatherings.

The most recent contribution to our selection of sauces is salsa, a Mexican sauce that already is well known and extremely popular.

One of them might be a recipe your grandma or grandpa might have made. The ingredients they used are still with us today, so give one a try.

Why do Italians steadfastly insist on calling tomato sauce *gravy*?

I would like to speculate on this question.

Italian cooks stubbornly insist they are making *gravy* when everyone knows that it's properly called a sauce. The answer may lie in patriotism and history.

When the early waves of Italian immigrants settled in southern New Jersey in the late 19th century and early 20th century, English and northern European cooking still retained a stronghold on the cooking style. French cuisine would have been understood and consumed by the few in upper class society. Whereas the French adorned their food with elaborate, time-consuming elaborate sauces, the English lavished gravies made from the flavorings of meat, which formed the mainstay of their diet. Before our colonial era, this sauce versus gravy matter took the form of frequent barbs back and forth across the English Channel, neither culture to budge from their ways.

The early Italians arriving on our shores were intensely patriotic—nothing was too American. As an example, it was all too common for the second-generation children to understand spoken village-dialect Italian, but speak only a few words. Being American, however, in no way meant losing the food traditions of the old country. Dishes were adapted to local ingredients, but not forsaken.

When Italian homemakers learned the word for tomato sauce, the English presence would have deferred to their word, gravy. French cooking was years away from the teachings of Julia Child with her *The French Chef* television series.

That is why we please grandma when we tell her we love her gravy.

Gravy, you see, *is* American.

Jersey Beach Plum Sauce

Makes one quart

We have a native shrub growing in southern Jersey many don't know about. Along the Jersey coast and back bays, the beach plum, Prunus maritima, flourishes. The six feet tall shrub tolerates drought, is salt tolerant and takes to full sun. In mid- to late-April, fragrant white blossoms appear, from which intensely flavored purplish berries ripen in September. The one-inch size berries harbor a large seed within, leaving them suitable only for cooking rather than eating out of hand. But oh what a wild taste they have! While the traditional preparation had been to make a beach plum jam or jelly, here we will share a recipe for making a sauce. It's far easier for anyone to do, and the sauce freezes well.

In our family, beach plum sauce has been used with pancakes and in desserts where June strawberries might have been used, but are out of season. The sauce is also excellent with venison and pork dishes. Some might choose to refer to this sauce as a puree.

```
2   quarts ripe beach plum berries
1   cup sugar
Juice of 1/2 lemon
```

Wash and pick over the berries, removing any stems.
Place in a three quart saucepan, add berries and sugar. Add water to barely cover. **Over** medium heat, bring to a boil, reduce to a slow simmer, and stir often with a wooden spoon, mashing as you stir. **Continue** cooking and stirring until all of the berries are soft and you have a thick mixture, about 20 minutes. Remove pot from the heat and pour into a medium-fine strainer over a larger bowl. With a spoon, mash as much of the berries through the strainer as is practicable. Discard the seeds. **Return** the strained sauce to the saucepan, add the lemon juice. Cook for another 5 minutes, stirring frequently. At this time add any additional flavorings you might prefer. Taste and adjust for sweetness. Allow to cool, place in a glass jar for storage in the refrigerator, where it will keep for one month, or in your freezer for longer keeping.
Variations: Lemon and orange zest contribute citrus notes, or add a tablespoon or two of a liqueur, such as orange-flavored Triple-Sec, Amaretto or Frangelico. All of the liqueurs would be added during the last three minutes of cooking.

Foraging and growing your own: Abundant as the beach plum shrubs are along the Jersey shore, ask for permission, whether public or private property. Beach plums are attractive bushes offering springtime flowering and fall harvests, if you can get to them before the birds. Beach plums can be started easily from seed, but since they don't take to transplanting easily, seedlings should be transplanted from container nursery stock. They prefer full sun in a site that is well drained. Fertilizing needs are minimal, if at all.

Chilaly

Makes about one and one-half cups

In culinary historian Andrew F. Smith's book, "Souper Tomatoes," in which he traces the development of soup through the ages, and, interestingly for us, the history of canning in New Jersey, Smith uncovered this recipe for Chilaly. Published in "Helps for the Hostess," (Camden, New Jersey: Joseph Campbell Company, ca. 1916), this recipe would be appreciated today. As yet, we have been unable to positively identify what "chilaly" actually means. Pilot bread, also known as hardtack, is a dense, unleavened bread.

In my trial I found Chilaly to offer itself as a hearty dipping sauce. Using the original ingredient proportions, I found this sauce too salty for today's taste, so see the note on our suggested changes.

1	tablespoonful butter
1/2	teaspoonful dry mustard and salt, see note.
1	teaspoonful Worcestershire sauce
2	tablespoonfuls chopped green bell pepper
1	tablespoonful chopped onion
1/2	cup Campbell's Tomato Soup
1/2	pound sharp cheese run through chopper
2	tablespoonfuls milk
1	egg

Cook butter with onions and pepper until brown. **Rub** mustard and salt together, add to tomato soup, then add to butter mixture. **Bring** to a boil; add cheese and Worcestershire. When cheese is melted, add milk and slightly beaten egg. **Serve** at once on hot pilot crackers. This is best cooked in the blazer of a chafing dish.

Our note: We suggest replacing the 1/2 teaspoon of salt with 1/2 teaspoon of sugar and serving with crackers, nachos or slices of crusty bread as an appetizer.

Tomato Catsup

Adele Baden's grandmother, Caroline Harmeter, wrote this recipe in 1889 for tomato catsup (her spelling) in the days when tomato catchup was one among other condiments that were made in the home kitchen. In those days when it was assumed you knew how to make catchup, there were no instructions. I interpret a dram to be an equivalent of a pinch.

To a 1/2 bushel of tomatoes, use the following:

6 oz. salt

6 oz. allspice

3 oz black pepper

1-1/4 oz. yellow mustard seed

6 drams cloves

3 drams nutmeg

2 drams red pepper

1/2 gall. vinegar

Greek Lemon and Olive Oil Sauce

Makes nearly one cup

When Tom Alexandridis owned his seafood restaurant, Alexander's Seafare, he found this sauce pleased his customers more than any other. Customarily, he would scatter this sauce on baked or broiled fish, but it enhances meats and vegetables as well. It lends itself to many variations, so after trying Alexandridis' version, go on to adjust it to your own liking.

> 1/2 cup extra virgin olive oil
> Juice of two lemons
> 1/4 cup chopped fresh or 2 tablespoons dried dill weed
> 2 tablespoons fresh parsley, chopped, optional
> Pinch of cayenne
> Salt and pepper to taste

Place all ingredients in a small jar, close the lid and shake well. Or, add the ingredients in a small bowl and mix well with a fork or small whisk. **Taste** for seasoning adjustment and keep in the refrigerator until ready for use. Best results are when this sauce is poured over the fillet at the end of the cooking, less of the lemon flavor is lost that way.

This sauce is best used within one week.

Variation: Consider adding oregano to the dill, or use oregano by itself.

Mexican Salsa
(Cooked)

Makes one cup

Several Mexican friends have suggested this straight-forward prep for salsa. The marriage of Jersey tomatoes and the remarkable cuisine of our American neighbor has been a happy pairing.

> 2 fresh green jalapenos, diced and seeded
> 2 ripe red tomatoes, round or plum, diced
> 1/4 teaspoon salt
> 2 garlic cloves, minced
> 1 tablespoon cilantro, chopped
> 1 small onion, chopped, white preferred

In enough water to cover, bring the jalapenos and tomatoes to a boil for 5 minutes. **Remove** jalapenos and tomatoes; blend them with 3 tablespoons of water, salt, and garlic. **Blend** until a coarse, rustic blend is achieved. **Add** in the cilantro and onions. **Resting** the salsa for a few minutes improvesits its flavor.

Barbecue or Marinade Sauce
from Haines Pork Store

Makes approximately two cups

When you need cooking help from a greengrocer or butcher, they respond by writing a proven and practical recipe over the counter on a spare slip of paper. Haines Pork Store in Mickleton will do just that. Here, they pass along a recipe that brings in a popular southern New Jersey ingredient, a crab boil seasoning, such as Old Bay.

- 1   cup ketchup
- 2   tablespoons vinegar
- 1   tablespoon Worcestershire sauce
- 1   tablespoon crab boil seasoning, such as Old Bay
- 1/2 cup sugar
- 1   tablespoon Dijon mustard

For a barbecue sauce, mix above ingredients; brush over barbecued pork or other meat towards the end of the cooking to avoid burning.

For marinating, add 1 cup of water.

Note: For either, cayenne pepper may be added.

Cranberry-Blueberry Sauce (Brenda Moore's)

Makes two quarts

This sauce took first prize at the 1988 Chatsworth Cranberry Festival. It's a good example of how local favorites, cranberries and blueberries, find their way into a sauce that compliments many dishes, both savory and sweet.

- 2   cups water
- 2   cups sugar
- 4   cups fresh or frozen whole cranberries
- 1/2 cup fresh or frozen blueberries

Heat water and sugar in a saucepan until boiling.

Add cranberries, lower heat to simmer and cook 5 minutes, stirring often.

Remove saucepan from the heat; mash cranberries with a potato masher until you reach a desired consistency.

Add blueberries and chill.

Serve with turkey, chicken or other meats.

Honey Mustard Sauce

Variable

I tasted this sauce when enjoying pub grub in Millville's Old Oar House Tavern. It fits in as a tangy sauce ideally matched for our favorite seafoods from our Delaware Bay and offshore fisheries. It's especially suited for shad, bluefish and mackerel. It's also a good choice for pork, sausage and chicken dishes.

Chef John O'Hara said that once you prepare this yourself, you won't bother to buy jarred honey mustard sauces. I agree! Once you make it, you can tailor the proportions to your liking.

Note that the sauce is a 3-2-1 ratio, so make as much or as little as you need.

> 1/2 cup (8 tablespoons) whole grain mustard
> 1/4 cup (4 tablespoons) honey
> 2 tablespoons apple cider vinegar, or other mild
>   vinegar such as white wine or rice wine vinegar

Combine all ingredients together, stir well and serve at room temperature. This sauce keeps well in the refrigerator, covered.

Orange-Basil Sauce for Ravioli and More

Makes nearly 1/2 cup sauce for 1/2 pound of ravioli

This recipe may not yet be Down Jersey, but it should be. It's a wonderful alternative to having ravioli with tomato sauce.

> 2 tablespoons butter
> 1/4 cup extra-virgin olive oil
> 2 tablespoons orange marmalade
> 6-8 fresh basil leaves, chopped, or 1 tablespoon dried
> 1 tablespoon paprika
> 1 tablespoon grated Parmesan or Romano cheese
> 2 tablespoons parsley, chopped
> 1/2 pound cooked cheese ravioli

In a saucepan over medium-low heat, add the butter; heat until the foam stops. **Add** the olive oil, orange marmalade, basil, and stir. Don't worry if the marmalade doesn't mix in thoroughly. Turn off the heat and add the cheese and parsley; stir in. **Arrange** ravioli on a flat platter and pour the sauce over the ravioli. Use parsley as a garnish if you like. Give one last stir before serving. **Variation:** Add hot red pepper flakes to the sauce. Some may prefer serving Romano cheese at the table for additional sprinkling. **Note:** This sauce is excellent over other pasta dishes and chicken.

Salem Lemon Butter Spread

Makes four cups

Since colonial times when lemons were carried northward on ships sailing from the Caribbean, lemon butter has been a popular sauce to serve and used as a spread over bread and other baked goods. It continues strong at the Quaker Church suppers near the Salem area. We thank Edith Pancoast-Davis for this recipe. Incidentally, both sur names-- Pancoast and Davis--are family names recorded as early settlers. A Pancoast, for example, had been the first recorded Sheriff of Burlington County.

Though local usage favors the name lemon butter, it might be more properly referred to as lemon curd. Bridgeport's Nancy Pedrick--another notable name associated with Pedricktown-- said that lemon butter goes to every picnic and is served as a side dish to eat with a spoon or spread on rolls. "Very good spooned over unfrosted yellow cake," she added.

5-6	large eggs
3	cups sugar
7/8	cup water
1	cup lemon juice
	Grated rind of 2-1/2 medium lemons
1/4	teaspoon salt
1/4	pound butter

In a mixing bowl, add the eggs; beat well. **Add** the remaining ingredients, except the butter; stir in. **Add** ingredients in top pan of a double boiler over simmering water. **Stir** constantly with a wooden spoon until mixture thickens. **Remove** from the stove, add 1/4 pound of butter and stir in. **Allow** lemon butter to cool, give one more stir, and pour into storage jars or sauce boat.

Fresh Cranberry Sauce

Makes three cups

Paula Rodgers of Woodbury, has her favorites that she prepares for her husband. This one, she admits, comes from a bag of fresh cranberries, yet is so healthy and liked by her family that she repeats it each year at Thanksgiving. "The orange rind in the recipe makes it special, I think," Mrs. Rodgers said.

1	cup water, plus 1 cup sugar
1	(12-ounce) package of fresh cranberries
1	teaspoon pumpkin pie spice
3-4	slices orange peel, thinly sliced

Heat the water and sugar mix to boiling. **Stir** in cranberries and 3 or 4 slices of thinly sliced orange peel and pumpkin pie spice. **Cook** for 10 minutes and serve with poultry, pork or chicken.

Sauces..... 233

Fresh Salsa

Makes one cup

Also called salsa cruda, which means raw, not crude, this sauce takes full advantage of the richness of our Jersey tomatoes. This is the sauce you are most likely to encounter at Mexican restaurants. If you don't care to use cilantro, use 1/2 teaspoon of cumin instead.

- 2 medium round tomatoes, unpeeled, diced
- 2 cloves garlic, minced
- 1 long, hot green pepper or 1 jalapeno, seeded and minced (keep hands away from eyes)
- 1/2 small white onion, diced
- 2 tablespoons cilantro, chopped
- Salt
- Juice of one lime or 1 tablespoon white vinegar
- 2 tablespoons water

Combine all the ingredients, starting with 1/4-tablespoon salt and adjust seasoning to taste. **Resting** the salsa for 20 minutes improves its flavor. This salsa doesn't freeze well.

Bruschetta Topping

Makes one cup

Bruschetta, a roasted bread traditionally topped with garlic and olive oil, has taken to a salsa topping. The use of plum tomatoes gives a drier, sturdier texture to this recipe. Of course, use regular tomatoes if that's what you have. It is especially important with salsa to use a sharp knife to avoid crushing the tomato pulp. While it certainly can be served over garlic bread, this topping has enough flavor of its own to be served over plain Italian bread.

- 6-7 plum tomatoes, unpeeled
- 2 cloves garlic, minced
- 1/4 teaspoon hot red pepper flakes, or a dash of cayenne
- 1/2 small onion
- 2 tablespoons parsley, finely chopped
- 1 tablespoon extra-virgin olive oil
- 2 tablespoons Romano or Parmesan cheese, grated

Combine all the above ingredients. Test for need of salt as the cheese may add sufficient saltiness.

Serve over slices of French or Italian bread, toasted or untoasted as you wish. This topping doesn't freeze well.

Today's Spaghetti Gravy

Useful for 1 to 1-1/2 pounds of pasta

Of course it isn't properly called gravy, but that's what Nona called it, and so, so do we. But until recently, gravy from a store-bought bottle didn't come close enough to consider using seriously; the only choice was to prepare hours-long sauces. Simply impractical for today's working home cooks to prepare from scratch, we now have bottled sauces available that are at least worthy of being used as a base, or starter.

Use as a base here means that by adding fresh ingredients, and more importantly, ingredients in proportion to the dish at hand and your own family's likes, you elevate the jar's contents to a respectable level. For example, in order to be competitive at the supermarket, few commercial sauces use extra-virgin olive oil, and they tend to err on the safe side with only modest seasoning. You can uplift the sauce as far as you want in seasonings. The principle at work here is that we tend to regard a dish from its freshest and best ingredients, as long as the base doesn't distract. Starting with a meatless marinara sauce insures that you won't have unwelcome flavors to contend with, and you can add you own meat during simmering if you choose.

We have a suggested a sauce doctored-up from a store-bought bottled base that will impress you, and one which you can then go on to tailor to your own family's inclinations. Note that we are suggesting to infuse the garlic in the olive oil and removing it to avoid the chance of burning, all too easy to do.

1 (32-ounce) jar of commercial marinara sauce
4 tablespoons of quality extra-virgin olive oil
3 cloves garlic, smashed
6-8 leaves of fresh basil, or 1 tablespoon dried
1/2 Red bell pepper, or 3 long sweet, diced, optional
1/4 cup dry red wine, optional
Pinch of ground cloves, optional

In a large, heavy bottom saucepan over medium-low heat, add the olive oil and garlic. Sauté the garlic until golden and discard.

Stir in the basil and add the peppers, if using. Simmer for one minute, stirring.

Pour in the jarred sauce and bring to a low simmer, stirring occasionally.

Add the wine, stir and simmer for 5 minutes until the alcohol has dissipated.

Add the cloves and simmer 5 minutes more, stirring occasionally.

Test for seasoning, perhaps addition of salt and black pepper, commercial sauces seldom need sugar added to balance excessive acidity.

Serve over your choice of pasta, or refer to the seafood chapter for Sicilian Tuna and Pasta.

"An Italian who doesn't dip his bread, is an Italian who has arthritis of the shoulder,"
Pat Cooper

Sauces..... 235

Quick Summer Tomato Sauce
with Angel Hair Pasta

Serves six

Carmen Zampaglioni, who owns Carmen's Deli in Paulsboro, said that this quick-to-make sauce is his family's favorite during the summertime. His mother, Antonia, learned this dish when she cooked for her family back in the mountain town of Condico in the province of Reggio Calabria in Italy. Since Antonia Zampaglione was the eldest of the children, she was expected to cook and take care of her younger siblings while the rest of the family worked their farm in the hills of Calabria. Judging by this recipe, she served her family well.

Jersey's tasty plum tomatoes help to keep this family favorite going.

4	tablespoons extra-virgin olive oil
1	medium onion, diced
2	cloves garlic, thinly sliced, not minced
6-8	ripe plum tomatoes, blanched, peeled, cored and coarsely cut or squeezed
5	leaves fresh basil, chopped, stems removed
1/4	cup Romano cheese
1	pound angel hair pasta, cooked till barely tender

In a large heavy pan, preferably cast iron, over medium heat, sauté onions until golden in 2 tablespoons of olive oil.

Add the garlic, stir for 1/2 minute and add the tomatoes.

Reduce heat to low; simmer, stirring occasionally, until the tomato color darkens to a maroon, which is called the breaking stage.

Add the fresh basil leaves, stir in and add the angel hair pasta. Stir over low heat for about 1 minute to allow the pasta to absorb the tomato sauce.

Remove from the heat and add the Romano cheese.

Transfer to a serving bowl and drizzle the remaining 2 tablespoons of olive oil on the pasta.

Gardener's Note: While plum tomatoes are usually favored for use in sauces due to their lower acidity and higher solid matter content, gardeners can opt for either plum or round tomatoes. Their are a few round slicing tomatoes noted for their higher solid content and thus are more versitile. One of these would be the variety *Pick Red,* and there are others, too. Canners, too, want more solid tomato that yields a higher pack-out.

Tomato Sauce
from Virginia Sorantino's Tomato Gravy Recipe

Makes two quarts

This recipe passed along by Paul J. Ritter recalls his grandmother's "gravy" that the Sorantino's enjoyed at family gatherings. The Sorantinos, farmers for over eighty years in the Cedarville area, have since retired from farming but have kept their foodways. Virginia Sorantino's maiden name, Aceto, (which means vinegar), she has from a family that came from the town of Ioggi in the province of Calabria in the "toe" of Italy. Calabria is known for a spicier style of sauce influenced by centuries of earlier spice trading with the Arabs.

1/4	cup extra-virgin olive oil
2-3	cloves garlic, chopped
1	heaping tablespoon chopped onions
1	(6-ounce) can tomato paste

Dash of ground black pepper

6	ounces water
2	(28-ounce) jars of crushed tomatoes
1	teaspoon sugar
4-5	leaves of fresh basil
3	tablespoons parsley, chopped

About 1 pound of cooked chicken thighs or browned
     ground beef
Parmesan or Locatelli cheese, grated

Cover the bottom of a 6-quart pot with the olive oil. "Buy the best even if it costs a little more."

Add the onions and sauté for 3 minutes, stirring so that the onions do not brown. Add the garlic, stir in the oil and onions; cook for 30 seconds.

Add the tomato paste, black pepper and water.

Next add the jars of crushed tomatoes and the sugar, which will balance the acidity of the tomatoes. **Add** the fresh basil and parsley.

Simmer the gravy for a couple of hours with the lid on, stirring occasionally with a wooden spoon.

Add the cooked chicken thighs or browned ground beef after 1-1/2 hours.

Simmer for another half hour. **After** the heat source is turned off, add the grated Parmesan or Locatelli Romano to your taste..

Note on addition of sugar: In the Sorantino's recipe a meager one teaspoon of sugar is called for to reduce the acidity of the tomatoes. While this is a good practice, the same tanginess that Jersey tomatoes boast of works against a mellowness in sauces. However, should you be using fully ripe paste tomatoes, most likely at the end of the season, then you may not need to add sugar. That's because as tomatoes ripen, their acidity lowers and their natural sweetness increases.

Jersey Tuscan Tomato Sauce

Makes about two and a half cups

Classically Tuscan in its simplicity, this sauce was introduced to a local cook, Anthony Battaglia who shared this one with me. The incomparable Jersey tomato surely brought out its best qualities. By putting to use a food mill, there is no need to core, peel or dice the tomatoes. Notice that the ingredient list calls for a bit more olive oil than you might anticipate for a sauce, but it's part of the balance of flavors and adds a welcome level of creaminess.

The ingredients are few, so don't try to add any more, with the exception of hot red pepper flakes.

- 4 tablespoons extra-virgin olive oil
- 3 pounds ripe round or cherry Jersey tomatoes, coarsely chopped
- 1 small onion, diced
- 6-8 fresh basil leaves, chopped
- Salt and pepper

In a heavy pan over medium heat, add 2 tablespoons of the olive oil. Add the onions and cook until clear, about 3 minutes. Add the tomatoes and basil, stirring occasionally to keep the tomatoes from scorching.

The tomatoes should become soft and broken down in about 10 minutes. Remove from heat and, using the smallest hole disk, put the mixture through a food mill.

Return to the pan and cook over medium heat for about 7 minutes more, uncovered, stirring occasionally. If a thicker sauce is desired, continue cooking a few more minutes.

When finished, add the remaining 2 tablespoons of the olive oil and stir in.

Note: This sauce is excellent served with cooked rigatoni.

LONG HANDLED SAUCE PAN

This historic reproduction by Peter Goebel shows a long-handled saucepan common in hearth cooking. It was reproduced from a period example circa 1747 notably, "The Convalescent's Meal" by Chardin.
Dated: 18th century
Origin: French
Drawing courtesy of Goosebay Workshops

Note: See page 157 for Holiday Oyster Sauce.
See page 141 for White Clam Sauce (with Pasta).
See page 206 for Blueberry Sauce.

Chapter 10
Our Lenni Lenape

Our Native Americans gave us and the rest of the world a great number of wholesome, nutritious foods that are an important part of our diets today. Corn, potatoes, squash, beans, sweet potatoes, peppers and other foods have found their way into our cuisines. Corn, for example, is now the most widely grown grain in the western hemisphere. Potatoes, once they traveled to Europe, had become a sustaining staple there and found their way back to the northern hemisphere to become a mainstay food. Fortunate for us in southern New Jersey, the tomato of Central America and the lima bean of South America made the transition to our climate to become regional favorites.

The Lenni Lenape, which means *original* or *first people*, became known to the early settlers as the Delawares, with the designation is long out of use. The name Delaware included the Nanticokes who resided across the River, now centered around the southern Delaware town of Millsboro. Anthropologists have identified over 44 subdivisions of the Lenape people who inhabited their ancestral homeland (Lenapehoking). In the southern part of New Jersey, the Little Siconese occupied the land along the Cohansey River, the Sewapose, the Maurice River, and the Alloways, as well as the Salem Creek and its tributaries. As the Delawares were uprooted off their land, they migrated more or less westward on what is remembered today as the trail of tears. Most of the Delawares eventually resettled in Indian Territory, now the state of Oklahoma. This is mentioned as, in our pursuit of Lenni Lenape foods, some of the traditions of our southern New Jersey Indians have been stored in the memories and traced back to the "Delawares" in Oklahoma. And, due to intermarriages, the Lenape cooking in southern New Jersey has been recently influenced by the Nanticoke Lenape of Delaware.

While we clearly understand the foods the Lenape contributed to us and, to a lesser extent, the food that they cooked, unfortunately we have relatively few written recipes to draw upon.

Lenni Lenape..... 239

It would be a mistake to assume that Lenape cooking would have meant a diet of gruel made from corn. John Heckewelder, a Moravian evangelist and keen observer of the American Indians, who crisscrossed the Allegheny Mountains in his travels and adventures from 1754 to 1813, noted[1] that when the women cooked dishes from pumpkin, they were particular in their choices of pumpkin and in the manner of cooking them.

In bringing forward the Lenape cooking today, I aim to reconstruct their foodways immediately prior to the Europeans arrival in the early 17th century. Many so-called recipes tagged "Indian" were ones that have as a primary ingredient corn, yet went on to include white wheat flour, baking powder and so on. I avoided them as much as possible in working toward reconstructing the recipes they would have cooked. Ingredients suggested are those that are close to the items the Lenape would have had and those which we can reasonably find today.

Though historical references will be made to their common use of coals and ashes in cooking, such as ash baked potatoes, we will defer from open fire-cooking recipes as few of use will attempt such cooking means.

INDIANS "BROT" CRANBERRIES TO EARLY SETTLERS

Providing us with one of the earliest written references to cranberries in New Jersey, one of the first settlers in Burlington, N. J., Mahon Stacy, wrote a letter to his brother in England dated April 26, 1680. It read in part:

"We have from the time called May until Michaelmas a great store of very good wild fruits as strawberries, cranberries and hurtleberries. The cranberries, much like cherries for color and bigness, may be kept until fruit comes in again. An excellent sauce is made of them for venison, turkeys and other great fowl and they are better to make tarts than either gooseberries or cherries. We have them brot to our homes by the Indians in great plenty."

---

1   John Heckewelder, *History, Manners, and Customs of the Indian Nations Who Once Inhabited Pennsylvania and the Neighboring States.* Salem, New Hampshire: Ayers Company, Publishers., p 143.

Tomato Popcorn Soup

Serves two

Our Lenni Lenape are not known to have used tomatoes, even though they could have come up from Central America where the European first learned of them. On the other hand, the Lenape certainly developed the culture of growing and using popcorn. Rather than popping the corn and eating as we would out of hand, they would grind the corn in a mortar and add it to their stews and soups. Mint would have been a seasoning used by the Lenape in their cooking.

    1   (15-ounce can) tomato soup
    1   can milk, or 1/2 can water, 1/2 can milk
    1   cup ground popcorn,
3-4   mint leaves, chopped

In a soup pot or sauce pan heat the tomato soup and the milk to a gentle simmer. **Add** the ground popcorn and mint leaves, and stir in. **Simmer** for another minute. **If** you like, garnish with a few mint leaves in each soup bowl.

The clay cooking pots shown here represent types of pots used by the Lenni Lenape. By far, most of the pots found by archaelogists are the conical-bottom shape pictured on the left. Archaelogists suggest that the conical shape was in use because it distributed heat from the hot coals more efficiently and would less likely crack when exposed to the heat during cooking. Flat-bottomed pots were believed to be from an earlier era. Information and drawing courtesy of **Alan E. Carman,** Curator of the Cumberland County Prehistoric Museum in Greenwich, where such Lenape artifacts can be viewed. Also, a permanent display of cooking pots found by archaelogists can be seen at the Woodruff Museum at the Bridgeton Public Library.

Butternut and Pemmican Soup
with Sage Seasoning

Serves six

Winter squash, such as pumpkin and other hard-skinned squash, were staples of the Lenape diet. Today, year round availability of butternut squash stands in quite well for pumpkin in soups. Pemmican was often used in soups (it would have had bear grease as part of its makeup), along with a wild herb seasoning such as sage. Here we use vegetable oil or bacon fat.

The technique for this recipe isn't true to the Lenape tradition of using hot rocks tossed into the water to bring it to a boil. Likewise for sautéing the sage, a feat not likely in clay pots that would have cracked with such attempts. But still, I think this reconstructed recipe pays homage to their use of ingredients and style of their cooking as best as we know and can replicate.

> 1 tablespoon vegetable oil
> 8 fresh sage leaves, diced fine, or 1 teaspoon powdered
> 1 medium size squash, about 2 to 2-1/2 pounds, peeled, seeded and cut into bite size cubes
> 4 ounces pemmican, or see substitute below
> Salt to taste
> 2-1/2 quarts water
> Squash seeds, toasted, optional as a garnish

In a 6-quart soup pot over medium heat, add the vegetable oil and briefly sauté the sage until its aroma is released, about 30 seconds after oil is hot.

Add the pemmican, stir in for a moment, and add the squash cubes. Stir occasionally until the squash begins to very lightly brown.

Add a light amount of salt, being mindful that the pemmican can be salty.

Add the water, bring to a boil, and reduce to a simmer.

Cook, stirring occasionally for 20 minutes, or until squash is tender.

Meanwhile, optionally toast squash seeds on a baking sheet in a 350-degree F. oven about 10 minutes, until fragrant.

When soup is finished, adjust salt, add more water if a thinner consistency is desired, and serve. Garnish with toasted squash seeds, if you wish.

Note: If you haven't made pemmican, you can use as an alternative 4 slices of crisply cooked bacon, diced, along with about 2 ounces of dried berries, such as raisins, blueberries or cranberries. Craisins, a brand of sweetened dried cranberries, used in my pemmican recipe, has sufficient sugar for this soup. The Lenape would have used maple syrup to sweeten their soups.

Parched (Roasted) Corn

Parching corn is one of many ways the Lenape used corn, as they had many ways to prepare corn, or Mother corn, as they called it. By parching corn, usually a field corn, they found it light and nutritious as trail food. Today, we might recognize a more processed version called corn nuts.

I had the opportunity to grow Delaware Blue Corn, a corn variety that traveled with the Delawares to Oklahoma where it was saved over the generations and eventually became available from the Eastern Native Seed Conservancy. This is the corn I used to pan roast.

The recommended corn for parching is field or flint corn; Delaware Blue would be considered a flour corn. Nevertheless, the corn burst upon the heat and became rather pleasing when eaten. Unlike popcorn which explodes to a puffy texture, parched corn is rather crunchy.

Our Lenni Lenape would have taken fresh ears, pulled back the husk, removed the silk, tied or braided the husks together and hung them to dry. It would have taken a few weeks. When ready to parch, the Lenape would have heated the dried corn over hot flat rocks.

Today, we would try to select an heirloom corn and follow their method, or dry frozen shoepeg corn in a warm oven by placing on an ungreased baking sheet, stirring occasionally. Yet another way would be to dry the corn in a dehydrator. When we parch corn in a modern method, instead of heated flat rocks, we would use a cast iron pan on a stove. Those with the opportunity to parch corn in a pan outdoors would be encouraged to do so. By heating them over hot, glowing embers, fragrant smokiness will impart it's flavor, which is more in keeping with the Lenape tradition. Parched corn will keep for months, less so with added oil.

Heat a cast iron pan with a light film of vegetable oil or bacon grease. **Place** an amount of kernels to fill the pan in one layer. Stir often until most of the corn has popped. **At** that time they will darken and puff up slightly. Though the Lenape might not have salted the parched corn, we might find it more agreeable doused with a light sprinkling of salt. The corn will be pleasingly crunchy and quite nice to chew. For added flavor, douse with a light amount of maple syrup.

If straight butter were used instead of vegetable oil, it would probably burn. However, butter mixed 50/50 with vegetable or olive oil will raise the burning temperature and lessen burning.

Lenni Lenape Stew

Serves six to eight

In John Heckewelder's chapter on Food and Cookery in his book, "History, Manners, and Customs of the Indian Nations Who Once Inhabited Pennsylvania and Neighboring States," he writes:

> The Indians have a number of manners of preparing their corn. They make an excellent pottage of it, by boiling it with fresh or dried meat (the latter pounded), dried pumpkins, dry beans, and chestnuts.

From the above account, I have reconstructed a recipe that approximates what might have been cooked by the Lenape, but without the benefit of smoke from a fire's embers. I have used dried Delaware Blue Corn with seed grown and obtained from the Eastern Native Seed Conservancy, P.O Box 451, Great Barrington, MA 01230, www.ensc.org.

In a bow to modern cooking, I suggest to brown the meat before continuing the stew to develop a welcome extra layer of flavor. As to the dried pumpkins in the recipe, today one can substitute dried butternut squash, which is in the same winter squash family and much easier to process for drying.

6 ounces (about 3/4 cup) dried pinto or kidney beans,
    soaked overnight
2 tablespoons vegetable oil
1/2-3/4 pound chuck or brisket beef, cubed
8 ounces (about 1 cup) shoepeg corn
1 cup dried pumpkin or other winter squash, chopped
Salt to taste
3 tablespoons maple syrup, optional

In a 6-quart soup heavy pot over medium heat, add oil and when hot, add meat, turning the meat to brown on all sides. **Add** the beans with 2 quarts of water and bring to a boil. **Reduce** to a low simmer and cook until tender, partially covered, about 1 hour. **Stir** occasionally and add more water as needed. **Add** the corn, pumpkin, salt, and maple syrup, if using. **Simmer** for another 5 to 7 minutes, stirring occasionally.
Adjust for salt or syrup and serve.

Drying squash: Use any winter squash such as pumpkin (eating type, not carving), butternut, cheese, buttercup, kabocha or delicata. Use a potato peeler to remove the skin, or if the skin is to tough, cut into sections and remove with a pairing knife. Cut into thin 1/8-slices and lay on a drying screen or baking pan. Place in a dehydrator or in an oven set to a warm temperature. Monitor and turn over occasionally until the squash is dry but not quite brittle. They should be a bit pliable when bent. Store in a sealed jar in a cool, dark location.

Corn Pone

Makes one dozen fritters

Many food historians agree that corn pone is the precursor to hush puppies. In another take off on corn, the Indian custom of frying on a griddle evolved into fry bread. It sprung from the U.S. Government's distribution of white wheat flour to the western reservations. Because neither white flour nor the baking powder in fry bread were used by the Native Americans before the Europeans arrived, I have attempted to reconstruct a recipe that would have likely been prepared. In the interest of holding the fritter together, I had to use a small portion of white flour, but it is predominately based on cornmeal.

The Native Americans used bear grease often; here we will use bacon for its grease and its flavor. Use lard, if you prefer. As salt was difficult to obtain in the Delaware Valley, it wasn't used often in cookery. Maple syrup, however, was at hand and was used in many dishes.

Admittedly, this recipe makes for a coarse fritter, but it does represent an approximation of how it might have been made. Though it may not be authentic, add a pinch of salt if you wish.

1	cup stone ground whole grain cornmeal
1/2	cup all-purpose flour
2	tablespoons maple or corn syrup
3/4	cup water
3	strips regular thinly sliced bacon

Combine and mix the corn and white flour. **Mix** in the maple syrup. **Add** the water gradually until the consistency of a thick pancake batter is achieved. Set aside. **Cut** the bacon in diced pieces. In a heavy griddle pan over low heat, render the fat out of the bacon. **When** the bacon becomes crisp, remove and stir it into the the batter mixture. There should be a layer of bacon fat remaining in the pan. **Bring** the pan to medium heat. Using a tablespoon, drop in the batter and cook until the bottom side is lightly browned, **Turn** over and repeat for other side. Add more vegetable oil if necessary. **Remove** to a platter lined with a paper towel. **Variation:** Crumble the corn pone into boiled or steamed lima beans.

Hemispherical Kettle, circa 1550-1650, a style of kettle that was commonly used by the Dutch for several hundred years. It was probably one of the main trading items the Dutch traded with the Indians in exchange for furs. The clay pots in use by the Lenni Lenape at that time were extremely fragile, so obtaining durable copper kettles would have been worth the trade.

Frances Blackwood

Frances Blackwood, a long-time resident of Salem County, had a previous commentary from John Fenwick and John Bartram's recorded encounter with the Lenape customs. This is excerpted from the Alloway Centennial Committee's book, *Alloway Remembers*.

We know John Fenwick's meeting with the Indians under Salem's old oak tree was a friendly one. Perhaps watching in the shadows of bush and tree, Indian women felt a sympathetic bond with the Quaker ladies who also listened and watched the proceedings in the background. It is not stretching the imagination too far to believe the native women must have sensed that the strangers' first need would be something to eat. This seems to be the universal thought of women the world over.

It is a pleasant thought that after the men completed their pledge of peace they, together with the Indian braves who had accepted them, hunted for wood to make their temporary shelter for the night and the women joined in what must have been the white man's introduction to the barbecue.

There may or may not have been rabbit or venison at that first meal. But certainly there must have been pots of soup bubbling away in kettles hung on tall tripods. The eastern Indians were accustomed to eat just one big or true "meal" a day. But even if Fenwick's landing came after the noon meal had been enjoyed, hospitality was one of the first rules Indian women learned in childhood and there was rarely a lack of food. John Bartram, visiting Indians not far from Philadelphia, described a meal served as consisting of "Three huge kettles of Indian corn soup (or maybe it was a thin hominy?) with dried eels and other fish cooked in it and a kettle full of young squash (with their flowers cooked together), and last of all a big bowl of Indian dumplings which consisted of young corn cut from the cob and some boiled beans combined and wrapped in corn leaves then roasted a few moments in the fire to heat thoroughly."

Besides the wide variety of meats available for the expert Indian hunter, some of the most important vegetable foods of today were used by the Indian women-not cultivated to the degree of perfection as those known by us, but quite possibly with considerably more vitamin and mineral content than those of today: Tomatoes, squash, maize (corn), cranberries, blueberries, peppers, and beans.

Lief Ericsson noted in his tale of discovery that natives here used wild grapes. It is common knowledge that the natives here cultivated corn; in fact we could truthfully assert that if those friendly natives had not shared their knowledge of this grain and its uses, civilization of this continent would have had a far different history.

Old Original Lenape Succotash

Once you see the ingredient list, this may appear to be a contradiction. Yet, by studying the accounts of Lenape and other Native Americans, they would have likely cooked succotash this way. Since bear grease is not available to us today, and we are not sure which type of corn the Lenape would have used, we have approximated the closest ingredients we can access today and maintain respect for the ways of their past before the settlers began trading and influencing their cookery.

The Lenape may have parched dried corn over smoky embers; here we suggest pan roasting fresh or frozen corn to heighten the corn flavor.

> 1/4 pound bacon, sliced in 1/2-inch pieces
> 1/2 pound (about 1-2/3 cups) shoepeg corn
> 1/2 pound lima beans
> 2 tablespoons maple syrup, optional
> Indigenous herb for further seasoning, see note below

In a 2-3 quart saucepan over medium heat, cook the bacon until the fat releases and becomes clear in the bacon. **Add** the corn and cook, stirring occasionally, until the corn begins to brown and caramelize. Remove corn with a slotted spoon and set aside.

Add the lima beans, stir in, and cook for 10 minutes, stirring occasionally.

Return the corn to the saucepan, stir in, and cook for 5 minutes more.

Add and stir in the maple syrup and herb seasoning, if using, and simmer a few seconds more. Remove and serve.

Note: The Lenape were known to use a number of indigenous plants to season their cooking. Among them would have been sweet bay magnolia leaves, coltsfoot, mint, wild mustard leaves and seeds, spicebush, wild ginger and wintergreen.

The Reverend John Heckewelder, a Moravian missionary, in the 1760's gives us one of the few accounts of Native American cooking. In this excerpt, it's clear that the Lenape's foodways were more sophisticated than we would have imagined:

> They also prepare a variety of dishes from the pumpkin, the squash and the green French or kidney bean; they are very particular in their choice of pumpkins and squashes, and in their manner of cooking them. The women say that the less water is put to them, the better dish they make, and that it would be still better if they were stewed without any water, merely in the steam of the sap which they contain. They cover up the pots in which they cook them with large leaves of the pumpkin vine, cabbages, or other leaves of the larger kind.
>
> John Heckewelder, *History, Manners and Customs of the Indians*
> *who once inhabited Pennsylvania*
> Historical Society of Pennsylvania, Philadelphia, 1876

Down Jersey Lenape Style Succotash

Serves four to six

We need only to pause a moment to recall that succotash is decidedly a Native American preparation that pairs corn and lima beans together. Certainly they are two ingredients that are abundant from local farms and gardens even today. In this second version a style practiced in the Down Jersey area today and graciously passed on to us by Elizabeth Munson from Millville. I have altered the ingredients to lower the butterfat and shorten the cooking time in keeping with contemporary taste.

As the Lenape's traditional use of bear grease for a cooking fat would be unlikely for us, we have accepted the alternatives of butter and bacon fat. Country Gentlemen corn, also known as shoepeg corn, would be the closest alternative corn, and is commonly found in supermarkets today.

> 3 tablespoons butter
> 1 tablespoon maple syrup or sugar
> 1/2 pound (about 1-2/3 cups) frozen shoepeg corn
> 1/2 pound fresh or frozen lima beans, smaller pole beans being the preferred
> Salt and black pepper to taste

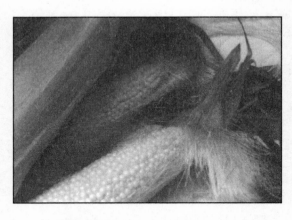

An heirloom variety corn with kernels arranged irregularly, **Country Gentleman**, has deep and narrow kernels, hence its alternate name, "Shoepeg." It's full flavor and current availability frozen at markets renders it ideal for use in Lenape cooking.

In a 3-quart saucepan over medium heat, melt the butter until the foam subsides. **Add** and stir in the lima beans, 1/3- cup of water, salt and pepper. Reduce the heat and simmer for 10 minutes, stirring occasionally. **Add** the corn and maple syrup, stir in, and cook at a simmer for 5 minutes more, stirring occasionally. Add more water as needed. **Test** for doneness; adjust seasonings and serve.

Note: Elizabeth Munson said that turkey is their favorite meat to serve with their succotash. She prefers to simmer her for 3/4 to 1 hour.

Elizabeth said her mother-inlaw, mother-in-law, from the Delaware Nanticoke Indian tribe, prefers the saltier addition of ham to her succotash. Others, I understand, opt to use diced bacon.

Shëwahsapan
(Grape Dumplings)

Makes approximately one dozen

The Lenape made good use of the native grapes, often called fox grapes. Today's closest variety would be Concord grapes often made in juice and available at food stores. The Lenape would boil their grapes, strain, and use them in soups, stews and in dumplings like this one below. For convenience, we have adapted a recipe from the book, "Lenape Indian Cooking with Touching Leaves Woman."

       1   cup flour
    1-1/2 teaspoons baking powder
       2   teaspoons sugar
      1/4   teaspoon salt
       1   tablespoon shortening or butter
    4-1/2 cups grape juice

In a mixing bowl, combine the flour, baking powder, sugar, shortening, and salt. **Add** 1/2 cup of the grape juice to the dry mix and mix until you have a dough a bit thicker than biscuit dough. **On** a floured board, roll out the dough to 1/4 inch thick. Cut these into 3/4-inch wide strips, and cut the strips into 3-inch long pieces. **Add** the remaining 4 cups of grape juice to a soup pot and bring to a boil. Adjust heat to a medium boil. **Add** 1/2 of the dumplings, one at a time. Boil slowly for about 15 minutes. **Repeat** for the second batch, adding more water as necessary.

Blue Shackamaxon Bean: This heirloom pole bean has a historical link to William Penn's Pennsbury Manor. Mahon Moon, a Morrisville, PA horticulturist who distributed seeds to members of the Friends Historical Association in 1906, had saved the seeds that were encountered when a group in 1683 went up the Delaware River to picnic on the site of Pennsbury Manor. The seeds were grown and saved by the Thomas family of Chester County, PA and were given to food historian and book author William Woys Weaver[1] who shared some with me. These beans were believed to be of Lenape origin.

This bean, which grows to a height of 3-1/2 to 4 feet high, has rose-pink flowers.. The pods are stripped with red, turn garnet red at the shell stage when the beans are deep navy blue. At maturity, the pods turn purple-blue as do the beans.. Weaver reports that the Lenape used this bean as a flour bean with blue cornmeal and stewed it as a shelly bean with "green"[2] corn. This bean may originally have had ceremonial purpose, now lost.

---

1   William Woys Weaver, *Heirloom Vegetable Gardening.* New York: Henry Holt and Company.
2   The Lenape referred to fresh corn as "green" corn.

Pemmican

Many of us already recognize pemmican as Native American food that combines pounded dried meat and sweet fruit mixed with fat. The meat often would have been bison or venison, the fruit choice for our Lenape might have been blueberries or cranberries, and the fat, bear fat. This combination of sugar and fat to coat dried, pounded meat has the effect of inhibiting bacteria growth. That is a storage factor extremely important for those whose food supply was always in doubt, and for hunters on long journeys traveling light.

Incoming Europeans quickly learned the value of pemmican as a high energy food that would keep almost forever, ideal for hunters and fur trappers on the trail. Today, trekkers have drawn on pemmican as highly nutritious trail food for much the same reason as our Native Americans.

In an attempt to recreate as faithfully as possible a type of pemmican our Lenape might have made, I located products at the supermarket that come close to what might have been made. Knauss, a locally available brand of dried beef, can be used as the meat with a bit of preparation. For the fruit, dried cranberries have recently been marketed as Craisins, which have been sugared. I chose to use natural leaf lard as the fat, but beef suet would have been the other readily available alternative. I lowered the fat portion somewhat as we aren't as concerned about long-term storage with refrigeration at hand, and as a matter of taste.

6   ounces (2 Knauss packages) dried beef
4   ounces Craisins
2-3 ounces pork or beef fat, leaf lard preferred

Further dry the beef in a warm oven on baking trays or dehydrator screens for 1-1/2 hours until crisp in order to finely chop or grind. At the same time set the Craisins in the warm oven to dry further as well as to make them easier to mince. When the beef is brittle to the touch, finely chop, or preferably use a small coffee or herb grinder to pulverize the beef.

The Craisins may require a few more minutes to lose moisture sufficiently to mince easily. Remove from the oven, allow to cool a few minutes to further firm, and mince with a knife or use a mechanical chopper. Combine with the dried minced beef.

Render the pork or beef fat in a heavy pan by adding water to start the release of the fat. Set heat to low, cover to avoid splattering and stir occasionally. Keep observing for the time when the fat starts to brown; at that time turn off the heat and remove the chitlings bits. Pour a portion of the hot fat over the beef and cranberry mixture. Stir the fat in until you reach a desired level of fat coating. You may not want to add all the fat from the pan. Mix thoroughly and allow to cool

Store the pemmican in zipper lock plastic bags, excluding as much air as possible. Store in the refrigerator for extra assurance of safety.

Corn Preparations
by the Delaware Indians

Alan E. Carman, a long-time amateur archaelogist in southern New Jersey and currently curator of the Prehistoric Museum in Greenwich, passed along to me this recorded history regarding the Delaware Indians' various uses of corn. Though we understand that corn was a mainstay in their diet, this listing of the numerous uses penned by George Loskiel, a Moravian Minister, bring home the point further.

1) Boiling corn in the husk.
2) Parboiling it, rubbing off the husk, and boiling it again.
3) Roasting the whole ear in hot ashes, as it came off the stalk.
4) Pounding it small and then boiling it soft.
5) Grinding it as fine as flour, by means of a wooden or stone morter and pestle, clearing it from the husks, and making a thick pottage of it.
6) Kneading the flour with cold water, making a cake about a hand's breath and an inch thick, enclosing this in leaves, and baking it in hot ashes under live coals. That was their bread.
7) Mixing dried blackberries with the flour to give the cakes better relish.
8) Chopping roasted or dried deer flesh, or sometimes smoked eels, and boiling this with the corn.
9) Boiling coarsely ground corn with fresh meat.
10) Letting unripe corn swell in boiling water, drying it, and laying it by for later use as soup or salad.
11) Roasting the whole corn when well grown, but still full of juice.
12) Roasting corn in hot ashes till it becomes thoroughly brown, then pounding it to fine flour, mixing it with sugar, and pressing it forcibly in a bag.

Reference: Wallace, Paul A., *Indians in Pennsylvania*, The Penn Historical and Museum Commission, Harrisburg, PA., 1968; Pages 33-34.

A Closing Page on Muskrat

In the remote reaches of deep Down Jersey, there is a tradition that runs deep and enduring. Nothing competes with the muskrat for delectable fare that will bring out the home crowd. Outreached and known to the broader region and the nation from the newspaper coverage of the annual muskrat fund-raising dinners, the days ahead for this unique custom remain in doubt. As to the announced dinners, the scarcity of this meadow meat has brought cancellation, or nearly so, of dinners in the last few years.

Some would venture to say the meat tastes like beef, others would simply say that muskrat has a sweet, delicious taste. Surely, it is a you-like-it-or-you-don't morsel. It doesn't taste like chicken. Muskrat fanciers agree that the meat must be cooked right to remove the gamy taste.

In sourcing muskrat, called rats by locals and marsh rabbits in polite parlor rooms, the catch unquestionably has been on the decline. First the prices of the fur, the main incentive for trapping muskrat, declined dramatically in the mid-80's. Following that, leg-hold traps were banned, which put another impediment on daily catches. More recently, veteran trapper Richard Finlaw said that a number of critters have been decimating the muskrat population. "You can count on many predators out there in the meadows attacking them, including mink, fox, raccoon, eagles and owls." Richard said.

Where once there were several hundred muskrat trappers wading knee-deep in the meadows during the official season that runs from December 1 to March 15, now there are less than two dozen stomping in meadows, in season, setting traps. As far as the locals are concerned, the onslaught of regulations protecting the environment brings about more and more challenges to their way of life, so much so that ratting may be heading for extinction.

Harry Beal, a Lower Alloways Creek resident now in his 60's, said that when he was growing up, trapping was how school-aged children managed to earn money. "It was how we got money to buy clothes and the things we needed for school, otherwise we couldn't go," Harry said.

Perhaps you may be lucky enough to land a ticket to one of the sought-after muskrat dinners; it's getting such that attendees now, after enjoying a dinner, buy a ticket for the next year's event.

For your interest, I have written down how Richard Finlaw prepares muskrat meat for his own family:

> First, you want to soak the meat in cold water with added salt for a day or two to draw out the blood. Then the meat is cut into edible portions, bone in, and par-boiled with celery and onions (others may add mustard seed) to simmer for one to one and a half hours, until about three-quarters done. Then the meat is removed, patted dry and fried until browned, most certainly, Finlaw says, in a cast iron pan.

The major distinction from home cooking at the community events is that they deep-fry the muskrat meat instead of pan sautéing, although the Rotary of Salem pan fries them in butter. There may exist recipes for muskrat that include ingredients such as tomatoes, but you won't find them at the fund-raising dinners.

Glossary of Down Jerseyspeak

The Block: The farmers refer to the Vineland Produce Auction as "the block" where their produce is auctioned off to brokers.

Breaker: A tomato that is showing the first breaking color sign of turning to red.

Bridger: A resident of Handcock's Bridge in Salem County.

Chigaudia: Italian slang for dandelion, a beautiful, delicious lawn flower, not a weed.

Crick: A small stream, as in a crick in your back, not the creak in your knees.

Cricker: A proud, native-born resident of LAC, which is Lower Alloways Creek (Crick) Township.

Frying peppers: The long, thin sweet peppers that are green or mature red and that are preferred for sautéing over the more bitter bell peppers that are more suited used raw.

Grass: No, not the funny stuff; it's asparagus, a major crop for southern New Jersey.

G' head: Locals knew Clint Eastwood wasn't from Down Jersey when he uttered his famous line, "Go ahead, make my day!" Here, we would have said, "G' head..."

Gun control: To the local hunters, it means a steady hand.

Jersey Lighting: Hard cider.

Jersey redskins: No, not a football team, it's our dry, dull red-skinned sweet potato that's a bit sweeter than the moist varieties and with a chestnut-like flavor.

Knobs: Farmer's slang for cucumbers so oddly shapen that they are sold cheap to the processors for pickling.

Marsh rabbit: A polite euphemism for muskrats, otherwise called, simply, rats.

Medda: In the Salem area, that means, of course, meadow, an environmentally correct name for swamp.

Might could have: A clearer way of saying maybe.

Nancy Hall: No, not a suffragist, but an heirloom variety of sweet potato that farmers here grow for their local customers who know how good they taste.

Pickle: A small cucumber, usually sold unwaxed at local farm markets. The name came about, it is speculated, from the huge amount of cucumbers grown for shipment to pickle processors, some as far away as Boston.

Proggers: Those who wrest their living from muck, such as those that progged for fallen cedar trees.

Route 40 divide: The border, below which, residents have seriously mulled over seceding from New Jersey. Also, the mecca for roadside barbecue stands. Anything north of Rt. 40 is considered North Jersey.

'Scarole: Local dialect for escarole made famous by Italian wedding soup.

Scunnions or scullions: To everyone else, they are green onions. Used especially near the Vineland area where Italian farmers predominate.

Stripers: It could mean striped bass, known as rockfish over in the Chesapeake region, or it could mean bell or frying peppers that are maturing from green to red, and in the process appear striped. Sometimes less expensive than either full green or red, they don't have the bitterness of green peppers.

The Shore: West coasters say "The beach," we say, "The shore."

Tired fish: Fishmongers slang for fish that, while still fresh, is off its peak.

Uncle Dupee: In the vacinity of Dupont's Chamber's Works in Carney's Point, they might happen to say, "Gotta go get my paycheck from Uncle Dupee."

Wastonians: Old slang for residents of Woodstown in Salem County.

Weakies: Slang for weakfish, known across the Bay in the State of Delaware and elsewhere as seatrout. It gets its name not from weak flesh, but from having weak mouth tissue that tears easily upon hooking.

—Compiled with assistance from Ron LeHew, Down Jersey's Official Town Crier

Author's note: This glossary was done without the assurance of any spell check

A

Abruzzo Style Oven Green Beans, 64
American Vegan Society. 176
Anderson, Captain Fenton Anderson, 99
Apples(s), 25, 200
    Apple Bread Crumb Topping with
        Cabbage, 184
Arugula, 19
Asparagus, 20
    and eggs poster, 47
    and eggs sandwich, 50
    history, 50
    South Philly, 65
    Roasted, 66
    Stir-Fry, 66

B

Baltimore & Ohio (B&O)
    Bayside schedule, 45
    Curry of Chicken Soup, 45
    Omelette, 62
    Pork Chops Normandy, 119
    Wheat Cakes, 223
Baden, Adele, 229
Barbecue Sauce, 231
Basil, 20
    with Orange Sauce, 232
Battaglia, Freed, Porkette, 128
Bayside (Caviar), 172
Beach Plum Sauce, Jersey, 228
Beans, green, 20
    Abruzzo Style, 64
    and Greens, 182
    and Potato Stew, German Style, 127
    Sautéed inSoy Sauce, 68
Beef
    Braciole, 108
    Irish Beef and Guinnes Stew, 103
    Pan-Grilled Steak, 100
    Pennsgrove Roast Beef Sandwich, 99
    Oyster Boat Beef Stew, 97
    Steak and Kidney Pie, 101
    Sunday Meatballs, 105
    Beer Batter, Waterman's Seafood, 134
Beets, 20
    in Borscht, 34
Biscotti, 203
Biscuits,
    Basic Buttermilk, 51
    Easy Mix, 51
Blackwood, Frances, 246
Blueberries, 25, 205
    and Ricotta Dessert, 205
    in Yummy Muffins, 214
    Sauce, 206
    Tea Cake,207
Bok Choy, also Pak Choy, 20

Booze, Edmund G., 154
Bot Boi Noodles, 115
Boxty, 69
Braciole, 108
Bread and Tomato Salad, 189
Broccoli, 20, 72
    Anytime Pancake, 70
    Lemon Dill, 72
    Sautéed, 71
    with Crab and Rice, 144
Broccoli Rabe, 20
    With or Without Pasta, 109
Brown, Mary, 90
Brown, Patti, 157
Bruschetta, 49
Brussels Sprouts, 21
    Bright and Best, 73
    with Mustard Butter, 73
Buckalew, Bill "Bucky," 163
Bulgarian Shopska Salad, 188
Butter Sauce, 209
Buttermilk Biscuits, 51
Butternut and Pemmican Soup, 242

C

Cabbage, 21
    Cheesy German, 74
    Napa, 41
    Oriental Sweet and Sour Sauce, 71
    Polish Panned, 75
    Prussian Style Red, 76
    Red, What's with?, 78
    with Apple Breadcrumb Topping, 184
Cajun Portabella Sandwich, 60
Campbell's V8, with Tuscan Lima Beans, 82
Carman, Alan E., 241
Carrots, 21
Cauliflower
    Farm Market Baked, 77
    Old Bay Cauliflower, 77
Cheese Balls, 52
Cheese, Tomatoes and, Sandwich, 55
Cheesey German Cabbage, 74
Cider, with Sausages, 130
Conch Seaville, 143
Cookies, Thumbprint, 210
Corn Bread, South Jersey, 208
Crane, Steve, 170
Cranberry Pudding, 209
Chicken
    Barbecue, 117
    Bot Boi, 114
    Congo Moambé, 120
    Curry of, 45
    Ginger, Japanese Style, 124
    Fricassee, German, 122
    in Chocolate Mole Sauce, 123

Index..... 255

Chicken, *continued...*
    in Corn and Chicken Soup, 35
    Liver Paté, 53
    or Turkey in Chestnut Wine Sauce, 118
    Parmesan, 112
    Pot Pie, 113, 114
    Ruby, 119
Chickpea, and Spinach Stew, 179
Chilaly, 229
Chittara, 64
Cider, Ruby, Mulled, 225
Cinnamon, Crispy Cucumbers, 79
Clam(s)
    Rhorman's Family Clam Pie, 137
    Salem County Deviled, 140
    Seabrook, 139
    Shucking, 36
    Wilsson Clam Pie, 138
    with White Clam Sauce and Pasta, 141
Clam Chowder, see stews
Colanero, Raymond, 215
Corn, 21
    and Clam Soup, 37
    Dried, Curried Corn and Clam Soup, 38
    Fritters, 52
    Paprika or Curried with Red Pepper, 78
    Parched, 243
    Pone, 245
    Preparations, 251
Corn, Sweet, Guide, 78
Costaris, Charlene H., 30
Crab(s)
    in Corn and Crab Soup, 35
    Jersey Crab Cakes, 150
    Port Norris, 149
    Red Sauced, with Linguini, 145
    Sicilian Style, 146
    Vietnamese, 149
    with Rice Sticks and Broccoli, 144
Crabs, soft-shell
    Cleaning, 150
    Grilled, 147
    Sauté, 147
Crabmeat, Pasteurized, 35
Craisins, 218
Cranberry Sauce, Fresh, 233
Cranberry-Blueberry Sauce, 231
Cucumbers, 22
    Asian, 41
    Crispy Cinnamon, 79
    in Raita Salad with Taziki, 190
    in Seabrook Style Cucumber Salad, 196
Curried or Paprika Corn, 78
Curried Spinach, 88
    in Dried Corn and Clam Soup, 38
    Spinach Stuffed Clams, 139

Cumberland County Pickled Peppers, 85
D
Dandelion, 22
Dashi, 41
Delaware Bay Estuary, 67
DellaRova, Pat, 214
DeVitis, Anita, 203
Dill's Jersey Cioppino, 136
Dinshah, Freya, 177
Dodge's Market, 110
Down Jersey map, VI
Dumplings, Grape, 249
E
Egg Sauce, 167
Eggplants, 22
    and Tomato Soup, 177
    Sautéed Farm Market, 180
    Parmesan, 178
Eggs
    and Asparagus Sandwich, 50
    and Peppers Sandwich, 58
    in Tomato Egg Drop Soup, 45
Ekimaglou, Dennis, 43
Endive, 22
Escarole, 22
    in soup, 39
F
Fehlauer,Nancy, Werner, 207
Fennel, 22
Fergone, Cindy, John, 154
Fortescue Fries, 155
Fish
    Baked, with mayonnaise, 152
    Bluefish, Barbecued or Broiled, 135
    Cakes, 41
    Cioppino, 136
    Cod, Baccala Style, 142
    Flounder, Baked alla Vineland, 151
    Fluke, Greek, Baked, 153
    Mackerel, Broiled, with Honey Mustard, 135
    Salmon, Poached, 159
    Shad
        Baked, 163
        Broiled, Orange Liqueur, 163
        Filleting, trying to, 162
        Shad Roe, Salem Oak Diner, 161
        Slow Cooker, 166
        Stuffed, Marino, 165
    Striped Bass, 167
    Teriyaki Seafood Medley, 168
    Tuna, Sicilian, with Rigatoni, 169
    Weakfish Fingers, 170
    Whiting, 171

Foster, Al, XVII, 59, 61, 121
French Fries, Bay Style, 67
Fried Rice, 54

G

Gardenshire, Elnora, 43
Garlic, 22
　　　　Bread, 49
Garvey, 133
German Escarole Salad, 193
German Green Bean and Potato Stew, 127
Ginger Cookies, Soft, 210
Glossary Jerseyspeak, 253, 254
Gravy
　　　　Sausage, Biscuits and, 52
　　　　Gravy, Today's Spaghetti, 235
　　　　Gravy, why is it called?, 227
Greek
　　　　Lemon and Olice Oil Sauce, 230
　　　　Tomato Salad, 194
Greens and Beans, 182

H

Hackett's Fried Tomatoes, 83
Haines Family, 210, 231
Harmeter, Caroline, 229
Herring Salad, 195
Historic Foodways Society of Delaware
　　　　Valley, 130
Hog Shrimp, 154
Honey Mustard Sauce, 232
Honey Mustard, with Broiled Mackerel,
　　　　135
Hunter's Sweet Potato Casserole, 90

I

Irish Beef and Guiness Stew, 103

J

Japanese in Down Jersey, 125
Japanese Mandarin Orange Cake, 212
Jersey Best Brand, 155
Jersey Bounce (drink), 225
Jersey Devil (drink), 225
Jersey Fresh Logo, 19
Jerseyspeak, Glossary, 254, 255
Julkaka (bread), 219

K

Kale, 22
Kidney, and Steak Pie, 101
Kohlrabi, 22
Krullen, 216

L

Laird's
　　　　Black Bean Soup, 33
　　　　Chicken Liver Paté, 53
　　　　Jersey Devil Cocktail, 225
Ledden's Seeds and Plants, 92
Leeks, 22

Lemon Butter Spread, Salem, 233
Lemon Dill Broccoli, 72
Lenni Lenape Stew, 244
Lettuce, 23
Lettuce, Romaine, 187
Lima Beans,
　　　　Picking, 40
　　　　Pole, like no other, 80, 81
　　　　Pot Pie, 113
　　　　Pot Pie, German, 111
　　　　Tuscan Style, with Campbell's V8, 82
Linguini, with Red-Sauced Crabs, 145
Lower Alloways Creek
　　　　Historical Cabin, 196
　　　　Pork Sausage, 130

M

Macaroni and Cheese, 110Margarum, Noel, 98
Marino Family, 165
Mason Jar, 84
McAllister, William, 161
Meatballs
　　　　in Escarole Soup, 39
　　　　Prussian, Lemon Cream Sauce, 107
　　　　Sunday, 105
Melons, 23
Mexican Salsa, 228
Migliaccio, 214
Mincemeat Pie Filling, Old Original, 98
Molasses Cake, 213
Mole (sauce), 123
Moore, Brenda, 231
Moravian Sugar Cake, 224
Muffins, Three Seasons Fruit, 204
Munson, Jean and Bob, 134
Muskrat Board, 102, page, 252
Mussels, Marinated, 156

N

Nesser, Moyo "Mo," 104
New Bridge, 194
New Jersey Farmers' Direct Marketing Association,
　　　　52

O

O'Donnell's Restaurant, 43
Okra, and Tomatoes, 84
Omelette, 62
Onions, 23
Onion, Sautéed, Salad, 199
Orange-Basil Sauce, 232
Orange, Mandarin Cake, 212
Oriental Sweet and Sour Cabbage, 71
Oysters
　　　　Barbecued, 57
　　　　Boat Stew, 97
　　　　Creamed, 155

Oysters, *continued...*
>Down Jersey Oyster and Spinach
>>Stew, 56
>Fritters, 155
>Holuday, 157
>New England Style, 56
>Port of Call Restaurant Stew, 56
>"R" months, safe?, 57
>Scalloped, 158
>Southern Style Stew, 56

P

Pak Choy (Bok Choy), 20
Pancakes
>Broccoli, Anytime, 70
>Old Country, 59
>Swedish, 220
>Vegan, 175
Paprika
>What is?, 89
>with Pan-Browned Potatoes, 87
Parched (Roasted) Corn, 243
Parsley, 23
Parsnip Fritters, 74
Pasta
>and Tuna, Sicilian, 169
>with Broccoli Rabe, 109
>with Red-Sauced Crabs, 109
Paczki (Polish Doughnuts), 217
Pears, Pickled, 209
Peas, 23
Pemmican, 248
Pennsgrove Roast Beef, 99
Peppers
>and Eggs Sandwich, 58
>and Sausage, 130
>Cooking, 130
>Cumberland County Pickled, 85
>Hot, 23
>Hot, Appetizer, 59
>Red, with Corn or Paprika, 78
>Stuffed, 131
>Sweet, 23
>with Vegan "Steak," 185
Pizzelles, 215
Polish Doughnuts, 217
Pork
>Porkette, 128
>Salem County Ribs, 104
Port of Call Oyster Stew, 56
Portabella
>Cajun, 60
>Grilled Sandwich, 183
Potatoes
>Comforting Soup, 186
>Griddle Cakes, Boxty, 69
>Pan-Browned with Paprika, 87

Red Pepper, Panned, 87

R

Ratatouille, 61
Ravioli,
>Butter Browned, 62
>with Orange Basil Sauce, 232
Ricotta Pie, 223
Riley, Sid, 162
Ritter (s')
>Chicken Barbecue, 117
>Farm Field Stew, 94
>Paul, J., 237
>Story, 117
Rodgers, Paula, 233
Rohrman, Albert C., Jr., 137
Romaine
>Hearts, 193
>Rollups, 189
Rumford Chemical Works, 33, 174

S

Salad(s),
>Cucumbers in Taziki Sauce, 197
>Cucumber Raita, 190
>Dandelion, 192
>Dandelion Salad Dressings, 191
>Fennel, Country, 190
>German Escarole Salad, 193
>Greek Tomato Salad, 194
>Juicy Tomato and Green Bean, 199
>Peasant Tomato and Bread, 189
>Sautéed Onion, 199
>Seabrook Style Cumber, 196
>Sillsallad, 195
>Tomato Salads, various, 198
>Waldorf, 200
>Wheaton Village Mixed, 188
Salsa
>Fresh, 234
>Mexican, Cooked, 230
Salem County Pork Ribs, 104
Santaniello, Carlotta, John, Mrs., 107
Sausage
>and Peppers, 129
>Biscuits and Gravy, 51
>Lower Alloways Creek, 130
Scallians (green onions), 23
Scallops, Carmalized, 160
Schaeffer, Bonnie, 41
Shad, see Fish
Shewahsapan, 249
Shipping Sheds, 97
Shivler, Ruth, 157
Shrimp, Hog, 154
Sorantino, Virginia, 237

Succotash,

    Down Jersey Style, 248

    Old Original Lenape, 247

Soup

    Asparagus, Vegan, 174

    Asparagus, Springtime, 32

    Black Bean, Laird Family, 33

    Buttermut & Pemmican, 242

    Corn and Clam, 37

    Creamed Corn and Chicken, 35

    Escarole, 176

    Estonian Sauerkraut and Barley, 42

    Italian Wedding, 39

    Lima Bean, 40

    Polish Country Borscht, 34

    Potato, Comforting, 186

    Pumpkin or Butternut, 46

    Snapper, 43

    Sweet Potato, 44

    Tomato Egg Drop, 45

    Tomato and Eggplant, 177

    Tomato Popcorn, 241

Spaghetti Cake, 214

Sparkling Holiday Punch, 225

Spinach, 179

    Easy Curried, 88

Squash

    Drying, 242

    Winter, 25

Steak

    and Kidney Pie, 101

    Pan Grilled, 100

Stew

    Chickpea, 179

    Irish Beef and Guinness, 103

    Ritter Farm Field Stew, 94

Still, Dr. James, 121

Succotash, 248

Suet Crust, 102

Sukiyaki, 96

Swedish

    Christmas Bread, 219

    Glogg, 226

    Pancakes, 220

    Sweedish Meatballs, 95

Sweet Potato(es)

    Biscuits, Heavenly, 222

    Casserole, Hunter's 90

    Casserole, Mary Brown's, 90

    Fried, 89

    Pie, 221

    Rolls, 222

    Soup, 44

Swisschard, 25

T

Tea Scones, 218

Thumbprint Cookies, 210

Tierno, Joe, 221

Tofu, 41

Tomato(es)

    and Bread Salad, 189

    and Eggplant Soup, 177

    and Okra, 84

    Catsup, 229

    Farm market, 25

    First Sandwich, 48

    Hackett's Fried, 83

    in Greek Salad, 194

    Tomato and Cheese,

        Open Faced, 55

    Popcorn Soup, 241

    Sauce, Jersey Tuscan, 238

    Sauce, Quick, 236

    Sauce, Sorantino, Virginia, 237

    Salem Fried, 92

    Stewed, with Lima Beans, 91

    Today's Spaghetti Gravy, 235

    Tomato Savvy

    Cooking with, 29

    Cherry, 28

    in salads, 187

    plum, 28

    round, 27, 28

    selection at the market, 29

    storage, 29

Tomato staking, 30

Trinity Episcopal Church, 95

Turkey (or Chicken) in Chestnut

   Wine Sauce, 118

V

Vegan recipes, see individual

Vegetables for fried rice, 54

W

Weaver, William Woys, 247

Welch's Grape Juice Story, 211

Wheat Cakes, 223

Whitelam, Harry, 56

Wild Rice, 132

Wilson, Bob, Sharon, 138

Woodbury Daily Times, 65

Z

Zampaglione, Carmen, 193, 236

Zucchini, 25

All illustrations and photographs were either by the author or used by permission from other contributors.

A special gratitude is owed to Jody Carrara, photographer of the Maurice River cover photograph.

Joe Colanero, from his sleuthing and travels throughout the region cherished as Down Jersey, has written for most major newspapers in this area, from gardening columns to food and restaurant articles. He lives in West Deptford with his wife Loretta. When he is not cooking for family and friends, he spends much of his time pulling weeds in his organic vegetable garden.

In the garden

At the Pennsylvania
Convention Center

Pre-lunch tour with Julia Child

"Our reviewers were enthusiastic about the authenticity of the recipes in Down Jersey Cooking and praised the author's unique historical approach to the regional cuisine. Joe Colanero is a talented and creative chef, extremely knowledgeable..."

—John B. Bryans
Editor-in-Chief, Book Publishing Division
Plexus Publishing, Inc.
www.plexuspublishing.com